Sustainability and Smart Manufacturing

This book discusses three key aspects of business operations: sustainability, human factors, and smart manufacturing, which make up modern business. The authors share their experiences in the transformation of enterprises to Industry 4.0/5.0 and the sustainability of steel production, as well as the reorganization of human factors using the example of the steel sector. The steel industry is covered both from a global perspective (key producers in the global steel market), as well as from a local and sectoral perspective (the companies that make up the sector of metal and metal product producers, using Poland as an example).

This insightful book discusses how the steel industry can develop intelligent solutions to enhance sustainable performance and the challenges they must overcome, including policy and regulation. Case studies evaluate how steel companies are investing in new technologies that meet environmental requirements but also human resource development to enhance digital skills and competencies of the workforce.

The book will find an audience across disciplines but be of particular value to scholars of industrial, operations, and technology management.

Bożena Gajdzik is an associate professor in the Department of Industrial Informatics at the Silesian University of Technology, Poland. For over 20 years, she has been dealing with the economics of business entities, including company management and steel mills. Her output includes 650 publications in national and international publishers, including 30 books about company management and business environment and 6 monographs about the steel industry: restructuring process in the sector towards market economy in Poland and now about the transformation of the steel industry to Industry 4.0. She is on the Stanford's Top 2% Scientists list for all carrier and for 2023.

Radosław Wolniak is a full professor in the Department of Economics and Informatics at the Silesian University of Technology, Poland. For over 20 years, he has been dealing with the issues of quality management, including Industry 4.0. His achievements include over 650 publications in national and international publishers, as well as many undertakings and projects implemented in cooperation with the business environment. He is an author of about 25 books about company management and business environment, among them 2 books were printed in Routledge. He is on the Stanford's Top 2% Scientists list for 2023.

Wieslaw Grebski is Professor Emeritus at The Pennsylvania State University. He was an Engineering Faculty and Coordinator of the Engineering Program at Penn State Hazleton. His research interests evolved from computer-aided manufacturing to sustainable forms of energy. Professor Grebski was always promoting close cooperation between university and industry. Under his leadership, a new engineering program focusing on renewable energy was developed. He has coauthored two hundred publications and nine books. Professor Grebski promoted different unconventional methods for teaching and learning. He was the recipient of the Milton S. Eisenhower Award. (This is one of the highest recognitions at Pennsylvania State University.) He has also received 11 other awards for teaching and advising. He has also taught the dual enrollment class, *Introduction to Engineering Design,* as a form of promoting the engineering profession and recruiting students for the engineering program. He was a member of the Pennsylvania Academy of Science, American Society of University Professors, American Society of Mechanical Engineers, and American Association of Engineering Educators.

Jan Szymszal is an Academic teacher at the University of Occupational Safety Management, Poland, and an Associate Professor at the Faculty of Technical Sciences. He is a specialist in the field of statistics and its practical use in management, medicine, psychology, and pedagogy. He is also an expert on the use of optimization methods and operational research in logistics and materials engineering, the use of computer methods in science – especially mathematics and forecasting – and the practical use of econometric methods.

Michalene Eva Grebski has a multidisciplinary background combining masters' degrees in Psychology and Business Administration as well as a Doctorate in Management. From 2016 through 2020, she was a faculty member at Northampton Community College (Pennsylvania, USA). Presently she is a faculty member at Colorado Mesa University (Colorado, USA). Michalene Eva Grebski has co-authored ten books and sixty-one scholarly articles. She is a member of following academic societies: American Counseling Association, American Psychological Association, American Association of University Professors, The International Honor Society in Psychology/PSI CHI.Her research interest is connected with innovativeness and creativity in education and entrepreneurial networks. She has conducted research related to the development of innovative skills and attributes as well as a multidisciplinary holistic approach for enhancing innovative behavior. Dr. Michalene Grebski is a member of many professional societies.

Routledge Advances in Production and Operations Management

This series sets out to present a rich and varied collection of cutting-edge research on production and operations management (POM), addressing key topics and new areas of interest in order to define and enhance research in this important field. Bringing together academic study on all aspects of planning, organizing and supervising production, manufacturing or the provision of services, subject areas will include, but are not limited to: operations research, product and process design, manufacturing strategy, scheduling, quality management, logistics and supply chain management. Highly specialised and industry-specific studies are actively encouraged.

Supply Chain Operations in the Arctic
A Multi-Perspective Approach Towards Sustainable Development
Edited by Antonina Tsvetkova and Konstantin Timoshenko

Real-Time Visibility in Supply Chain Management
Theories, Technologies, and Tensions
Sławomir Wyciślak

Digitalization for Sustainable Manufacturing
Twin Transition in Norway
Edited by Sverre Gulbrandsen-Dahl, Heidi Dreyer, Håkon Raabe, Kristian Martinsen, Einar L. Hinrichsen, Gabor Sziebig and Halvor Holtskog

Sustainability and Smart Manufacturing
The Transformation of the Steelwork Industry
Bożena Gajdzik, Radosław Wolniak, Wieslaw Grebski, Jan Szymszal and Michalene Eva Grebski

For more information about this series, please visit: https://www.routledge.com/The-Routledge-Philosophers/book-series/RAPOM

Sustainability and Smart Manufacturing

The Transformation of the Steelwork Industry

Bożena Gajdzik, Radosław Wolniak, Wieslaw Grebski, Jan Szymszal and Michalene Eva Grebski

Routledge
Taylor & Francis Group
LONDON AND NEW YORK

First published 2025
by Routledge
4 Park Square, Milton Park, Abingdon, Oxon OX14 4RN

and by Routledge
605 Third Avenue, New York, NY 10158

Routledge is an imprint of the Taylor & Francis Group, an informa business

British Library Cataloguing-in-Publication Data
A catalogue record for this book is available from the British Library

ISBN: 978-1-032-69737-6 (hbk)
ISBN: 978-1-032-69731-4 (pbk)
ISBN: 978-1-032-69761-1 (ebk)

DOI: 10.4324/9781032697611

Typeset in Times New Roman
by codeMantra

Contents

1 The genesis, essence, and development of Industry 4.0

1.1 Creation and assumptions of the Industry 4.0 concept

The genesis of the Industry 4.0 concept is seen in the Fourth Industrial Revolution. The term, Industry 4.0, was introduced in 2011 by Henning Kagermann (2015), professor of physics and former CEO of SAP. It is assumed to be a very general development concept referring to the changes that are taking place in industry, based on the strong interplay of automation, processing, and exchange of Big Data and additive manufacturing technologies with autonomous robots and machine learning (Hermann et al., 2015; Kagermann et al., 2013). The term Industry 4.0 (original nomenclature in German) comes from the German government's High Tech Strategy document. The term, for the first time, was used at the Hanover Fair in 2011. In October 2012, a working group led by Siegfried Dais of Robert Bosch GmbH presented a set of implementation recommendations for the high-tech industry to the federal government. The final report 'Industry 4.0' developed by the group was presented on 8 April 2013 (Plattform Industry 4.0, 2014).

The German Federal Government presents Industry 4.0 as a new, emerging structure in which manufacturing and logistics systems in the form of cyber-physical production systems (CPPSs) intensively use the globally available information and communications network for an extensively automated exchange of information and in which production and business processes are matched (Lars et al., 2016).

The concept of Industry 4.0 is based on digital technologies (Kagermann, 2015) to which it adds the new technologies of the Fourth Industrial Revolution to create CPPSs, and the architecture was presented by Lee et al. (2015). Kagermann (2015) emphasized that digitalization is at the core of change. Manufacturing in Industry 4.0 is a synergy of the activities of state-of-the-art Operations Technology (OT) and innovative Informatic Technology (IT). Intensive use of both information and communication technologies (ICTs) is taking place in Industry 4.0 companies. ICT combines all available technologies and enables the transmission of information and its processing. The conceptual scope of ICT includes all communication media (Internet, wireless networks, Bluetooth networks, telephone, and audio and video communication technologies), devices enabling the storage of information (memory sticks, hard disks, CD/DVDs, tapes, etc.), and its processing (personal computers, servers, clusters, etc.). In addition, ICT technologies also include IT

DOI: 10.4324/9781032697611-1

applications and complex IT systems that enable the processing and transmission of data at a higher level of abstraction than hardware. Industry 4.0 needs autonomous and collaborative robots that perform repetitive tasks more accurately than humans and that communicate with each other. Robots in Industry 4.0 are becoming increasingly autonomous, flexible, and collaborative. Robots have an increasing range of capabilities. Robots are being designed that are able to interact with each other and work safely side-by-side with humans, learning from them (Bahrin et al., 2016). For the communication and learning process, Internet of Thing and Internet of Services (IoT and IoS) are needed. Industrial Internet of Things (IIoT) is constantly developing and supporting process improvement and automation, optimizing understanding of needs, customer service, and facilitating decision-making in businesses (World Economic Forum, January 2015).

Industry 4.0 is assumed to be the general concept of technical changes in the production environment with technologies typical of the Fourth Industrial Revolution. In the history of the development of civilization, there have been three industrial revolutions, characterized by disruptive changes in economic processes and resulting in productivity growth (this growth is assumed to be by leaps and bounds). The First Industrial Revolution involved activities related to the use of water power, which resulted in the creation of the steam engine and contributed to the development of mechanical tools. The Second Industrial Revolution was the result of the invention of electricity, which enabled mass production on production lines. The Third Industrial Revolution was a scientific and technological revolution consisted of the automation of production processes using electronics and IT tools. The Third Industrial Revolution developed into the Fourth Industrial Revolution in highly developed countries called the era of Industry 4.0. Grumpos (2021) writes that the First is named Mechanical Revolution, the Second Electrical Revolution, the Third Automated Revolution, and the Fourth Digital Revolution.

The industrial revolution of the fourth stage is caused by (Buxo, 2015):

- the introduction of ubiquitous digitization and development of Internet including IIoT,
- the reliance in decision-making processes on virtual simulations and real-time data processing,
- collaborative robots and artificial intelligence (AI),
- machine-to-machine (M2M) and machine-to-people (M2P) communication,
- horizontal and vertical systems integration, and
- augmented reality.

The Fourth Industrial Revolution is about the deep automation of production processes, but also of logistics processes, ordering supplies, personalizing products, collaborating with co-operators and consumer markets, and streamlining supply chains. In Industry 4.0, much of the production will be in smart and digitized factories. In such factories, computerized production systems equipped with network links to established digital twin systems communicate with other facilities and transmit data about the equipment itself. The networking of all systems leads to the emergence of 'cyber-physical production systems' and smart factories in which production systems, components, and people communicate via networks, and production takes place almost autonomously (Lasi et al., 2014).

Every industrial revolution changes the industries. In the steel sector under study, which has influenced human development for ages, industrial revolutions have also introduced many technological changes. The development of metallurgy accelerated with the construction of the steam engine. Although the birth of the modern steel mill was only in the 19th century. After the Second Industrial Revolution – the electrification of industrial processes – the productivity of steel production increased. In 1856, H. Bessmer designed the first pear-shaped converter for steel production (Bielański, 2002). In 1864, the French metallurgist Pierre-Émil Martin developed the process of smelting steel in a regenerative furnace (Encyclopedia, PWN, online). These innovations were very important because they paved the way for modern steelmaking technologies, referred to as Electric Arc Furnace (EAF) and Basic Oxygen Furnace (BOF), i.e. electric steel plants and integrated steel plants (blast furnaces and converters). In the Third Industrial Revolution, steelmaking technologies were combined with computers. An important step in the development of steelmaking processes was Computer Integrated Manufacturing (CIM), i.e. the integration of computers into planning and production processes to control the entire steelmaking process. Technological developments have led to significant automation of steel production, reducing manual labour and further increasing productivity. Technological change has been accompanied by changes in management methods. World Class Manufacturing (WCM), with its ten pillars (Gajdzik, 2013), expanded with Six Sigma and Lean Management, has influenced better organization of production by removing inefficient operations. In the ongoing Fourth Industrial Revolution, steel mills – world steel producers ranked by the World Steel Association – proceeded to build smart steel manufacturing (Gajdzik, 2022a,b). The word 'smart' is often used to describe technologies working in augmented reality in steel companies. Even the Fourth Industrial Revolution has become Industry 4.0 (Bonner, 2017). According to Groumpos et al. (2021) name Industry 4.0 has itself "revolutionized" the perception and understanding of major innovative scientific and technological achievements that drive each so-called "industrial revolution".

The concept of Industry 4.0 has its main pillars, which are described by the technologies of the Fourth Industrial Revolution (Table 1.1). In their works, authors of scientific publications, consultants, scientific institutes, and consulting companies describe different configurations of the Industry 4.0 pillars with their respective technologies or technological features (Sinderman et al., 2016; Erboz, 2017; Burrell, 2019; Senn, 2019; Rüßmann et al. from Deloitte, 2015; BCG, 2017; Machado et al., 2019; Bahrin et al., 2016). Some authors have mentioned nine main pillars of Industry 4.0 in their work (Senn, 2019; Burrell, 2019; Grumpos, 2021) and others more (Saniuk et al., 2020; Gajdzik, 2022a). Main pillars of Industry 4.0 are: Internet of Things and Internet of Services, Big Data and Big Data Analytics, Advanced Simulation, Cloud Computing, Cyber-Physical Systems, Universal Integration, Augmented Reality, Additive Manufacture (including Printing 3D, AI

Table 1.1 Essence of main pillars of Industry 4.0

Pillar	*Short description*
IoT	IoT gives us the ability to realize smart manufacturing. The Industrial Internet of Things enriches more and more devices with embedded computing. The Industrial Internet of Things allows field devices to communicate and interact both with one another and with a more centralized controller, as necessary.
Big data & analytics	Companies can manage data to optimize processes. Big data and analytics enable the collection and comprehensive evaluation of data from many different sources and customers to support real-time decision-making, optimize production process, save energy, and improve equipment service and product quality.
Cloud computing	Harvesting large quantities of data involves careful management, and providing a 'Data warehouse' facility to organizations is invaluable. As technology becomes more efficient, data and machine functionality will increasingly be deployed in the cloud. The cloud enables the use of services for the production system: sharing data between locations and company boundaries.
Advanced simulation	Complex algorithms and testing them allow for new projects. Simulations are leverage real-time data to mirror the physical world in a virtual model, which can include machines, products, and humans. This allows operators to test and optimize the machine settings for the next product in line in the virtual world before the physical changeover, thereby driving down machine setup times and increasing quality.
Autonomous systems	More systems in business are becoming autonomous and need less human intervention to provide effective results.
Universal integration	Integrating Factory Test equipment and a bespoke Manufacturing Execution System can enable remote access and feedback into product test yield, improving projections.
Augmented reality	By creating computer-generated perceptual information, it is becoming easier to train your staff, even in unique and difficult conditions. In manufacturing process, augmented-reality-based systems can support a variety of services, such as selecting parts in a warehouse and sending repair instructions over mobile devices.
Additive manufacture	Application of AM techniques to achieve fast market entry and creative solutions is becoming more important in a competitive environment. 3D printing is used for personal use in companies (e.g. the printing of spare parts) or for commercial purposes. Additive manufacturing methods can also be used in Industry 4.0 to produce small batches of customized products that offer construction advantages, such as complex, lightweight designs. High-performance, decentralized additive manufacturing systems will reduce transport distances and stock on hand.
Cyber security	Security of your infrastructure, both online and offline is a business critical factor. Bespoke systems design will ensure your organizations' Data Integrity. Communication and advanced identity and access management for machines and users must be secure. The importance of cyber security is increasing with increased connectivity and use of standardized communication protocols.
Autonomous robots	Human labour is getting more expensive, so robots are replacing humans. Humans are now collaborating with robots. Robots are becoming more autonomous, flexible, and cooperative. Robots will have a greater range of capabilities than those used in manufacturing today.

Source: Own elaboration based on: Burrell (2019), Bahrin (2016).

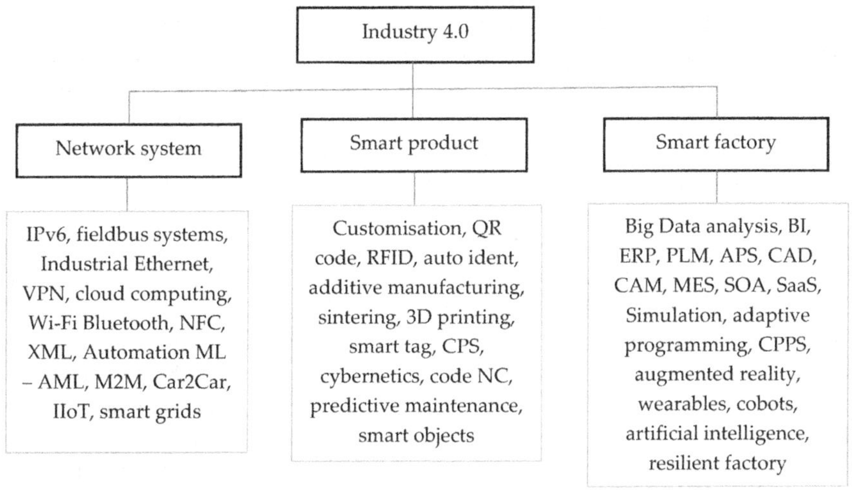

Figure 1.1 Key subtechnologies used within the Industry 4.0 concept in the company.
Source: Own elaboration based on Pieriegud (2016).

and Learning Machines, Autonomous Robots/Cobots) and Cognitive Computing, and Cyber Security.

According to Culot et al. (2020), Industry 4.0 is a set of technologies that consists of technologies connecting physical and digital objects, advanced networking solutions, data processing technologies, technologies relating to physical operations in processes, and digital process support. Industry 4.0 technologies work together and transmit, in the course of this collaboration, Big data. Advanced network solutions and data processing technologies require cloud computing, the Internet of Things, and cyber security systems. Technologies relating to processes enable, among other things, additive manufacturing. Simulation techniques are also used at this stage to improve processes and optimize them (Frank et al., 2019). Main Industry 4.0 technologies consist of sub-technologies or otherwise sub-pillars or sub-categories (Figure 1.1). The link for technological interaction is 'digitality'. The Internet in Industry 4.0 has taken on a new meaning by strengthening its role in creating new opportunities for producers, employees, and customers. In a network of vertical and horizontal relationships, collaboration using cyber technology in the global business space is being realized. Industry 4.0 is based on a potential IT/OT application that creates a cycle of relationships: physical-to-digital-to-physical (Sniderman et al., 2016). Collaborative technologies to ensure interoperability, decentralization, virtualization, modularity, and interoperability (Hermann et al., 2015).

After a decade since the concept of Industry 4.0 was introduced, it has become a capacious architecture for a new business model describing the principles of production of goods and services, which is characterized by moving towards the digitization and automation of production and service environments (Lee et al., 2014; Lasi et al., 2014; Oesterreich and Teuteberg, 2016; Sreedharan and Unnikrishnan,

2017). It has been noted that industrial automation systems enable the creation of new and innovative functions by accessing the networks and cyberspace to create entirely new business frameworks, processes, and deployment methods, which are having an increasingly powerful impact on the performance of organizations.

The idea of Industry 4.0 allows products, machines, components, people, and systems to form an intelligent network (Sreedharan and Unnikrishnan, 2017; Kamble, Gunasekaran and Gawankar, 2018) that can integrate systems cyber-physical to act quickly by combining information and memory physical with an intelligent network to serve customers more quickly and efficiently (Erol et al., 2016; Saldivar et al., 2015; Shafiq et al., 2016). Industry 4.0 can deliver smarter services and make processes seamless across different sectors of the economy. In addition, manufacturers can empower their customers by responding to their needs through technologies such as 3D printing, cloud applications, mobile devices, and big data, creating a whole new smart environment (Almada-Lobo, 2015; Hofmann and Rüsch, 2017). Customers collaborating with the manufacturer participate in the co-creation of the product. Products are personalized, i.e. designed and manufactured for specific customers according to their expectations, predispositions, and even dreams (Bauernhansl et al., 2014).

1.2 Sustainability as a priority for smart manufacturing

Climate change associated with global warming led to environmental degradation. This is the price that we are all paying for unsustainable practices. The general public is increasingly more aware of the situation, and more people are willing to purchase products manufactured in a sustainable manner. The manufacturing industry is responsible for 23% of the global greenhouse gas emissions. Sustainable manufacturing can make a major impact by slowing down environmental degradation. According to the Paris Climate Agreement (COP21), industry needs to lower carbon emissions by 45% by 2050 as well as eliminates waste and optimizes the supply chain and a product's lifecycle.

Smart manufacturing and the Internet of Things are making those tasks achievable. The governments of most countries support and enforce sustainability standards as well as provide financial incentives for the development of sustainable manufacturing practices. At the same time, more customers are likely to buy products manufactured using sustainable technologies. Sustainable manufacturing companies usually demonstrate a higher growth rate and higher profit.

Smart manufacturing is becoming a standard industry practice. The main benefits of smart manufacturing are the following (Bonilla et al., 2018):

- increased productivity,
- increased efficiency in the manufacturing process, and
- increased sustainability in the manufacturing process.

Smart manufacturing allows the company to make the product faster and less expensive as well as increases the variety of the product. Prior to smart manufacturing, those two goals could not be accomplished simultaneously. Presently a company can adjust the variety of products by analysing the sales data and prices in real time. The results of this analysis allow the company to maximize profit and minimize overproduction. This analysis also allows for more efficient use of raw materials. The efficient use of raw materials and minimizing waste increase the sustainability of the operation. The advanced smart-manufacturing technologies create a conducive environment towards ecofriendly practices (Pusavec et al., 2010).

Smart manufacturing creates opportunities to incorporate many environmentally friendly practices. In smart manufacturing, several key advantages come into play. First, real-time data collection and the Internet of Things facilitate the optimization of the supply chain. This not only leads to more efficient logistics but also reduces transportation costs and emissions. Another notable benefit is increased energy efficiency. By utilizing real-time monitoring systems, smart manufacturing can effectively manage and reduce energy consumption. Furthermore, the integration of Internet of Things technology and real-time data collection enables the optimization of maintenance plans. This, in turn, greatly extends the lifespan of machines and minimizes downtime, improving overall productivity. Additionally, smart manufacturing contributes to waste reduction through its ability to efficiently use raw materials and minimize waste production.

Implementing sustainable manufacturing needs to happen from the top down. Transformation to sustainable manufacturing is normally a three-step procedure:

1 Plan
2 Execute the plan
3 Reflect on the results

From the sustainability perspective, all manufacturing operations and processes need to be performed in environmentally friendly ways (Fleith de Medeiros et al., 2014). Industry 4.0 creates many opportunities to develop environment-friendly sustainable solutions while still generating a reasonable profit. Sustainable practices improve the company's image and attract clients who are concerned about the environment.

Manufacturing is improving the quality of life, but this often happens at the expense of the environment. It is necessary to learn better manufacturing methods which do not harm the environment. Industry 4.0 is being viewed as an opportunity to implement sustainable environment-friendly manufacturing methods. Smart manufacturing and collecting a large amount of real-time data allow for a better understanding of manufacturing processes from the perspective of energy consumption as well as waste and pollution generated by the process.

This mindset creates a great opportunity for developing a plan to eliminate waste as well as decrease energy consumption and any kind of pollution. The holistic approach increases the sustainability of manufacturing and decreases the negative environmental and social impacts of manufacturing.

Sustainable manufacturing is becoming a long-term goal for most progressive manufacturing companies. The benefits of sustainable manufacturing are as follows:

- Gaining public endorsement by improving a company's reputation
- Complying with future regulatory requirements
- Securing long-term economic growth and validity
- Reaching new environmentally conscious customers
- Improving manufacturing efficiency by the reduction of waste

More customers consider the environmental impact of the product that they are purchasing. Manufacturing companies take many measures and methods to improve sustainability of the processes (Rüßmann et al., 2015).

Manufacturers are actively working to reduce their environmental footprint by implementing strategies aimed at decreasing pollution. This includes using environmentally friendly materials such as non-toxic and biodegradable substances. Additionally, they are revising their manufacturing technologies to reduce or eliminate pollution, while enforcing strict procedures for handling hazardous materials. Real-time pollution-monitoring systems and pollution control measures are being deployed to monitor air and water quality and to install systems that control pollution of air and water from manufacturing plants.

Manufacturing companies are embracing the principles of a circular economy by developing plans to incorporate recycled materials into their processes. This not only reduces waste but also promotes sustainability by reusing resources efficiently. Additionally, waste management and recycling programmes are being established throughout the production process, ensuring that materials are properly managed and reused where possible.

Energy efficiency is a paramount concern for sustainable manufacturing. Manufacturers are investing in energy-saving equipment such as LED lights, energy-efficient HVAC systems, and motors. Real-time energy management systems are being implemented to monitor and control real-time energy consumption, ensuring that energy is used more efficiently. Furthermore, manufacturers are exploring renewable energy resources, such as solar, wind, and geothermal power generation systems, to reduce their reliance on non-renewable energy sources. Frequent energy audits are conducted to develop and implement energy-saving plans, further contributing to sustainability goals.

Efficiency is key in sustainable manufacturing. Manufacturers are implementing continuous quality improvement procedures, which involve regular assessments and incremental improvements to enhance both product quality and manufacturing processes. Optimizing manufacturing processes helps reduce production time and maximize efficiency. The lean manufacturing concept is also being embraced to reduce excess inventory and eliminate waste, promoting a more streamlined and sustainable production process.

Sustainable manufacturing starts from the product design (design for lean manufacturing). To conserve natural resources, the design process needs to consider repairability and remanufacturing ability of the product (Zawadzki and Zywicki, 2016). Remanufacturing is the process of reusing the parts of discarded products to make another product (Kishawy et al., 2018). This is part of *industrial symbiosis* (Rosen and Kishawy, 2012).

The manufacturing process needs to be optimized with fewer production steps to lower energy and labour costs (Shrouf et al., 2014). Sustainable manufacturing needs to produce sustainable products, but also needs to be sustainable from the social and environmental perspectives (Romero, 2020).

Manufacturing companies need to work with the suppliers to reduce or eliminate the waste of the packaging materials. Using local suppliers reduces the cost of transportation and reduces some of the needs for packaging.

Sustainable manufacturing not only protects the environment, but also decreases the cost of the manufacturing process. The state government in many states in the United States offer help and incentives to sustainable manufacturing companies moving into the area. The Environmental Protection Agency (EPA) in the United States defines sustainable manufacturing as follows (Sobaszek et al., 2017):

- reducing the use of energy, water, and other resources;
- reducing the waste of raw materials and other resources;
- providing increased workplace safety for employees; and
- reducing emissions and pollution.

Distribution and shipment of the product is also taking a negative toll on the environment. The shipping industry contributes significantly to global carbon emission. COVID-19 demonstrated the inefficiency of the supply chain. The general public became more aware of the inefficiency of the supply chain and the shipping industry (Jasiulewicz-Kaczmarek and Saniuk, 2015). Sustainable manufacturing is making considerable progress increasing efficiency and reducing the number of steps in the supply chain as well as reducing the number of suppliers.

Changes in the manufacturing industry directly affect the shipping industry (Müller et al., 2018). Sustainability of the supply chain as well as sustainability of the shipping industry are at the forefront of the change. Shippers are looking for various methods to enhance sustainability in daily operations. Analysis of fuel usage and emissions of carbon dioxide is usually the first step in addressing the sustainability of the shipping industry. Approximately 35% of the time trucks are driving empty.

Eliminating and reducing empty miles is very important for increasing the sustainability of the shipping industry. Automated dispatch software allows for better flexibility in making last-minute adjustments needed to eliminate empty miles. Eliminating empty miles also creates safer conditions for the drivers. Empty trailers are hard to control in bad weather conditions.

In the United States *Smart Way Transport Partnership* is an organization with the objective of helping to manage logistics more efficiently and sustainably. Sustainability of the shipping industry is also being improved by changing packaging materials into organic ecofriendly and biodegradable. Research is being conducted in bioplastics produced from vegetable fats and other biodegradable materials.

There are also initiatives to streamline marketing operations for the purpose of conducting marketing in more sustainable ways. Electronic databases are being used and updated frequently to replace very inefficient bulk mailing methods.

1.3 Human factor in Industry 4.0 towards creativity and innovativeness

In the last two decades, we have witnessed the changes associated with the Fourth Industrial Revolution. Advanced robotics, machine learning, artificial intelligence (AI), nanotechnology, genetics, and biotechnology have become part of our everyday life.

The advancements in technologies rapidly change the hard and soft skills requirements of the workforce. Those skill requirements are changing faster than ever before. The current and future workforces need to keep up and stay at the forefront of those changes (Zhou et al., 2015). The skills for the future were published in the Future of Job's Report: World Economic Forum 2020. The future's most critical job skills in this report were as follows:

- complex problem-solving ability,
- critical thinking skills,
- creativity,
- people management skills,
- ability to coordinate with others,
- emotional intelligence skills,
- judgment and decision-making skills,
- service orientation,
- negotiation skills,
- cognitive flexibility,
- entrepreneurial thinking,
- conflict-solving skills,
- analytical thinking,
- growth mindset,
- interpersonal communication skills,
- technology skills,
- virtual collaboration skills,
- data analysis and visualization skills,
- appreciation for diversity,
- social intelligence, and
- computational thinking.

This list will change rapidly as technology progresses (Benesova and Tupa, 2017). The Fourth Industrial Revolution will lead to the elimination of many jobs. Those are positions which are easy to automate. Simultaneously Industry 4.0 has created many opportunities for employment. Talent and human expertise cannot be automated.

The Fourth Industrial Revolution (Industry 4.0) like the previous three industrial revolutions is driven by the human side and is relying on human knowledge, expertise, and talent (Lorenz et al., 2015). Machines in smart factories are communicating with each other or even self-optimizing the manufacturing process and responding to market demands. Many people are concerned that highly automated *smart manufacturing systems* will be replacing human labour. This is not entirely true. Easily automated human labour will be eliminated and replaced by many new positions requiring advanced degrees and specialized skills (Liao et al., 2017). Those newly created positions are normally high-paying jobs. Smart manufacturing process allows the workforce to focus on the tasks that only humans can perform. Those tasks require creativity, imagination, innovativeness, and teamwork. Some of those new positions include the following (Mosconi, 2015):

- Equipment Systems Engineer
- Data Scientist
- Control Systems Engineer
- Automation Engineer
- Validation Engineer
- Systems Designer
- Project Manager
- Robotics Engineer

Digital transformation is only possible if the required high-skilled workers are available (Gorecky, 2014). Relocating existing employees to new positions within the company is a popular practice. Retraining the existing workforce for new positions is a major challenge for many companies. There is a prediction that in the United States, 40% of the production employees will need to be retrained for new positions within the next ten years. In the United States, community colleges play a major role in retraining the existing workforce to prepare them for new roles within the company.

The human side of Industry 4.0 is as important as ever before (Shafiq, 2016). The demand for highly skilled digital technology workers is constantly increasing and sometimes exceeds the number of jobs eliminated because of the process of automation. Highly automated intelligent production systems are still driven by humans and rely on human intervention. The need for human intervention became very interdisciplinary (Kagermann, 2015).

The highly automated digital production systems are vulnerable to cyberattacks as well as misinformation and misinterpretation of the collective data. There is an ongoing need for interpretation of the data collected by machines for management and decision-making purposes. The human side is always needed to supplement artificial intelligence (AI). Industry 4.0 requires ongoing sophisticated employee training to achieve *operational excellence* (Proctor and Wilkins, 2019).

Behind a smart manufacturing system and artificial intelligence, there is always a human side. Human talent and knowledge were needed to design and build smart manufacturing systems. Humans have also developed algorithms for machines to communicate with each other and learn. Humans are also responsible for entering the right data into the machines as well as analysing the business results (Bayram and Ince, 2018). Even though the machines are smart enough to communicate with each other, they fail periodically and need human intervention (Nardo et al., 2020). The main driving force in Industry 4.0 is still human involvement.

Elon Musk, CEO of Tesla, acknowledged in an interview that one of his mistakes was putting too much emphasis on digital technology and underestimating the human factor. Presently, after gaining experience in implementing Industry 4.0, more emphasis is being placed on the human factor and machine-human interaction.

There are many challenges in implementing Industry 4.0. Some of the challenges are as follows: (Kane et al., 2015).

- developing new business models and strategies,
- revising organizational processes,
- managing change and developing a new company culture,
- connecting different departments for the purpose of better collaboration, and
- securing the information technology (IT) system from the perspective of cyberthreats and data privacy protection.

Many manufacturing companies are adapting Industry 4.0 technology without a detailed plan of retraining existing employees to lower the skill gap created by the new technology (Saniuk et al., 2020a).

All the methods mentioned above have been proven to be effective. Selection of the reskilling method depends on the nature, requirements, and location of the company. It also depends on the company's budget and the age of the workforce. A hybrid approach combining two or three methods can be very effective.

In the era of Industry 4.0, the integration of smart technologies into manufacturing and industrial processes has brought about a transformative wave of benefits. These advantages, as outlined by Motyl et al. (2017), are not only reshaping the way industries operate but also improving their overall performance and competitiveness. One of the standout benefits of Industry 4.0 is the enhanced flexibility and agility it offers to businesses. With the integration of smart technologies, industries can quickly adapt to changing market conditions, customer demands, and unforeseen disruptions. This adaptability ensures that companies can respond swiftly to challenges and opportunities, ultimately improving their resilience in a dynamic business environment.

Smart technologies have proven to be catalysts for significantly increased productivity and efficiency in manufacturing. Automation, real-time data analysis, and optimized resource allocation streamline processes, reducing waste and increasing output. This boost in productivity often translates into higher profitability, as costs are minimized, and production capacity is maximized. Quality assurance is paramount in manufacturing, and Industry 4.0 empowers businesses to maintain a real-time focus on quality improvement. Through data-driven insights and real-time monitoring, companies can identify and rectify issues more swiftly, ensuring that the products they deliver consistently meet or exceed quality standards.

The use of smart technologies in manufacturing leads to improved product quality. Automated processes, precision manufacturing, and real-time quality checks reduce defects and errors, resulting in higher-quality products that meet or even exceed customer expectations. This, in turn, bolsters a company's reputation and customer trust. Industry 4.0 enables businesses to provide a more personalized and tailored consumer experience. With the data collected and analysed, companies can understand customer preferences, needs, and behaviours. Products and services can be more rapidly customized. This not only enhances customer satisfaction but also fosters brand loyalty.

Innovation is a cornerstone of competitiveness in modern business and manufacturing sites. Industry 4.0 technologies create opportunities for innovation by fostering the development of new products, processes, and business models. With increased connectivity and data-driven insights, companies can explore uncharted territories and stay at the forefront of their respective industries.

Industry 4.0 creates friendly environments towards innovativeness and attracts individuals with high innovative potential (Grzelczak et al., 2018). Richard Florida conducted research related to innovative people clustering together and creating highly innovative cities. Many of those innovative cities are in California. The state of California with Silicon Valley is the area where many modern smart technologies were developed (Florida, 2002).

The number of patents granted per 1,000 residents per year in some highly innovative cities reaches 50 patents per 1,000 residents per year which is 50 times higher than the national average of .96 patents per 1,000 residents per year. Highly innovative cities are always very prosperous. They have a much higher percentage of highly educated people (sometimes two times the national average). Those cities are normally very diverse with many immigrants, different nationalities, and minority groups. Diversity is conducive towards innovativeness, and innovativeness is conducive to diversity (Florida and Gates, 2001).

1.4 Steel management in a dynamic surrounding

Modern organizations operate in a very dynamic surrounding. The surrounding is a set of economic, social, legal, ecological, and other factors in which the business is realized (Griffin, 2002). There are several internal and external factors in the surrounding that can influence business decisions. Different combinations of these factors, like price, social changes, and market regulators, can influence the market where a business operates. The environment within which economic entities operate exerts a pivotal influence on organizational management decisions, significantly impacting the activities of modern organizations through interactive dynamics. Changes in the surrounding cause changes in the conditions of functioning of the organization. A characteristic feature of the modern economic surrounding is its volatility, high unpredictability, and the magnitude and parallelism of processes and transformations (Drucker et al., 2008; Griffin, 2002; Peters and Waterman, 2004; Porter, 2008; Listwan, 2008). Each organization has to adapt to changes to keep a good position in your market. Change is something inevitable. For an organization, it is a necessity, but also an opportunity for growth. The changes that occur in a company's surroundings are visible in its structure and strategy. For companies to survive and compete in a competitive market, they must quickly and effectively adapt to, follow, and even anticipate emerging changes.

In the Fourth Industrial Revolution, the surrounding in which the organizations conduct business are packed with new intelligent and high technologies. Along with the growing automation and autonomy of production, new business organization opportunities are emerging. Factories turn into smart factories, i.e. companies based, to a large extent, on digital assets. The challenge for every industry is the transition from a hierarchical, multi-level company structure to an organization where internal units communicate with each other directly, regardless of the organizational level. These units will also communicate with the outside digital world as well as with other devices, enabling the development of the Internet of Things. In addition, as part of Industry 4.0, each product in its life cycle will have a digital representation – from design, testing, through production, service, and even to recycling according to the model of production and consumption that is called "circular economy" (Circular Economy Action Plan, Brussel, 11 March 2020).

Industry 4.0 is expected to influence four long-term relationship paradigm shifts that are going to change the landscape of the European Manufacturing (Santos et al. (2017) based on EFFRA, 2013): (1) Factory and Nature, (2) Factory and Local Communities, (3) Factory and Value Chains, and (4) Factory and Humans. In the first area are expected improvements in resource efficiency and sustainability of manufacturing systems. In the second area, new technologies can increase geographical proximity and acceptance of external customers in design and manufacturing processes. The changes in the third area concern the new forms of chains that will be formed by distributed and responsive manufacturing through collaborative processes, enabling mass customization of products and services. Fourth areas are human-oriented interfaces and improved work conditions (Santos et al., 2017). The concept of Santos's relations was adapted to the steel sector (industry) and presented in Figure 1.2. Now the relations are: (1) Steelworks and Nature, (2) Steelworks and Local Communities, (3) Steelworks and Value Chain, and (4) Steelworks and Humans. The individual areas of the relationship are connected by the "lens" of sustainability. The image using the "lens" reflects the key direction of changes in the ongoing transformation of the steel industry in the EU. The challenges for the European steel industry are the following (Branca et al., 2020; Gajdzik et al., 2023, McKinsey, 2001):

- Ensuring continuous reaction of steelworks to market needs and securing the position of European steelworks on the global steel.
- Maintaining the competitiveness of the steel industry in the highly developed countries of the European Union thanks to efficient processes and cost and resource savings – the principle: maximizing steel production efficiency and minimizing production costs.

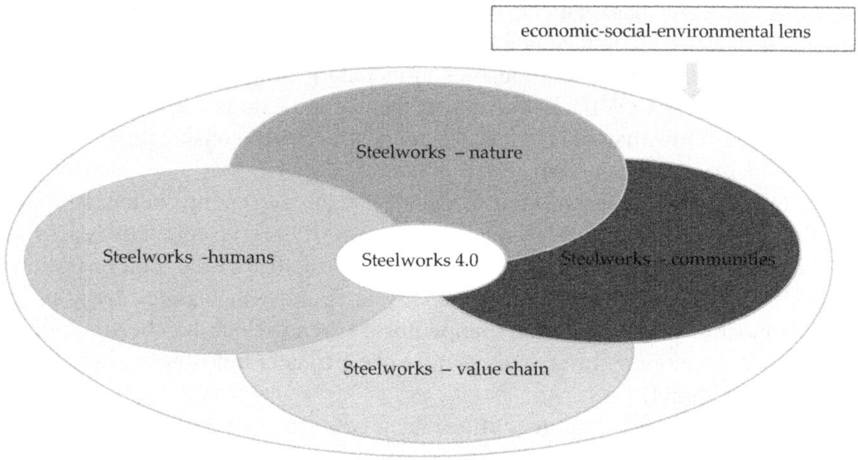

Figure 1.2 Relationship paradigm for steelworks in Industry 4.0.

Source: Own elaboration based on Santos's classification.

- Achieving higher quality of steel products through the use of advanced manufacturing technologies – directions: smart steel manufacturing (SSM) and customization of steel products.
- Activation of steel capital (especially from EU countries) on the global steel market through investments in new low-emission (even zero-emission) steel production technologies – direction: deep decarbonization in the steel industry, market, sharing production assets, or jointly producing inputs such as hydrogen or DRI by world steel producers.
- Maintaining the flexibility of steel production and ensuring the validity of supplies in a dynamic and labile environment – direction: resilience in the steel supply chain.
- Protection of the European market against the strong competition of steelworks from the Asian market and the dominance of the Chinese steel industry on a global scale under the conditions of continuation of a strong environmental protection policy – direction: sustainable steel production (a proposal of the Global Forum on Steel Excess Capacity (GFSEC) (BMWi, 2020).
- Development of new market segments: electric vehicles or electrical steel for use in electric motors, grids, renewable energy plants, new constructions for buildings, etc.
- Spreading digitization across operational and commercial functions – digital transformation across the value chain – from procurement (for example, predictive pricing algorithms and automated contract management) to production (such as digitally enabled maintenance and automation of internal logistics) to sales and the go-to-market approach, in which B2B customers are increasingly buying online and becoming less loyal and more demanding of a smooth customer journey.

- Costs and cash management, including raw-material flexibilization steel producers may need to renegotiate their sales contracts with automotive, machinery and equipment, and other industries to include floating instead of fixed prices (after the fall of COVID-19 and during the war in Ukraine (in the first months), the prices of raw materials in the steel market increased considerably, which led to an increase in production costs).
- Reducing energy consumption in the steel industry (energy intensive industries (EII), energy costs are one of the main drivers of competitiveness for the EU steel sector. Energy costs represent up to 40% of the total operational costs of steelmaking. European industry is faced with higher energy prices than most of its international competitors, a trend which has been amplified by price development in recent years) (The EU steel industry: website of the European Union).
- Reducing martials – resources efficiency (access to raw materials is crucial for the steelmaking industry and resources are scarce in Europe) – more on policy and strategy for raw materials: COM2016 https://single-market-economy.ec.europa.eu/sectors/raw-materials/policy-and-strategy-raw-materials_en. (coking coal is on the list of critical raw materials CRMs in EU: COM2023).

The key area of influence of the steel industry is the natural. Although sustainability has been a strategic direction for many economies in the world since the 1970s, there is still much to be done (Report of the World Commission on Environment and Development: "Our common future" [Brundtland report]. New York: UN, 4 Aug. 1987). The purpose of the smart steelworks (synonymous name: steelworks 4.0) in this relationship is to reduce the negative impact of metallurgical technologies on the environment. In the European steel industry, reducing the negative impact of steel plants on the environment is the basic direction of climate neutrality policies. The determinants of steelwork sustainability are, above all, low-emission CO_2 and resource efficiency and, in particular, the reduction of energy intensity in the sector. Green steel (the project: Green Steel for Europe acronym: GREENSTEEL) is included in the European Green Deal (11 Oct. 2019, COM/2019/640). In sustainable steel production, the emphasis is on achieving lower levels of carbon dioxide emissions by steelworks, and even zero emissions by 2050. The steel industry is responsible for around 5% of CO_2 emissions in the EU and 7% globally (IEA, 2020). CO_2 emissions and energy use in European steel production have already been halved since 1960, and the sector aims to achieve further cuts of 80–95% by 2050 (IEA, 2020), compared to 1990 levels (Vogl et al., 2018).

The priority programmes on the EU market are considered to be European Union, projects to reduce carbon dioxide emissions and renewable energy sources (programmes: RFCS, Europe Horizon). Since the conventional Blast Furnace – Basic Oxygen Furnace production route is highly CO_2-intensive (usually with a carbon footprint of 1.6–2.0 tonnes of CO_2 per tonne of crude steel produced) and most EU steel mills are operating close to optimum efficiency, the industry is increasingly focussing on hydrogen-based steelmaking to decarbonize the sector. The production of low-carbon steel requires the development of new metallurgical technologies.

The future belongs to new steel plants with steel production processes based on the direct reduction of iron using hydrogen. The REPowerEU plan (launched in May 2022) helps the Union: save energy, produce green energy, diversify energy supply; highlights that around 30% of the primary steel production in the EU is expected to be decarbonized by 2030 using renewable hydrogen according to EU climate targets (JRC news, 15 June 2022). European research into applied technologies for reducing carbon dioxide emissions focuses on three areas: Carbon Direct Avoidance (CDA), Process Integration (PI), and Carbon Capture, Storage, and Usage (CCSU).

European plans and programmes are reflected in the strategies of the corporations (strong steel groups). Companies strategies of sustainability are usually a part of corporate social responsibility (CSR). The European Union has been promoting CSR and sealing the scope of reporting on this activity for years (EC, 2001). In the current industrial transformation, steelworks are actively involved in activities for socially responsible business. The largest steel companies (strong capital groups on the global steel market) annually report their results for the benefit of the environment, society, employees, and other stakeholder groups. Sustainable development is based on the concept of eco-efficiency. Economy and ecology are combined as a win-win concept. Ecological innovations are carried out in the case of simultaneous economic advantages. The goal is to reduce costs due to an increased efficiency of resources (materials and energy) and reduced amounts of wastes and emissions. In sustainability management, innovation, productivity, and cost savings are necessary for business (Baumgartner, 2014). In the Fourth Industrial Revolution, the scope of responsibility should be extended to the wise implementation of smart technologies. Applying the method of detailed evaluation and evaluation of the effectiveness of the measures will serve to achieve the objectives.

A multitude of conditions are created for what needs to be done to create a way to quantify what the benefits of these solutions might be. In fact, it is difficult to find universal means of use in all conditions, so each time you should carefully analyse the effects and effects of the action with the final effect. Companies must exercise due diligence in doing business. According to Governance 4.0, a world proposal for new model governance, i.e. the primacy of society and nature, must be at the core of any new governance system (Davos Agenda, 2022). On the level of corporation, good corporate governance can mean generally better relationships with all stakeholders. This helps improve social and labour relationships and aspects such as environmental protection and can help further reduce poverty and inequality (Claessens and Yurtoglu, 2012). In January 2021, the European Commission prepared new assumptions for the development of industry called Industry 5.0. Within the European perspective on Industry 5.0, emphasis is placed on the imperative of incorporating sustainability considerations into corporate strategies at the board level. It is crucial to establish clear, measurable, time-bound, and science-based sustainability objectives to gauge advancements toward these goals, as outlined in the concept of "Corporate Governance 5.0" within the European document titled "Industry 5.0, ESIR Policy Brief No. 3." What is the difference between Industry 4.0 and Industry 5.0: while Industry 4.0 is more concerned with the application of disruptive technologies, Industry 5.0 is focused on allowing a Society 5.0, with a sustainable human-centred society, by the use of those technologies from Industry 4.0.

By using technologies that are the pillars of Industry 4.0, companies (factories) will be more flexible, which will result in smart connections with other participants in the supply chain (Agile Supply Chains). The changes must concern both the manufacturing operations carried out in the Smart Factory (Chen et al., 2017) and the logistics operations that combine them, such as transport, warehousing, or service in distribution centres (Hofmann and Rüsch, 2017). It will take many years to make changes to the chains. Supply chain readiness for Industry 4.0 means executing tasks related to streamlining the flow of physical resources (time compression), real-time resource data exchange, and personalizing products (Bentyn, 2017). On the way of evolution of Supply Chains towards Autonomous Logistical Systems, there are customers and their needs. He or she wants a product tailored to his or her needs – tailor-made. Digital technologies combined with intelligent algorithms of machines are able to "talk" with the customer and create a product according to his needs. The more the products are customized, the more personalized it is. With the development of smart factories, individual personalization will turn into mass or hyper-personalization (Wang et al., 2017). The processes of personalization and customization enable better matching of products to the specific market of the recipient of products. When co-creating a product with a customer, there may be problems related to the protection of intellectual property or crossing the boundaries of fair business in the quest of manufacturers to acquire new customers. The issue of social responsibility in the context of Industry 4.0 can be a very broad area of research due to the variety of problems that may arise during the implementation of new technologies of the Fourth Industrial Revolution (Saniuk et al., 2020a, 2020b).

In the ongoing technological transformation, existing supply chain models such as the traditional one based on independent cooperation of chain participants (IMP) and the strategic one resulting from planned capital actions and strategic alliances (Ebers, 2002) will transform into spatially dispersed supply chains that will bring together new technologies. Wireless data transfer technologies together with RFID (Radio Frequency Identification) tags enable control of the position of goods in the warehouse and during transport. The spread of this technology is associated with the development of the Internet of Things. In the chains will be a growing number of objects and products having the ability to generate, transmit, and process data. The effect of this capability is the interaction between the chain links and the parent system(s) controlling the flow of resources (Schmidt et al., 2015). The increased dynamics of product lifecycles, resulting in the need to build flexible solutions across multiple stages of production and supply chain asset logistics, makes it necessary to increase the visibility of assets in the supply chain. This facilitates control and decision-making based on real-time data (Nanterme and Daugherty, 2017). This transformation involves implementing advanced IT technologies and outfitting manufacturing devices with communication modules that interface with a superior system to monitor the status and conditions of processes throughout the production chains.

The connection of the data circulation system begins at the stage of production design, through manufacturing processes, distribution, and service, and ends with the implementation of product recycling. In Industry 4.0, the chain is supported by IoT, Big Data, Data Analytics, embedded sensors, robots with great autonomy and flexibility, advanced manufacturing techniques (e.g. 3D printing), and smart products and devices that can communicate and interact with each other (Porter, and Heppelamm, 2014). Potentially, Industry 4.0 may bring about a change from isolated manufacturing activities to automated, optimized, and fully integrated product and data flow within (global) value chains (Strange and Zucchella, 2017; Zucchella et al., 2019). Industry 4.0 organizes suppliers, manufacturers, and customers in a virtual, vertically, and horizontally integrated, value chain (Nagy et al., 2018, Stock and Seliger, 2016). The next-generation digital supply chain, in Industry 4.0, is called "Supply Chain 4.0" (McKinsey, 2016, Frederico et al., 2019), and in Industry 5.0, it is called "Supply Chain 5.0" (Frederico, 2021). According to Frederico (2021) "supply chain 5.0 is a trend which will involve three main perspectives: collaborative work between humans and robots (cobots), mass customization, and personalization to customers, and a super smart society (Society 5.0)" (name "Society 5.0" was proposed by Japan in 2016) (Carayannis et al., 2020).

Under the powerfully popularized concept of Industry 4.0, the steel industry cannot stand still. Steel producers with other participants in value chain must build a new chain with Industry 4.0 technology. In modern companies, the role of innovation is growing significantly (Gajdzik, 2022a, 2022b). Companies are still focused on improving production and related processes to reduce costs and increase productivity (BCG, 2015; Dubey et al., 2022). Steel producers – leaders in the global steel market – started to build smart manufacturing. Their technological investments are being made with a strong connection to the needs and expectations of their customer markets, in particular, the expectations of the automotive and construction sectors. So the value chain in the steel sector is becoming increasingly smart.

Steel mills are strongly linked to steel product customers. Final consumers are the automotive industry (the production of cars, bodies, and car parts), construction (buildings, roads, pipelines, cable lines, and steel structures), the machine industry (e.g. mining, construction machinery, agricultural), the transport equipment industry (ships, naval constructions, and rolling stock), and the household appliances industry (washing machines, refrigerators, cookers, etc.). The demands of the steel product consumers, who are themselves, producers, are increasingly high. The processes of the steelworks and the customers of steel products are dependent on each other. Demand data for steel products makes it possible to meet consumer needs. There must be flexibility in the cooperation between producers and consumers. In the steel chain, the flexibility that comes from B2B cooperation can be bimodal, trimodal as well as multi-modal. Steel consumers, working with steel mills, initiate the process of change in steel products to adapt them to markets (Ranjan and Read, 2016). They (steel consumers) are the beneficiaries of steel product innovation, but in the innovation process, the steel mills bear the greatest risk of innovation changes (the time from design to testing to implementation of new production technologies is long, and technological investment in steel mills is very capital intensive) (Axelson et al., 2021; Richardson-Barlow et al., 2022).

In the concept of industrial transformation – Industry4.0/5.0 – technologies, no matter how advanced, cannot exist without human intervention. It serves people, and it is created and used by them. With technological progress, automation and robotization are leading to a gradual reduction in the share of the human factor in industry. Digitization of industrial plants allows you to shift the scope of activities related to broadly understood data processing and analysis towards machines. This does not change the fact that people play a decisive role in running an industrial plant. Technology can only complement human activities by freeing people from jobs where human involvement is too costly, inefficient, or dangerous. Man is subject to certain limitations both in terms of physical fitness and the ability to process information, hence the tendency to transfer the process of data collection and processing to computers. The human mind is a valuable tool, so if there is an opportunity to save this extraordinary resource by automating certain activities. Planning for the implementation of Industry 4.0 solutions should start with a reorganization. The human factor must be prepared for change. After all, plant workers will use the new systems, and the better they make use of them, the more they will believe in their implementation (Pauceanu et al., 2020).

The role of the Fourth Revolution Technology Operator is multi-tasking. An operator can be a device user, a solution mentor, a process controller, a robot assistant, a machine programmer, a mobile robot manager, a data analyst, a link between machines, an artificial intelligence teacher, and a virtual advisor (Ruppert, 2018). The scope of each role depends on the type of tasks and the type of technology supported or the types of communication and communication systems. Employee interactions with new technological solutions reduce physical effort. Working with smart machines seems to be easier than with traditional machines. The advantage of using new technologies in metallurgy is the ability to replace the metallurgist in heavy work performed under conditions particularly burdensome to his health, e.g., high or low temperature, noise, mechanical vibration, dust, and blast furnace gases. Autonomous technologies are able to perform tasks even under extreme conditions. Intelligent device sensors detect threats in their working environment. IoT devices and hybrid solutions allow you to monitor and send information about working conditions (Lee and Seppelt, 2012).

In the old systems, many activities such as perception, cognition, learning, analysis, decision-making, control, and operation were performed by employees. For example, when machining with conventional machine tools, operators had to closely observe, analyse, manipulate, and control the process. New additive technologies have much greater precision and repeatability capabilities, and products manufactured with additive technologies have higher parameters than products manufactured with traditional technologies (Bajaj et al., 2019).

Nowadays, the EU steel industry supports nearly 2.5 million jobs in the forms: direct employment: 308,000, indirect: 1,530,000, induced: 706,000 (Eurofer, 2022). The EU steel industry creates around €134.5 billion of Gross Value Added including 23.4 billion in steel mills (Eurofer, 2022). Developing a modern and competitive steel industry requires a skilled and educated workforce. In the framework of the future 'New European Skills Agenda', the Commission, in close cooperation with Member States and social partners, will seek to build a shared commitment to invest in people and their skills. The European Globalisation Adjustment Fund and the European Social Fund support workers and local communities by reducing the negative social impact of relocation – The European Software Skills Alliance (ESSA).

The most important level of change technological transformation is the functioning of enterprises in business and non-business ecosystems. Business organizations are part of an ecosystem that integrates different sectors, not just members of a particular sector. The Industry 4.0 business ecosystem should encompass a broad range of interdependencies of communities of industry, governments, industry associations, and others, extending beyond the boundaries of traditional industrial relations. Industry 4.0 is not only smart manufacturing in smart factories, but also smart cities with smart urban planning and smart housing systems, equipped with smart energy, eco-friendly materials, and smart products (more in: Stock and Seliger, 2016; Stock et al., 2018; Bonilla et al., 2018; Tuttokmaği, 2018).

Integrating the business environment, technology, communities, and governments that support industrial transformation is a key opportunity for changing companies to gain a competitive advantage. Large opportunities for organizational innovation and the diversity of organizations in ecosystems are changing the nature of economies and societies. The spatial scope of change is unlimited, meaning that local ecosystems are evolving into global ecosystems in individual business areas. Figure 1.3 shows an illustrative diagram of the impact structure of Industry 4.0 on steel mills in the broader ecosystem.

Referring to the scope shown in Figure 1.3, companies are looking for answers to the questions: How to manufacture? What to produce? For whom to boil? The technological levels of change (presented in Figure 1.3) are geared towards smart steel manufacturing. This is a level strongly linked to production engineering, planning, and operations management. The product lifecycle level coexists with the engineering design. The next level – value creation networks – requires reference to the organizational context of the business with an emphasis on business networks. This level is linked to such disciplines as business economics and knowledge management. Ecosystems of the Fourth Industrial Revolution are characterized by rapid change, radical innovation, dispersed and diverse organizational knowledge (managerial and technological), value virtualization (intangible world using ICT), existing but constantly changing objects (cyber-physical systems), expanding cyberspace, and virtual reality (Brettel et al., 2014). The last level is global conditions, i.e. the global impact of production on achieving sustainable development (Bonvoisin et al., 2017). At this stage, attention should be paid to the impact of production and

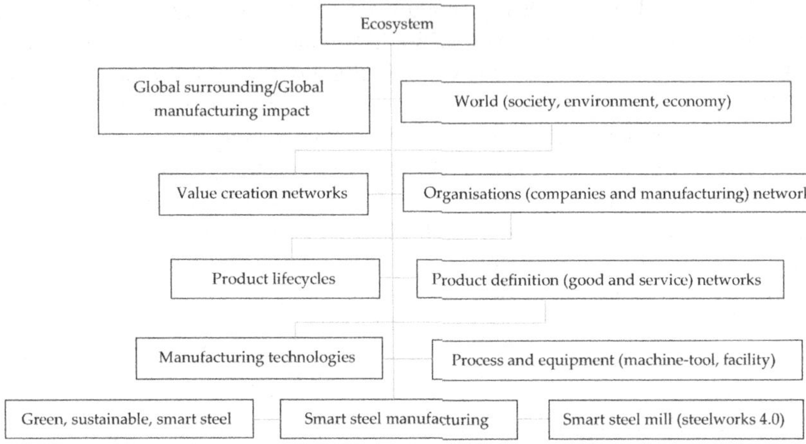

Figure 1.3 Space for steelworks 4.0.

Source: Own elaboration.

new technologies of the Fourth Industrial Revolution on the world, including on the environment, society, and economy.

According to Shmeleva and Shmelev (2019), we should still be asking ourselves: How sustainable is smart and how smart is sustainable? Companies in the Fourth Industrial Revolution should take into account the intrinsic capacity to actively co-create the business ecosystem by influencing the external environment and vice versa by exploiting the opportunities offered by the global ecosystem. From building cyber-physical systems in smart factories to creating ecosystems on a global scale, many decades will pass. The future must be sustainable, human-centric, and resilient (Industry 5.0). The modern ecosystem is strongly concentrated on the problems of sustainable development. The implementation of sustainable development (business, ecology, society, and aspects at the interface of these components) involves the attribution of management problems, and then the selection of the decision-making mechanism before selecting decisions appropriate to the situation (creative solution). Operating in an ecosystem may require a hybrid approach from businesses. A hybrid enterprise has the ability to combine the logic of action based on multiple models of dealing with tensions. The hybrid enterprise is dynamic in scopes (Battilana and Dorado, 2010): (i) ability to understand (sense) the business surrounding, (ii) ability to seize opportunities. In a highly dynamic and even periodically labile surrounding ("black swan"), companies are constantly adapting to change.

1.5 The concept of sustainable green steel

Steel is the most versatile industrial material in the world. Thousands of different grades and types of steel developed by industry make the modern world possible. Steel is 100% recyclable and therefore a fundamental part of the circular economy.

Steel, as a basic engineering material, is also an important factor in the development and implementation of innovative technologies that reduce CO_2 emissions, increase resource efficiency, and support sustainable development in economies. Unfortunately, the traditional steel production process, Blast Furnace-Basic Oxygen Furnace (BF-BOF), requires the use of large quantities of coal in blast furnaces, which contributes to an unfavourable CO_2 balance (two tonnes of carbon dioxide per tonne of steel produced). The global steel industry is responsible for 7%–9% of global CO_2 emissions (IEA, 2020; McKinsey and Company, 2020). The BF (Blast Furnace) process currently dominates the ironmaking technologies and is responsible for 80% of the total CO_2 emissions from primary iron and steel production (Nurdiawati and Urban, 2021).

Reducing the negative impact of the steel industry on the environment has been included in the economic programmes. Standards, protocols, initiatives, and government policies have an important role to play in decarbonizing the global steel industry. Recent years have seen a significant increase in the number of policy documents aimed at reducing CO_2 emissions from iron and steel production. "Green Steel" has been included in "Green Steel for Europe" (ESTEP, https://www.estep.eu/.). This project is part of the 2030 climate and energy policy and the long-term strategy for a climate-neutral Europe by 2050. "Green Steel for Europe" builds on the long-term decarbonization pathway of the steel industry. The pathway is in line with the Paris Agreement. According to the agreement, the steel industry must cut CO_2 emissions by 93% by 2050. The project is called the net zero strategy. Coal must be withdrawn from The Blast Furnace-Basic Oxygen Furnace (BF-BOF) technology. Now coal is used in the Blast Furnace-Basic Oxygen Furnace (BF-BOF) technology because it provides the thermal energy to smelt iron from iron ore lumps in a blast furnace and also provides the necessary chemical reaction.

The blast furnace (BF) process has been the major method of iron production for over 600 years (Strassburger et al., 1969). Now about 75% of the world's steel is produced in the Blast Furnace-Basic Oxygen Furnace (BF-BOF) (WorldSteel, 2022). The CO_2 emissions in primary steelmaking (BF-BOF) is 2,227 kg CO_2/tonne steel (Orth et al., 2007). Particular stages of steel manufacturing are responsible for the following shares of CO_2 emissions: ore and coke preparation emits ~20% of the total CO_2 in the BF-BOF route and the BF contributes ~70%, the steelmaking only ~11% of the total emissions (Orth et al., 2007). Moreover, the BF process is energy intensive and requires a high capital cost as it entails large infrastructure. The BF consumes around 78% of the total energy required in the BF-BOF route (Worrell et al., 2008).

In the process of deep decarbonization – the strategy "net zero" – new technologies are proposed for the steel industry. Instead of adding a mixture of ore and coke to the blast furnace and blowing finely ground coal dust, steelmakers want to blow hydrogen into the blast furnace. Because hydrogen is extremely reactive, it extracts oxygen from iron oxide and combines with it to form H_2O. Water as steam can even be used as heat energy for heating. The temperatures needed to melt iron would be provided by an electrically generated arc at the base of the blast furnace

(Sohn et al., 2016). This new technology is called DRI-EAF (Direct-Reduced Iron Technology – Electric Arc Furnace). Hydrogen is used as a reducing agent instead of natural gas. The resulting reduced iron (DRI) is further processed into green crude steel in an electric arc furnace using environmentally friendly electricity. Hydrogen is therefore crucial in the production of crude steel. The precondition is that the energy used for melting in the electric arc furnace and for the production of hydrogen by electrolysis has been generated without CO_2 emissions. The most desirable process is combustion (of course, at high temperature) of "green" hydrogen, but "blue" will also be tolerated. "Blue" hydrogen is produced from fossil fuels using carbon capture and storage technology, but "green" is result of the electrolysis of water from renewable electricity. It consists of the decomposition of water (H_2O) into oxygen (O_2) and hydrogen (H_2) under the influence of a direct electric current flowing through the electrodes in the water. "Green" hydrogen is a pure fuel (more about the perspective of "green" hydrogen in Salam et al., 2023; Al-Ghussain et al., 2023; Singh et al., 2023; Martins and Carton, 2023). Another way is to directly use renewable energy sources from suppliers instead of "black" energy. The latter option allows to reduce the import of iron ore since it mainly uses scrap metal (melted by heated electrodes). As it turns out, it is not the technologies themselves that are the problem, but all the consequences that their introduction into general use will entail.

Steelworks must decarbonize to radically reduce CO_2 emissions according to world sustainable development. The most frequently quoted definition of sustainable development is from a report of the World Commission on Environment and Development titled "Our common future", commonly known as the Brundtland Report (1987): "sustainable development is development that meets the needs of the present without compromising the ability of future generations to meet their own needs" (UN, 1987). Referring to this definition, sustainable steel production meets the needs of the present without compromising the ability of future generations to meet their own needs. In the late 1990s, the European Union published the emission standards BAT (IPPC) – Council Directive 96/61/EC on 24 September 1996 – and Reference Document for Iron and Steel Production for key environmental aspects of the steel industry by the technology used (Industrial Emissions Directive 2010/75/EU) (see: Eur-lex, 21.12.2022). In this Reference Document, direct reduction (DR) was mentioned as the future technology for the steel industry (Reference Report, 2013). A few years later, DRI (Direct Reduction Iron) technology and renewable energy plants (so-called Green Hydrogen) were mentioned in the European strategy "net zero" strategy. The development of DRI technology and clean hydrogen (carbon-free) are part of the Green Steel World and the European Steel Industry Climate Policy as part of the 2050 climate neutrality objective. The adaptation of steel companies to the requirements of Industry 4.0 is carried out using advanced technologies, which are referred to as sustainable steel production, due to the need to meet high standards of emissions of pollutants and consumption of natural resources. In practice, this means that large furnaces will be replaced by electric furnaces. For a transitional period, these technologies would operate side by side in parallel, after which the blast furnace would be completely replaced.

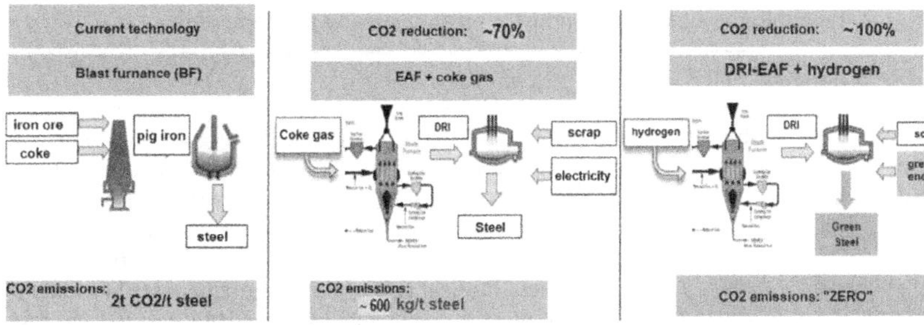

Figure 1.4 Decarbon process in metallurgy in the perspective of 2050.

Source: From presentation of Polish Steel Association, Poland, Katowice, 2021.

The development of DRI-EAF technology can lead to a reduction in direct carbon dioxide emissions of up to 95% compared to blast furnace technology. During the transition to DRI technology, it will be necessary to use solutions based on natural gas and coke gas. Technology EAF+coke gas reduces about~70% CO_2 emissions. Ultimately, however, DRI will be based on the use of green hydrogen in the process. The process lines will consist of electric furnaces supplemented by other installations (EAF/LF/CC). Figure 1.4 presents the key steps of metallurgical decarbonization in the perspective of 2050.

The new steel melting technology – DRI – is already being used worldwide but still to a limited extent. Few countries have one, two, or three mills with DRI technology, e.g. Iran has three steel mills. Globally, DRI technology is used in 20 countries in addition to India, which is the market leader in DRI technology. In the European Union market, DRI technology is used by Germany and Sweden. Total steel production using DRI technology is low. In recent years, total steel production in DRI technology was less than 100 million tonnes (WorldSteel, 2022).

Two steps (scenarios) presented in Figure 1.5 in the process of deep decarbonization are proposed by Gajdzik et al., 2023; Barlow et al., 2022; Nurdiawati et al., 2021; Tata Steel, 2020; Cirilli et al., 2019; Różański et al., 2022. The first step is based on modification of existing blast furnace-basic oxygen furnaces (BF+BOF) to use pulverized coal and iron ore known as HIsarna technology (Tata Steel, 2020) while installing Carbon Capture Utilisation and Storage (CCUS) technology to capture CO_2 in aquifers or inactive oil and gas reservoirs. The second step called Hydrogen Direct Iron Reduction (H_2-DRI) uses green hydrogen produced via water electrolysis along with electric arc furnaces (EAF). Based on these two key strategies (key directions of change in steel industry technologies in strategy "net zero"), further sub-strategies (sub-directions) are being developed and are the subject of scientific research (see, for example, BCG, 2022; Shahabuddin et al., 2023). Table 1.2 shows the possible directions of change according to the base technologies of the steel sector currently in use, BF and EAF, and Table 1.3 presents the key scenarios based on realized projects with the strategic direction of changes.

Table 1.2 Technologies of the steel industry on the pathway to green steel

Type of technology	*Key change/changes*
Technology BF-BOF with BF gas as fuel and biochars	The blast furnace (BF) is fed with iron ore, limestone and coke to produce liquid iron. Steel production is realized in BOF process but BOF partially reuses BF gas as fuel. Much of the gas is sent to other processes. A feature of this technology evolution is biochars, which can partially replace metallurgical coke. Biochars are expected to reduce the use of metallurgical coke by up to 10%, resulting in less CO_2 going into the air (1.5–2.2 t CO_2/t steel)
EAF with fossil fuels biofuel	In the process of steel manufacturing, energy comes from chemical sources (fossil fuels: natural and coal). Fossil fuels account for the dominant share of total energy. In new solutions, the fossil fuels could potentially be replaced by biofuels. In this scenario furnaces must be new-generation.
DRI-EAF	The reducing agent is natural gas. Iron is not melted but is solid. Solid iron is called as sponge iron. The sponge iron is a steelmaking product (examples: Midrex, HYL III). In this technology, steelworks can achieve from 40 to 60% CO_2 reductions. Products from Direct Reduced Iron (DRI) are high in iron content and low in copper and other undesirable metals – tramp elements – and nitrogen content. It is used to make a broad range of steel products. Its physical and chemical characteristics make it desirable for use in the electric arc furnace (EAF), blast furnace (BF), and basic oxygen furnace (BOF). In Midrex technology plants can be designed to switch from one DRI form to another with no disruption of product flow – cold DRI (CDRI) to hot briquetted iron (HBI), CDRI to hot DRI (HDRI), or HDRI to HBI. Products can be produced simultaneously in any combination.
Blast furnace (BF) with the waste gas from the smelting unit and from biomass (biosyngas)	Smelting reduction with or without CCS(U). Ores are partially reduced in the pre-reduction unit by using the waste gas from the smelting unit. Final reduction and smelting take place in the smelting unit. BOF technology allows the full use of biomass substitutes. Example of technology: HIsarna (Tata Steel). HIsarna technology is currently being tested without CCS(U). This technology can reduce CO_2 emissions by 35%. However, if CCS(U) were introduced in addition, CO_2 emissions would fall to 80%.
BF with CCS(U)	Top-gas recycling blast furnace with CCS(U): Carbon Capture, Utilisation and Storage). When we compared this using CCS(U) with technology without CCS(U), we obtained 35% CO_2 reduction (technology without CCS(U) predicts 25% less CO_2 and with CCS(U) up to 60% less CO_2). According to the programme Tata Steel (ULCOS-BF) modification of the conventional blast furnace reduces by 50% emission CO_2 per 1 tonne of steel.

(*Continued*)

Table 1.2 (Continued)

Type of technology	*Key change/changes*
H_2 DRI-EAF	In this process, hydrogen (H_2) is used instead of natural gas. Realized projects: HYBRYT, GrINHy, H2Future, SuSteel (Sustainable Steelmaking), SALCOS. In these projects, hydrogen replaces coke, coal, or natural gas. Hydrogen is an ore-reducing agent, plasma is used to simultaneously reduce iron ore and melt it into raw steel in a special direct current electric arc furnace. The advantage of using green electricity and hydrogen as a reducing agent is completely avoiding carbon dioxide emissions (by 95%).

Source: Own elaboration based on: (Gajdzik et al., 2023; Nurdiawati et al., 2021; Chen et al, 2022; Xylia et al., 2018; Carpenter, 2012; Vogle et al., 2018; Axelson et al., 2018; Somers, 2022, Zaini et al., 2023; Cirilli et al., 2018; Pei et al., 2020; Bhaskar et al., 2020, and projects: HIsarna, SuSteel, GrINHy, Hibrit, Midrex, H2future, HYL, IGAR, SALCOS, and Horizon 2020, EU, 2017).

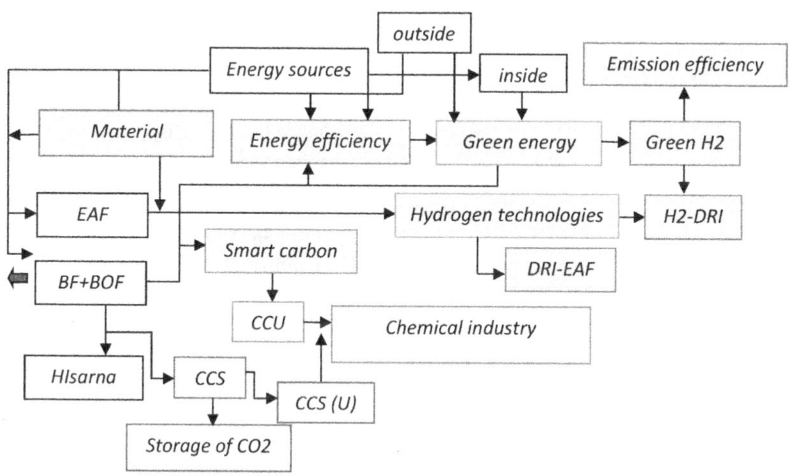

Figure 1.5 The way of the steel industry to decarbonization.

Source: Own elaboration. The map was prepared by B. Gajdzik.

On the pathways of the steel industry to climate neutrality in Europe by 2050 (reduction of CO_2 emissions by about 95% compared to 1990), there are some projects based on key results:

- Elimination of fossil coal from metallurgical process
- Use of green hydrogen
- Implementation of direct reduction processes using hydrogen
- Maximizing the share of electric process of producing steel from scrap and iron from direct reduction

Table 1.3 Technologies in steel manufacturing decarbonization based on key scenarios

Technology	*About technology*	*Changes and project examples*	*Current time project*
DRI-EAF – Direct-Reduced Iron Technology Electric Arc Furnace/	Electric steel melting process (currently used) will replace BOF process (also currently used) but will be enhanced with DRI technology	• Hybrid technology: DRI-EAF, • Technology uses natural gas and coke oven gas • Technology uses hydrogen	• Is realized
EAF-DRI – Direct-Reduced Iron Technology and green H_2	Technologies with ecological H_2 Installations: • HDRI (hot DRI) • CDRI (cold DRI)	• Technology uses green hydrogen (pure fuel) The most well-known option for producing green hydrogen is the electrolysis of water from renewable electricity. It consists of the decomposition of water (H_2O) into oxygen (O_2) and hydrogen (H_2) under the influence of a direct electric current flowing through the electrodes in the water.	• Projected development 2040–2050
CDA – Carbon Direct Avoidance	The technology uses reduction of iron ore by hydrogen (produced by H_2O electrolysis) and using biomass gas and reduction of Fe by electrolysis.	• HYBRIT: the first project in which hydrogen completely replaces carbon as a reducer in crude steel manufacturing. • GrInHy in this project the key innovation is the production of green industrial hydrogen through reversible design, production and operation of high-temperature electrolysis.	• Is realized • Projected development: 2040

(*Continued*)

Table 1.3 (Continued)

Technology	*About technology*	*Changes and project examples*	*Current time project*
CCU – Carbon Capture, Storage, and Usage	A set of technological solutions for different methods of carbon capture based on chemical and biological processes of CO_2 conversion and CO_2 capture by mineral raw materials. CCU technology focuses on converting industrial CO_2 into value-added chemicals and plastics.	• Carbon4PUR –this project demonstrated that industrial waste gases, mixed CO/CO_2 streams, can be converted into semi-finished products for the production of polyurethane plastics useful for rigid foams and coatings. • Steelanol, FresMe and M_4CO_2 – these projects aimed at recycling coal into bioethanol (advanced bioethanol).	• Is realized (first stage)
BF without CCS(U) or with CCS(U)	Smelting reduction with or without CCS(U). Ores are partially reduced in the pre-reduction unit by using the waste gas from the smelting unit. Final reduction and smelting take place in the smelting unit. BOF technology allows the full use of biomass substitutes.	• HIsarna (Tata Steel): the HIsarna test installation was built on the Tata Steel site in IJmuiden in 2010. The programme consisted of the next period: 2010–2014, 2016–2018, and 2018–2019, and the actual programme is on the period 2020 and further. One test plant is already in operation in India, another, the second, is being implemented.	• Is realized

Source: Own elaboration based on: (Branca et al., 2020; Gajdzik, 2022b; Monograph, Polish Steel Association, 2021).

- Furnaces powered by renewable energy, application of CO_2 capturing and storage as well as capturing and utilization processes (CCU, CCS)
- Production of iron by electrolysis
- Use of electricity from renewable sources, etc.

The creation of a market for steel produced by less carbon-intensive production processes, here called 'green steel', has been identified as a means of supporting the introduction of breakthrough emission reduction technologies into steel production. We can say that results of climate changes will be "green" steel. Green steel is often called ecological steel or ecological steel products. How to understand the concept of Green Steel? Today, there is no generally accepted definition of the term and it is most often used to describe steel products that are manufactured sustainably (e.g. high recycling rate of steel at the input of production or use of green energy in the manufacturing process) (Draxler et al., 2021; Muslemani et al., 2021).

In the last 50 years, the steel production process has been significantly improved. Steel production meets many radical environmental standards. The global metallurgy consumes less raw materials and energy. Here are examples of the environmental sustainability achieved by the global steel industry in the last 50 years (website: invest-tech.pl., "Green Steel for Europe" project, acronym GREENSTEEL – reports) (see also some results in the last 20 years prepared by Remus et al., 2013 based on BAT reports):

- Ninety percent of the water used in steel manufacturing is purified, cooled, and returned to the source.
- The energy used to produce one tonne of steel has been reduced by about 60%.
- Steel is the most recycled material in the world, around 630 million tonnes recycled annually.
- The global material efficiency index is high – in 2021 the recovery and use of steel industry by-products reached 98%.
- Steel is the main material used to build renewable energy infrastructure: solar, tidal, geothermal, and wind.

In technological transformation of the steel industry (Tables 1.1 and 1.2), the term green steel refers primarily to new steel production technologies that reduce CO_2 emissions per tonne of steel. Iron ore steel is usually produced using a blast furnace. The reference point for green steel is the concept of carbon footprint (Montoya-Torres et al., 2015). The Product Carbon Footprint (PCF) determines the total greenhouse gas emissions generated by a product, from the extraction of raw materials to the end of its life. It is measured in carbon dioxide equivalents (CO_2e). Green steel means reducing the carbon footprint by implementing alternative production technologies based on blue hydrogen and ultimately on green hydrogen. The product's total carbon footprint (PCF), which includes emissions across the third supply chain (under EU corporate reporting rules), is considered the leading KPI for assessing how green a steel product can be. This KPI must be determined through a thorough life cycle analysis (LCA) "from cradle to gate" according to globally accepted standards (e.g., ISO 14067), and then verified by a third party, e.g., by the international certification body DNV, as was the case for the steel production under the name "bluemint Steel", the ThyssenKrupp concern, which applied steel production technology to reduce its CO_2 balance by 70% per tonne of steel.

On the steel market, some relations build the concept of "green steel" (1) between products manufactured through a primary vs secondary steelmaking route, (2) between 'green' and traditional, 'brown' steel, (3) with other substitutable materials, and (4) between steel producers and consumers of steel. According to Gajdzik (Monograph, 2022) among all steel consumers, nowadays the automotive industry is a likely candidate for green steel demand, where a market could be supported by price premiums paid by willing consumers, such as those of high-end luxury and heavy-duty vehicles. According to Muslemani et al. (2021) however, numerous details remain under-explored, including exactly what 'green' entails in the context of steelmaking, the likely competitiveness of green steel products in domestic and international markets, and potential policy mechanisms to support their successful market penetration.

Companies and researchers try to classify the green steel. Green steel can be classified according to the degree of reduction of the negative impact of the production technology on the environment. Klöckner&Co has published a one-dimensional concept that divides steel products into five categories from "start" to "prime". This categorization is based only on the total PCF of the steel product, covering emissions in ranges 1, 2, and 3. Klöckner & Co does not accept carbon offset or credit and emphasizes the importance of external certification. However, the German Steel Federation has published a two-dimensional concept that defines five labels for 'green steel' from A to E. These labels are based on two parameters: Total PCF of the steel product including upstream emissions of ranges 1, 2, and 3 and the share of steel scrap (%) used in the production of the final steel product (website: metaltrade.pl; Draxler et al., 2021).

For steel mills to be able to produce green steel, they need to change their manufacturing technology or build new green steel mills from scratch. The location for a new versus 'green' steelworks must be somewhere that has nearby renewable energy sources (powering an arc furnace or producing 'clean' hydrogen) with sufficiently high capacity to reduce the cost of transferring energy or hydrogen to the steelworks. Today's steel mills, which have relied on the modification of blast furnaces and eclectic furnaces (the new generation of electric furnaces have higher efficiencies and lower energy intensity than those produced only a decade ago), have to cooperate with the environment – the energy sector, which is a key supplier of energy for them. This sector is also undergoing a process of decarbonization, turning black energy (energy produced from coal) into green energy (Blazquez et al., 2019, SEforALL, Gunnarsdóttir et al., 2020, Ligus et al., 2021). Metallurgical plants must have the availability of hydrogen and associated infrastructure. Low-emission hydrogen and strategic zero-emission "green" are still difficult to access, making it impossible for steel companies to accurately and realistically plan the profitability of new plants. Steelworks, in the future, could be self-sufficient in energy but now need green energy suppliers (Różański et al., 2022).

The pathways to green steel are strongly involved with smart carbon pathways. Reducing CO_2 emissions in metallurgical processes requires the elimination of coal as a fuel and reducer in steel manufacturing. Two ways are proposed from the European steel industry: (i) the capture and use (CCU – carbon capture and usage) or sequester (CCS – carbon capture and storage) of the gas, (ii) direct carbon avoidance (CDA) in the production of steel from iron ore can be implemented using hydrogen metallurgy processes and processes using electricity obtained from renewable or emission-free sources. According to Research Fund for Coal and Steel (RFCS, 2022), on the pathways to smart carbon there are some projects (Table 1.4). Particular projects have nowadays different levels of maturity estimated by the Technology Readiness Level (TRL). TRL is a scale from 1 to 9. The scale is used in the estimation of technology maturity in engineering. The TRL level presents the differences between the ordinal and resulting coefficients of the project (Conrow, 2009).

Decarbonization is based on radical technological innovations (so-called: deep decarbonization). New industrial technologies are strongly linked to sustainable world targets. The key carbon-free (natural, green, ecological) technologies presented in the chapter will be pursued in parallel with sub-innovation, the essence of which is to reduce material and energy consumption by increasing material efficiency through structural modifications that, for example, increase product life or enable reuse, or the production of high-strength, lightweight steel. During a "green" transformation, a key block of change and the life cycle of steel enables recycling through end-of-life disassembly and streamlined scrap handling. For steel consumers, innovations in the steel manufacturing increase product value and services (Wyns et al., 2018).

The market in decarbonization challenges green products, including 'green' steel. Steel mills start their pathways to reducing CO_2 emissions until net zero according to the 2050 climate neutrality. The implementation of many investments has the support of governmental organizations (key investments for the economy). A source of revenue (investment support) can be the CBAM 'tax'. Without government support, it will be difficult for steel mills to make new investments. Steel mills need to move from smart carbon to hydrogen technologies implementation (DRI-EAF) with government support. Governments can provide financial incentives and support to businesses to invest in new technologies and infrastructure, while businesses can collaborate to invest in shared infrastructure, such as pipelines for transporting hydrogen or carbon dioxide. Supportive policies and regulations can incentivize the adoption of low-carbon alternatives by the steel industry. The concept of this chapter is visualized in Figure 1.6.

Table 1.4 Green steel and smart carbon in two pathways of decarbonization

CCU+CCS			*CDA*		
Iron bath reactor smelting reduction	Reducing agent	Carbon	Hydrogen-based direct reduction	Reducing agent	Hydrogen
	Current TRL	6		Current TRL	6–8
	Project examples	HIsarna		Project examples	HIBRID, Salcos, Hyfor
Gas injection into the blast furnace (BF)	Reducing agent	Carbon	Hydrogen plasma smelting reduction	Reducing agent	Hydrogen
	Current TRL	5–8		Current TRL	5
	Project examples	ULCOS		Project examples	SuSteel
Alternative carbon source	Reducing agent	Carbon	Alkaline iron electrolysis	Reducing agent	Electricity
	Current TRL	2–7		Current TRL	5–6
	Project examples	SHOCOM, GreenEAF2		Project examples	SIDERWIN, IERO, ASCoPE
Increased scrap usage	Reducing agent	(Carbon)	Molten oxide electrolysis	Reducing agent	Electricity
	Current TRL	4–8		Current TRL	2
	Project examples	FlexCharge, AdpatEAF		Project examples	ULCOS, IERO, VALORCO
Carbon oxide conversion	Reducing agent	(Carbon)			
	Current TRL	8 (conversion) 4–5 (implementation)			
	Project examples	Steelanol, Carbon2Chem			

Source: (Climate-neutral Steelmaking in Europe, Decarburization pathways – Investment needs – Policy Conditions – Recommendations. European Research Executive Agency (REA), Research Fund for Coal and Steel RFCS, 2022. [Online] Available at: https://op.europa.eu/en/publication-detail/-/publicati on/89cda1b2-b169-11ec-83e1-01aa75ed71a1/language-en/format-PDF/source-254269180); SIDERWIN (2019).

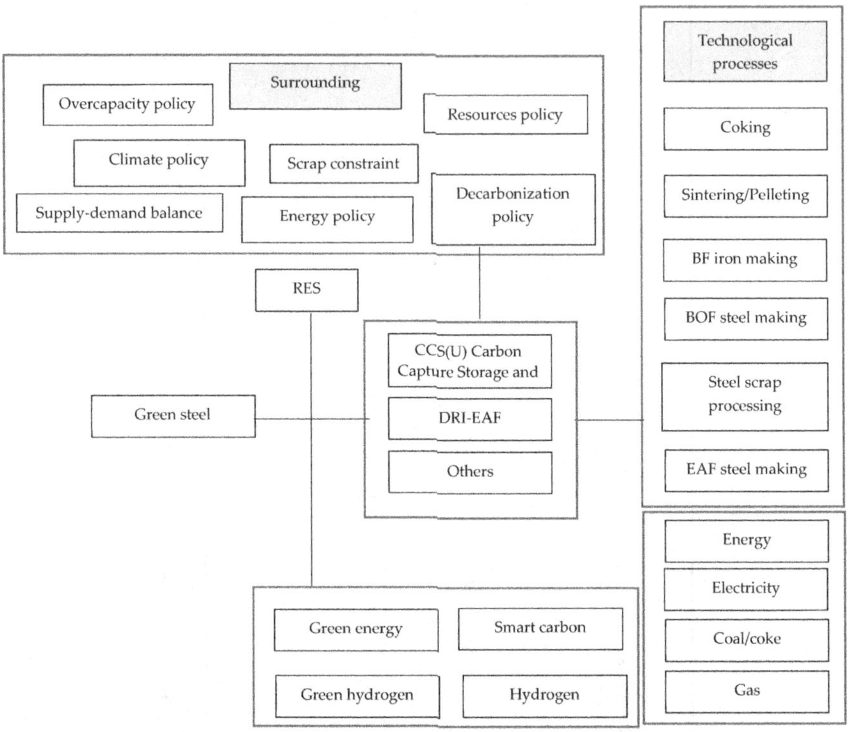

Figure 1.6 Constructs of the steel industry decarbonization.

Source: Own elaboration based on: Li et al. (2023).

Bibliography

Alamda-Lobo, F. (2015). The Industry 4.0 revolution and the future of manufacturing execution systems (MES). *Journal of Innovation Management*, 3(4), 16–21.

Al-Ghussain, L., Ahmad, A.D., Abubaker, A.M., Hassan, M.A., Annuk, A. (2023). Techno-economic feasibility of hybrid PV/wind/battery/thermal storage trigeneration system: Toward 100% energy independency and green hydrogen production. *Energy Reports*, 9, 752–772.

Axelson, M., Oberthür, S., Nilsson, L.J. (2021). Research and analysis. Emission reduction strategies in the EU steel industry. Implications for business model innovation. Publisher Wiley. *Journal of Industrial Ecology*, 25, 390–402. https://doi.org/10.1111/jiec.13124.

Axelson, M., Robson, I., Khandekar, G., Wynys, T. (2018). *Breaking through Industrial Low-CO_2 Technologies on the Horizon.* Brussels: Institute for European Studies, Vrije Universiteit Brussel.

Bahrin, M.A.K., Othman, M.F., Azli, N.H.N., Talib, M.F. (2016). Industry 4.0: A review on industrial automation and robotic. *Jurnal Teknologi*, 78, 6–13, 137–143. https://doi.org/10.11113/jt.v78.9285.

Bajaj, P., Hariharan, A., Kini, A., Kürnsteiner, P., Raabe, D., Jägle, E.A. (2019). Steels in additive manufacturing: A review of their microstructure and properties. *MSEA*, 2019. https://doi.org/10.1016/j.msea.2019.138633.

Barlow, C.R., Pimm, A.J., Taylor, P.G., Gale, W.F. (2022). Policy and pricing barriers to steel industry decarbonisation: A UK case study. *Energy Policy*, 168, 113100. https://doi.org/10.1016/j.enpol.2022.113100.

Battilana, J., Dorado, S. (2010). Building sustainable hybrid organizations: The case of commercial microfinance organizations. *Academy of Management Journal*, 53(6), 1419–1440.

Bauernhansl, T., Hompel, M., Vogel-Henser, B. (2014). *Industrie 4.0 in Produkten. Automatisierung und Logistik*. Springer Fachmedien: Wiesbaden.

Baumgartner, R.J. (2014). Managing Corporate Sustainability and CSR: A Conceptual Framework Combining Values, Strategies and Instruments Contributing to Sustainable Development. 21(5) Special Issue on Managing Corporate Social and Environmental Responsibility - From Strategies to Implementation September/October 2014 258–271, https://doi.org/10.1002/csr.1336.

Bayram, B., Ince, G. (2018). Advances in robotics in the era of Industry 4.0. In *Industry 4.0: Managing the Digital Transformation*. Springer Series in Advanced Manufacturing (Book Series: SSAM). Springer: Cham, 187–200. https://link.springer.com/chapter/10.1007/978-3-319-57870-5_11.

BCG: Boston Consulting Group. (Hg.) (2015). *Industry 4.0: The Future of Productivity and Growth in Manufacturing Industries*. München. https://www.bcg.com/publications/2015/engineered_products_project_business_industry_4_future_productivity_growth_manufacturing_industries, Access data [27.10.2023]

BCG: Transforming the steel industry may be the ultimate climate challenge | BCG. https://www.bcg.com/publications/2022/steel-industry-carbon-emissions-challenge-solutions, [access data: 27.10.2023].

Benesova, A., Tupa, J. (2017). Requirements for education and qualification of people in Industry 4.0. *Procedia Manufacturing*, 11, 2195–2202.

Bentyn, Z. (2017). Adaptacja łańcuchów dostaw do potrzeb przemysłu 4.0 (title in English: Adaptation of supply chains to the needs of Industry 4.0). *Autobusy*, 6, 1317–1321.

Bhaskar, A., Assadi, M., Somehsaraei, H.N. (2020). Decarbonization of the iron and steel industry with direct reduction of iron ore with green hydrogen. *Energies*, 13, 75813. https://doi.org/10.3390/EN13030758.

Bielański, A. (2002). *Podstawy chemii nieorganicznej*. T. 2. Warszawa: PWN, 921.

Blazquez, J., Fuentes-Bracamontes, R., Manzano, B. (2019). A road map to navigate the energy transition. https://www.oxfordenergy.org/wpcms/wp-content/uploads/2019/10/A-road-map-to-navigate-the-energy-transition-Insight-59.Pdf, [access data: 27.10.2023].

BMWi: Für eine starke Stahlindustrie in Deutschland und Europa!: Handlungskonzept Stahl, Bundesministerium für Wirtschaft und Energie (BMWi), July 2020, bmwi.de, [access data: 27.10.2023].

Bonilla Silvia, H., Silva Helton, R.O., da Silva, M.T., Gonçalves, R.F., Sacomano, J.B. (2018). Industry 4.0 and sustainability implications: A scenario-based analysis of the impacts and challenges. *Sustainability*, 10, 3740. https://doi.org/10.3390/su10103740 www.mdpi.com/journal/sustainability, [access data: 27.10.2023].

Bonner, M. (2017). What is Industry 4.0 and what does it mean for my manufacturing? *Saint ClaireSystems,* 2017.https://blog.viscosity.com/blog/what-is-industry-4.0-and-what-does-it-mean-for-mymanufacturing, [access data: 29.12. 2018].

Bonvoisin, J., Stark, R., Seliger, G. (2017). Field of research in sustainable manufacturing. In Stark, R., Seliger, G., Bonvoisin, J. (Eds), *Sustainable Manufacturing: Challenges, Solutions and Implementation*. Springer International Publishing. Sustainable Production, Life Cycle Engineering and Management: Cham. https://doi.org/10.1007/978-3-319-48514-0.

Branca, T.A., Fornai, B., Murri, M.M., Streppa, E., Schröder, A.J. (2020). The challenge of digitalization in the steel sector. *Metals*, 10(2), 288. https://doi.org/10.3390/met10020288, [online:] https://www.mdpi.com/2075-4701/10/2/288/htm, [access data: 27.10.2023].

Brettel, M., Friederichsen, N., Keller, M., Rosenberg, M. (2014). How virtualization, decentralization and network building change the manufacturing landscape: An Industry 4.0 perspective. *International Journal of Mechanical, Aerospace, Industrial, Mechatronic and Manufacturing Engineering*, 8(1), 37.

Bungart, S. (2014). Industrial Internet versus Industrie 4.0. Produktion – Technik und Wirtschaft für die deutsche Industrie, 2014. http://www.produktion.de/automatisierung/industrial-internet-versus-industrie-4-0/print, [access data: 1.12.2014]

Bürger, T., Tragl, K. (2014). SPS-Automatisierung mit den Technologien der IT-Welt verbinden. In Bauernhansl, T., ten Hompel, M., Vogel-Heuser, B. (Eds), *Industrie 4.0 in Produktion, Automatisierung und Logistik. Anwendung, Technologien und Migration.* Springer Fachmedien, Wiesbaden, 559–569.

Burrell, D. (2019). *Principles of Industry 4.0 and the 9 pillars*, 7th February 2019. https://www.plextek.com/insights/insights-insights/industry-4-0-and-the-9-pillars/, [access data: 27.10.2023].

Buxo, A. (Nov. 2015). Digital transformation will scale in 2016, IDC FutureScape predicts. https://www.linkedin.com/pulse/digital-transformation-scale-2016-idc-futurescape-predicts-buxo, [access data: 08.11.2023]

Carayannis, E.G., Draper, J., Bhaneja, B. (2020). Towards fusion energy in the industry 5.0 and society 5.0 context: Call for a global commission for urgent action on fusion energy. *Journal of the Knowledge Economy*, 1–14.

Carpenter, A. (2012). *CO_2 Abatement in the Iron and Steel Industry; CCC/193*. IEA Clean Coal Centre: London.

Castelo-Branco, I., Amaro-Henriques, M., Cruz-Jesus, F., Oliveira, T. (2023). Assessing the Industry 4.0 European divide through the country/industry dichotomy. *Computers & Industrial Engineering*, 176, 108925. https://doi.org/10.1016/j.cie.2022.108927

Chen, B., Wan, J., Shu, L., Li, P., Mukherjee, M., Yin, B. (2017). Smart factory of Industry 4.0: Key technologies, application case, and challenges. *IEEE Access*, 6, 6506–6519.

Chen, D., Li, J., Wang, Z., Lu, B., Chen, G. (2022). Hierarchical model to find the path reducing CO_2 emissions of integrated iron and steel production. *Energy*, 258, 124887.

Cheng, J., Westman, J. (2020). Effects of digitalization in steel industry: Economic impacts and investment model. Degree project in industrial engineering and management, second cycle, 30 credits Stockholm. KTH Industrial Engineering and Management Industrial Management: Sweden. https://www.diva-portal.org/smash/get/diva2:1460881/FULLTEXT01.pdf, [access data: 27.10.2023].

Circular Economy Action Plan, Brussel, 11 March (2020). https://ec.europa.eu/commission/presscorner/detail/en/ip_20_420, [access data: 27.10.2023].

Cirilli, F., Mirabile, D., Bianco, L., Baracchini, G., Rekersdrees, T., Marcos, M., Sommerauer, H., Griessacher, T., Echterhof, T., Reichel, T. (2018). Biochar for a sustainable EAF steel production (GREENEAF2). Final Report. Research and Innovation. EUR 29517 EN. https://www.researchgate.net/publication/334625171_Biochar_for_a_sustainable_EAF_steel_production_GREENEAF2, [access data: 27.10.2023].

Cirilli, F., Stubbe, G., Overbeck, T., Borlée, J., Pierret, J.-Ch., Draxler, M., Sormann, A., Wang, Ch., Lundberg, T., Granbom, H. (2019). CO_2 mitigation in electric arc furnace steelmaking. In: Workshop: GreenSteel by EAF Route: A Sustainable Value in the EU Circular Economy Scenario. Bergamo, Italy. 13–14 November.

Claessens, S., Yurtoglu, B. (2012). Corporate Governance in Emerging Markets: A Survey. January 15, pp. 1–77. Electronic copy http://ssrn.com/abstract=1988880, [access data: 27.10.2023].

COM. (2013). Communication from the commission to the parliament, the council, the European economic and social committee and the committee of regions. Action Plan for a Competitive and Sustainable Steel Industry. Document 52013DC0407: COM/2013/0407 final https://single-market-economy.ec.europa.eu/sectors/raw-materials/related-industries/metal-industries/steel_en, [access data: 27.10.2023].

Conrow, E.H. Estimating Technology Readiness Level Coefficients. AIAA SPACE (2009). Conference & Exposition. Published by the American Institute of Aeronautics and Astronautics, Pasadena, CA. 14–17 September 2009.

Culot, G., Nassimbeni, G., Orzes, G., Sartor, M. (August 2020). Behind the definition of Industry 4.0: Analysis and open questions. *International Journal of Production Economics*, 226, 107617.

Culot, G., Orzes, G., Sartor, M., Nassimbeni, G. (2020). The future of manufacturing: A Delphi-based scenario analysis on Industry 4.0. *Technological Forecasting and Social Change*, 157. https://doi.org/10.1016/j.techfore.2020.120092.

Dais, S. (2014). Industrie 4.0 – Anstoß, Vision, Vorgehen. In: Bauernhansl, T., ten Hompel, M., Vogel-Heuser, B. (Eds), *Industrie 4. 0 in Produktion, Automatisierung und Logistik*. Anwendung, Technologien und Migration, 625–634.

Davis, J., Edgar, T., Porter, J., Bernaden, J., Sarli, M. (2012). Smart manufacturing, manufacturing intelligence and demand-dynamic performance. *FOCAPO*, 47, 145.

Davos Agenda 2022: Global governance, World Economic Forum, K. Schwab (Founder, Executive Chairman, World Economic Forum). https://www.weforum.org/agenda/2022/01/this-is-what-governance-4-0-could-look-like/, [access data: 27.10.2023].

Doyle-Kent, M., Kopacek, P., Doyle-Kent, M., Kopacek, P. (2021). Do we need synchronization of the human and robotics to make Industry 5.0 a success story? In Durakbasa, N.M., Gençyılmaz, M.G. (Eds), *Digital Conversion on the Way to Industry 4.0*. ISPR 2020. Lecture Notes in Mechanical Engineering. Springer: Cham.

Draxler, M., Sormann, A., Kempken, T., Hauck, T., Pierret, J.-Ch., Borlee, J., Di Donato, A., De Santis, M., Wang, Ch. (March 2021). Green Steel for Europe, Technology Assessment and Road Mapping. [Online] https://www.estep.eu/assets/Uploads/D1.2-Technology-Assessment-and-Roadmapping.pdf, [access data: 27.10.2023].

Drucker, P.F., Maciariello Joseph, A., Jim, C. (2008). *Management*. Harper Collins Publ.: USA. ISBN-10.0061252662.

Dubey, G., Gupta, R.K., Kumar, S., Kumar, M. (2022). Study of Industry 4.0 pillars and their uses in increasing productivity and reducing logistics defects. *Materials Today: Proceedings*, 63, 85–91.

Ebers, M. (2002). Explaining inter-organizational network formation. In Ebers, M. (Ed), *The Formation of Inter-organisational Networks*. Oxford University Press: Oxford.

EFFRA. (2013). *Factories of the Future: Multi-annual Roadmap for the Contractual PPP under Horizon 2020*. Brussels.

Encyclopaedia, PWN, entry: Marten process. https://encyklopedia.pwn.pl/haslo/martenowski-proces;3938127.html, [access data: 27.10.2023].

Erboz, G. (2017). How to define Industry 4.0: Main pillars of Industry 4.0. In: Conference Paper (PDF Available) November 2017 *with* 16,509 Reads Conference: 7th International Conference on Management (ICoM 2017), Nitra, Slovakia. https://www.researchgate.net/publication/326557388_How_To_Define_Industry_40_Main_Pillars_Of_Industry_40, [access data: 27.10.2023].

Erol, S., Jäger, A., Hold, P., Ott, K., Sihn, W. (2016), Tangible Industry 4.0: A scenario-based approach to learning for the future of production. *Procedia CIRP*, No. 54, https://doi.org/10.1016/j.procir.2016.03.162.

ESTEP, UE, Brussel, https://www.estep.eu/green-steel-for-europe/, [access data: 27.10.2023].

Eur-Lex. (21.12.2022). Opinia Europejskiego Komitetu Ekonomiczno-Społecznego „Rola technologii usuwania dwutlenku węgla w dekarbonizacji europejskiego" (opinia z inicjatywy własnej) (2022/C 486/08). Dziennik Urzędowy, EU, C 486/53, https://eur-lex.europa.eu/legal-content/PL/TXT/PDF/?uri=CELEX:52022IE1057&from=EN), [access data: 27.10.2023].

Eurofer, European Steel in Figures 2022, Data Covering (2021). Brussels. https://www.eurofer.eu/assets/publications/brochures-booklets-and-factsheets/european-steel-in-figures-2022/European-Steel-in-Figures-2022-v2.pdf, [access data: 27.10.2023].

European Commission. (2001). *Promoting a European framework for Corporate Social Responsibility*, COM 366 final, 18.07.2001. EC: Brussels.

European Green Deal, COM/2019/640 Final. (2019). Communication from the commission to the European parliament, the European council, the council, the European economic and social committee and the committee of the regions. The Document 52019DC0640. https://eur-lex.europa.eu/legal-content/PL/TXT/?uri=CELEX%3A52019DC0640&qid=1653851156228, [access data: 27.10.2023].

Evans, P.C., Annunziata, M. (2012). Industrial Internet: Pushing the Boundaries of Minds and Machines. http://www.ge.com/docs/chapters/Industrial_Internet.pdf, [access data: 6.11.2014].

Fleith de Medeiros, J., Ribeiro, J.L.D., Cortimiglia, M.N. (2014). Success factors for environmentally sustainable product innovation: A systematic literature review. *Journal of Cleaner Production*, 65, 76–86.

Florida, R. (2002). *The Rise of Creative Class: And How It's Transforming Work, Leisure, Community and Everyday Life.* Basic Book: New York.

Florida, R., Gates, G. (2001). *Technology and Tolerance: The Importance of Diversity to High -Tech Growth.* Brookings Institution, Center for Urban and Metropolitan Policy: Washington, DC.

Frank, A.G., Dalenogare, L.S., Ayala, N.F. (2019). Industry 4.0 technologies: Implementation patterns in manufacturing companies. *International Journal of Production Economics*, 210, 15–26. https://doi.org/10.1016/j.ijpe.2019.01.004.

Frederico, G., Garza-Reyes, J.A., Anosike, A., Kumar, V. (2019). Supply Chain 4.0: Concepts, maturity and research agenda. *Supply Chain Management: An International Journal*, 25, 262–282.

Frederico, G.F. (2021). From Supply Chain 4.0 to Supply Chain 5.0: Findings from a systematic literature review and research directions. *Logistics*, 5, 49. https://doi.org/10.3390/logistics5030049.

Gajdzik, B. (2013). World Class manufacturing in metallurgical enterprise. *Metalurgija*, 52, 131–134.

Gajdzik, B. (2022a). Diagnoza kierunków transformacji przemysłu stalowego w Przemyśle 4.0, Title in English: Diagnosis of the steel Industry transformation direction in the Industry 4.0. Monograph no. 945. Publisher: Silesian University of Technology. Wydawnictwo Politechniki Śląskiej Gliwice 2022, 468pp.

Gajdzik, B. (2022b). Frameworks of the maturity model for Industry 4.0 with assessment of maturity levels on the example of the segment of steel enterprises in Poland. *Journal of Open Innovation: Technology, Market, and Complexity,* 8, 77. https://doi.org/10.3390/joitmc8020077.

Gajdzik, B., Wolniak, R. (2021a). Digitalisation and innovation in the steel industry in Poland—Selected tools of ICT in an analysis of statistical data and a case study. *Energies*, 14, 3034, 1–25. https://doi.org/10.3390/en14113034.

Gajdzik, B., Wolniak, R. (2021b). Transitioning of steel producers to the steelworks 4.0—Literature review with case studies. *Energies*, 14, 4109. https://doi.org/10.3390/EN14144109.

Gajdzik, B., Wolniak, R., Grebski, W. (2023). Process of transformation to net zero steelmaking: Decarbonisation scenarios based on the analysis of the polish steel industry. *Energies*, 16(2). https://doi.org/10.3390/en16020787.

Gorecky, D., Schmitt, M., Loskyll, M., Zuhlke, D. (2014). Human–Machine-Interaction in the Industry 4.0 Era. In: 2014 12th IEEE International Conference on Industrial Informatics (INDIN), 14718826.

Griffin Ricky, W. (2002). *Management*, Edition, 7. Publisher, Houghton Mifflin Company, Boston, MA.

GrINHy. https://salcos.salzgitter-ag.com/en/grinhy-20.html, [access data: 27.10.2023].

Grumpos, P.P. (2021). A critical historical and scientific overview of all industrial revolutions. *IFAC PapersOnLine* 54-13, 464–471. https://doi.org/10.1016/j.ifacol.2021.10.492

Grzelczak, A., Kosacka, M., Werner-Lewandowska, K. (2018). Employees competences for Industry 4.0 in Poland–Preliminary research results. In *DEStech Transactions on Engineering and Technology Research*. DEStech Publications, Inc.: Lancaster, PA, 130–144.

Gunnarsdóttir, I., Davidsdottir, B., Worrell, E., Sigurgeirsdóttir, S. (2020). Review of indicators for sustainable energy development. *Renewable and Sustainable Energy Reviews*, 133, 110294. https://doi.org/10.1016/j.rser.2020.110294.

H2future Project, EU. https://h2future-project.eu/technology, [accessed data: 10.3.2023].

Hermann, M., Pentek, T., Otto, B. (2015). Design Principles for Industrie 4.0 Scenarios. A Literature Review, Working Paper No. 01, Technische Universität Dortmund Fakultät Maschinenbau, http://www.iim.mb.tu-dortmund.de/cms/de/forschung/Arbeitsberichte/Design-Principles-for-Industrie-4_0-Scenarios.pdf, [access data: 3.07.2023].

Herzog, K., Winter, G., Kurka, K., Ankermann, R., Binder, M., Ringhofer, A., Maierhofer, Fick, A. (2017). The digitalization of steel production. *BHM Berg- und Hüttenmännische Monatshefte*, 162, 504–513. https://link.springer.com/article/10.1007/s00501-017-0673-9, [access data: 27.10.2023].

Herzog, K.W. (2017). The digitalization of steel production. *BHM Berg- und Hüttenmännische Monatshefte*, 162(11), 504–513.

HIsarna. (2020). TataSteel: HIsarna Factsheet nr. 2/2020. https://www.tatasteeleurope.com/sites/default/files/tata-steel-europe-factsheet-hisarna.pdf, [access data: 27.10.2023].

HIsarna Building a Sustainable Steel Industry. https://www.tatasteeleurope.com/sites/default/files/tata-steel-europe-factsheet-hisarna.pdf, [access data: 27.10.2023].

Hofmann, E., Rüsch, M. (2017). Industry 4.0 and the current status as well as future prospects on logistics. *Computers in Industry*, 89, 23–34. https://doi.org/10.1016/j.compind.2017.04.002.

Horizon 2020. (2017). *Green Industrial Hydrogen via Reversible High-Temperature Electrolysis*. EU: Brussel.

HYBRIT. (2017). *Fossil Free Steel*. HYBRIT: Stockholm.

HYL. Satyendra (April 22, 2017). HYL process for direct reduction of iron ore. https://www.ispatguru.com/hyl-process-for-direct-reduction-of-iron-ore/, [access data: 10.03.2023].

IEA. (2020). *Iron and Steel Technology Roadmap*. Paris. https://doi.org/10.1787/ 3dcc2a1b-en. https://www.iea.org/reports/iron-and-steel-technology-roadmap, [access data: 08.11.2023].

IGAR Project. (2023). ArcelorMittal. https://corporate.arcelormittal.com/corporate-library/reporting-hub/igar-reforming-carbon-to-reduce-iron-ore, [access data: 27.10.2023].

Industrial Emissions Directive 2010/75/EU (Integrated Pollution Prevention and Control) Best Available Techniques (BAT) Reference Document for Iron and Steel Production, Brussels, European commission. https://publications.jrc.ec.europa.eu/repository/handle/JRC69967, [access date: 08.11.2023].

Industrial Internet Consortium. (2013). Fact Sheet. http://www.iiconsortium.org/docs/IIC_FACT_SHEET.pdf, [access data: 3.12.2014].

Industrial Internet of Things: Unleashing the Potential of Connected Products and Services, World Economic Forum, January (2015). http://www3.weforum.org/docs/WEFUSA_IndustrialInternet_Report2015.pdf, [access data: 15.04.2016].

Industry 5.0: Towards a Sustainable, Human-Centric and Resilient European Industry. Publications Office of the European Union: Luxembourg, 7 January 2021. https://doi.org/10.2777/308407. https://research-and-innovation.ec.europa.eu/news/all-research-and-innovation-news/industry-50-towards-more-sustainable-resilient-and-human-centric-industry-2021-01-07_en, [access data: 08.11.2023].

Industry 5.0: A Transformative Vision for Europe. ESIR. Policy Brief No. 3. https://www.horizon-europe.gouv.fr/sites/default/files/2022-01/industry-5-0-pdf-5324.pdf, [access data: 27.10.2023].

Invet tech. https://invest-tech.pl/dlaczego-stal-nierdzewna-jest-materialem-eko [access data: 27.10.2023].

Jasiulewicz-Kaczmarek, M., Saniuk, A. (2015). Human factor in sustainable manufacturing. In: Antona, M., Stephanidis, C. (Eds), *Universal Access in Human-Computer Interaction. Access to the Human Environment and Culture*. Springer: Basel, 9178, 444–455.

Join Research Centre 15 June 2022. https://joint-research-centre.ec.europa.eu/jrc-news-and-updates/eu-climate-targets-how-decarbonise-steel-industry-2022-06-15_en, [access data: 27.10.2023].

Kagermann, H. (2015). Change through digitalization – Value creation in the age of Industry 4.0. In: Albach, H., Meffert, H., Pinkwart, A,· Reichwald R (Eds), *Management of Permanent Change*, Springer Fachmedien: Wiesbaden, 23–45.

Kagermann, H., Wahlster, W., Helbig, J. (2013). Securing the future of German manufacturing industry. Recommendations for implementing the strategic initiative Industrie 4.0. Final Report of the Industrie 4.0 Working Group, Forschungsunion, Acatech.

Kamble, S.S., Gunasekaran, A., Gawankar, S.A. (2018). Sustainable Industry 4.0 framework: A systematic literature review identifying the current trends and future perspectives. *Process Safety and Environmental Protection*, 117. https://doi.org/10.1016/j.psep.2018.05.009.

Kane, G.C., Palmer, D., Phillips, A.N., Kiron, D. (2015). Is your business ready for a digital future? *MIT Sloan Management Review*, 56, 37.

Kishawy, H.A., Hegab, H., Saad, E. (2018). Design for sustainable manufacturing: Approach, implementation, and assessment. *Sustainability*, 10, 3604.

KUKA. (February 2016). *Hello Industrie 4.0: Smart Solutions for Smart Factories*. KUKA Aktiengesellschaft: Augsburg. https://www.kuka.com/pl-pl/firma/prasa/news/2015/02/20150210_hello_industrie_40, [access data: 08.11.2023].

Lars, A., et al. (Feb. 2016). German Standardization Roadmap: Industry 4.0. Version 2. DIN e.V.: Berlin. https://sci40.com/files/assets_sci40.com/pdf/german-standardization-roadmap-industry-4-0-version-2-data.pdf, [access data: 08.11.2023].

Lasi, H., Fettke, P., Kemper, H.-G., Feld, T., Hoffmann, M. (2014). Industrie 4.0: Bedarfssog und Technologiedruck als Treiber der vierten industriellen Revolution. *Wirtschaftsinformatik*, 56(4), 261–264.

Lasi, H., Fettke, P., Kemper, H.-G., Feld, T., Hoffmann, M. (2014). Industry 4.0. *Business and Information Systems Engineering*, 6(4). https://doi.org/10.1007/ s12599-014-0334-4.

Lee, J., Bagheri, B., Kao, H. (2015). Research letters: A cyber-physical systems architecture for Industry 4.0-based manufacturing systems. *Manufacturing Letters*, 3, 18–23.

Lee, J., Kao, H.A., Yang, S. (2014), Service innovation and smart analytics for Industry 4.0 and Big Data environment. *Procedia CIRP*, 16. https://doi.org/10.1016/j. procir. 2014.02.001.

Lee, J.D., Seppelt, B.D. (2012). Human factors and ergonomics in automation design. In: Salvendy, G. (Ed), *Handbook of Human factors and Ergonomics*.Wiley: Hoboken, 1615–1642.

Li, Z., Andersson, F.N.G., Nilsson, L.J., Åhman, M. (2023). Steel decarbonization in China – A top-down optimization model for exploring the first steps. *Journal of Cleaner Production*, 384. https://doi.org/10.1016/j.jclepro.2022.135550

Liao, Y., Deschamps, F., Loures, E.F.R., Ramos, L.F.P. (2017). Past, present and future of Industry 4.0—A systematic literature review and research agenda proposal. *International Journal of Production Research*, 55(12), 3609–3629.

Ligus, M., Peternek, P. (2021). The sustainable energy development index – An application for European Union Member States. *Energies*, 14(4), 1117. https://doi.org/10.3390/en14041117.

Listwan, T. (2008). Contemporary Trends in Human Resources Management of Organizations. Prace Naukowe Uniwersytetu Ekonomicznego we Wrocławiu, no 31 Zarządzanie personelem jako kryterium doskonałości, pp. 23–33.

Longo, F., Nicoletti, L., Padovano, A. (2017). Smart operators in industry 4.0: A human-centered approach to enhance operators' capabilities and competencies within the new smart factory context. *Computers & Industrial Engineering*, 113, 144–159.

Longo, F., Padovano, A., Umbrello, S. (2020). Value-oriented and ethical technology engineering in industry 5.0: A human-centric perspective for the design of the factory of the future. *Applied Sciences*, 10, 4182.

Lorenz, M., Rubmann, M., Strack, R., Lueth, K.L., Bolle, M. (2015). *Man and Machine in Industry 4.0—How Will Technology Transform the Industrial Workforce through 2025?* The Boston Consulting Group. https://www.bcg.com/publications/2015/technology-business-transformation-engineered-products-infrastructure-man-machine-industry-4

Machado, C.G., Winrotha, M.P., da Silva, E.H.D.R. (2020). Sustainable manufacturing in Industry 4.0: An emerging research agenda. *International Journal of Production Research*, 58(5), 1462–1484. https://doi.org/10.1080/00207543.2019.1652777.

Martins, K., Carton, J.G. (2023). Prospective roles for green hydrogen as part of Ireland's decarbonisation strategy. *Results in Engineering*, 18, 101030.

McKinsey & Company. (2020). Decarbonization Challenge for Steel. https://www.mckinsey.com/industries/metals-and-mining/our-insights/decarbonization-challenge-for-steel. [accessed 31.05.2022].

McKinsey & Company. (March 2021). The Future of the European Steel Industry. A Road Map toward Economic and Environmental Sustainability. https://www.mckinsey.com/~/media/mckinsey/industries/metals%20and%20mining/our%20insights/the%20future%20of%20the%20european%20steel%20industry/the-future-of-the-european-steel-industry_vf.pdf, [access data: 27.10.2023].

McKnsey & Company. Supply Chain 4.0 – the next-generation digital supply chain October 27, 2016 | Article https://www.mckinsey.com/capabilities/operations/our-insights/supply-chain-40--the-next-generation-digital-supply-chain#/, [access data: 27.10.2023]

Metal Trade. https://metaltrade.pl/green-steel/, [access data: 27.10.2023].

Midrex Process. https://www.midrex.com/direct-reduced-iron/ [access data: 10.03.2023].

Miśkiewicz, R., Wolniak, R. (2020). Practical application of the industry 4.0 concept in a steel company. *Sustainability*, 12, 5776.

Montoya-Torres, J.R., Gutierrez-Franco, E., Blanco, E.E. (2015). Conceptual framework for measuring carbon footprint in supply chains. *Production Planning and Control*, 26, 265–279.

Mori, L., Saleh, T., Sellschop, E., Van Hoey, M. (January 2018). Digital opportunity map for a metal payer. In *Unlocking the Digital Opportunity in Metals. Metals and Mining Practice*. McKinsey&Company: Beijing, 4.

Mosconi, F. (2015). *The New European Industrial Policy: Global Competitiveness and the Manufacturing Renaissance*. Routledge: London.

Motyl, B., Baronio, G., Uberti, S., Speranza, D., Filippi, S. (2017). How will change the future engineers' skills in the Industry 4.0 framework? A questionnaire survey. *Procedia Manufacturing*, 11, 1501–1509.

Müller, J.M., Kiel, D., Voigt, K.I. (2018). What drives the implementation of Industry 4.0? The role of opportunities and challenges in the context of sustainability. *Sustainability*, 10, 247.

Muslemani, H., Liang, X., Kaesehage, K., Ascui, F., Wilson, J. (2021). Opportunities and challenges for decarbonizing steel production by creating markets for 'green steel' products. *Journal of Cleaner Production*, 315, 128127. https://doi.org/10.1016/J.JCLEPRO.2021.128127

Nagy, J., Oláh, J., Erdei, E., Máté, D., Popp, J. (2018). The role and impact of Industry 4.0 and the internet of things on the business strategy of the value Chain—The case of hungary. *Sustainability*, 10, 3491. https://doi.org/10.3390/su10103491.

Nanterme, P., Daugherty, P. (2017). *The Era of the Intelligent Enterprise. Technology for people*. Accenture. https://www.huffpost.com/entry/accenture-the-era-of-the-intelligent-enterprise_b_5887b422e4b05a82fd5b2fa2.

Nardo, M., Forino, D., Murino, T. (2020). The evolution of man-machine interaction: The role of human in Industry 4.0 paradigm. *Production & Manufacturing Research*, 8, 20–34.

Neef, C., Hirzel, S., Arens, M. (2018). *Industry 4.0 in the European Iron and steel industry: Towards an overview of implementation and perspectives*. Institute for Systems and Innovation Research ISI: Fraunhofer.

Nurdiawati, A., Urban, F. (2021). Towards deep decarbonisation of energy-intensive industries: a review of current status, technologies and policies. *Energies*, 14, 2408. https://doi.org/10.3390/en14092408.

Oesterreich, T.D., Teuteberg, F. (2016). Understanding the implications of digitisation and automation in the context of Industry 4.0: A triangulation approach and elements of a research agenda for the construction industry, *Computers in Industry*, 83. https://doi.org/10.1016/j.compind.2016.09.006.

Orth, A., Anastasijevic, N., Eichberger, H. (2007). Low CO_2 emission technologies for iron and steelmaking as well as titania slag production. *Minerals Engineering*, 20(9), 854–861.

Pacaux-Lemoine, M.P., Trentesaux, D., Zambrano Rey, G., Millot, P. (2017). Designing intelligent manufacturing systems through human-machine cooperation principles: A human-centered approach. *Computers & Industrial Engineering*, 111, 581–595.

Pauceanu, A.M., Nada, R., Ayman, M. (2020). Employability under the fourth industrial revolution. *Economics & Sociology*, 13(3), 269–283.

Pei, M., Petäjäniemi, M., Regnell, A., Wijk, O. (2020). Toward a fossil free future with HYBRIT: Development of iron and steelmaking technology in Sweden and Finland. *Metals*, 10(7), 972–982. https://doi.org/10.3390/met10070972

Peters, H. (2016). Application of Industry 4.0 concepts at steel production from an applied research perspective. In: Presentation at 17th IFAC Symposium on Control, Optimization, and Automation in Mining, Mineral and Metal Processing, [online:] https://tc.ifac-control.org/6/2/files/symposia/vienna-2016/mmm2016_keynotes_peters. PowerPoint-Präsentation (ifac-control.org), [access data: 27.10.2023].

Peters, H. (2017). How could Industry 4.0 transform the Steel Industry? Presentation at Future Steel Forum, Warsaw, 14–15.6.2017. [online:] https://futuresteelforum.com/content-images/speakers/Prof.-Dr-Harald-Peters-Industry-4.0-transform-the-steel-industry.pdf, [access data: 27.10.2023].

Peters, T.J., Waterman, R.H. (2004). *In Search of Excellence: Lessons from America's Best-Run Companies*. Harper Business Essentials: New York.

Pieriegud, J. (2016). Cyfryzacja gospodarki i społeczeństwa – wymiar globalny, europejski i krajowy. In: Gajewski, J., Paprocki, W., Pieriegud, J. (Eds), *Syfryzacja gospodarki i społeczeństwa – szanse i wyzwania dla sektorów infrastrukturalnych*. Instytut Badań nad Gospodarką Rynkową – Gdańska Akademia Bankowa: Gdańsk.

Plattform Industrie 4.0. (2014). Plattform Industrie 4.0, 2014: Industrie 4.0. Whitepaper FuE-Themen. http://www.plattform-i40.de/sites/default/files/Whitepaper_Forschung%20Stand%203.%20April%202014_0.pdf, [access data: 3.10.2022].

Polish Steel Association. (2021). (abbreviation in Polish: HIPH), *Historia i stan rozwoju technologicznego hutnictwa na świecie. Sytuacja sektora stalowego w Polsce*. Presentation prepared by S. Dzienniak, 18 August 2021, Conference: Restructuring of steel industry, PTE, Katowice, Poland.

Porter, M.E. (2008). *On Competition. Updated and Expanded Ed.* Harvard Business School Publishing: Boston.

Porter, M.E., Heppelmann, J.E. (November 2014). How smart, connected products are transforming competition. *Harvard Business Review*, 92(11), 64–88. https://www.hbs.edu/faculty/Pages/item.aspx?num=48195, [access data: 27.10.2023].

Proctor, M., Wilkins, J. (2019). 4.0 Sight—Digital Industry around the World. Technical Report, EU Automation. http://www.4sightbook.com/, [access data: 27.10.2023].

Pusavec, F., Kramar, D., Krainik, P., Kopac, K. (2010). Transitioning to sustainable production—Part II: Evaluation of sustainable machining technologies. *Journal of Cleaner Production*, 18, 1211–1221.

Ranjan, K.R., Read, S. (2016). Value co-creation: Concept and measurement. *Journal of the Academy of Marketing Science*, 44(3), 290–315.

Remus, R., Aguado-Monsonet, M.A., Roudier, S., Sanch, L.D. (2013). Title: Best Available Techniques (BAT) Reference Document for Iron and Steel Production. JRC REFERENCE Report. Publications Office of the European Union: EC, Luxembourg, 621pp. European Commission EUR 25521 – Joint Research Centre – Institute for Institute for Prospective Technological Studies. EUR – Scientific and Technical Research series – ISSN 1831-9424 (online), ISSN 1018-5593 (print), ISBN 978-92-79-26475-7 (pdf), ISBN 978-92-79-26476-4 (print). https://doi.org/10.2791/97469. https://eippcb.jrc.ec.europa.eu/sites/default/files/2019-11/IS_Adopted_03_2012.pdf, [access data: 27.10.2023].

REPowerEU plan: Joint European action for more affordable, secure and sustainable, European Commission, March 16, 2022, [Online]. https://www.globalcompliancenews.com/2022/03/16/european-commission-introduces-repowereu-joint-european-action-for-more-affordable-secure-and-sustainable-energy-10032022/, [access data 08.11.2023].

RFCS. (2022). Climate-neutral Steelmaking in Europe, Decarburisation pathways – Investment needs – Policy Conditions – Recommendations. European Research Executive Agency

(REA), Research Fund for Coal and Steel RFCS, 2022. [Online] https://op.europa.eu/en/publication-detail/-/publication/89cda1b2-b169-11ec-83e1-01aa75ed71a1/language-en/format-PDF/source-254269180, [access data: 27.10.2023].

Richardson-Barlow, C., Pimm, A.J., Taylor, P.G., Gale, W.F. (2022). Policy and pricing barriers to steel industry decarbonisation: A UK case study. *Energy Policy*, 168(C). https://doi.org/10.1016/j.enpol.2022.113100.

Romero, D., Bernus, P., Noran, O., Stahre, J., Fast-Berglund, Å. (2016a). The Operator 4.0: Human Cyber-Physical Systems & Adaptive Automation Towards Human-Automation Symbiosis Work Systems [in] APMS 2016, Advances in Production Management Systems. Initiatives for a Sustainable World; pp. 677–686; IFIP International Conference on Advances in Production Management Systems. [Online] https://link.springer.com/chapter/10.1007/978-3-319-51133-7_80, [access data: 27.10.2023].

Romero, D., Noran, O., Stahre, J., Bernus, P., Fast-Berglund, Å. (2015). Towards a human-centred reference architecture for next generation balanced automation systems: Human-automation symbiosis. *Advanced Production Management System*, 460, 556–566.

Romero, D., Stahre, J., Taisch, M. (2020). The Operator 4.0: Towards socially sustainable factories of the future. *Computers & Industrial Engineering*, 139, 106128.

Romero, D., Stahre, J., Wuest, T., Noran, O., Bernus, P., Fast-Berglund, Å., Gorecky, D. (2016b). Towards an operator 4.0 typology: A human-centric perspective on the fourth industrial revolution technologies. In: Proceedings of the International Conference on Computers and Industrial Engineering (CIE46), Tianjin, China, 29–31 October 2016; Volume 11, pp. 1–11.

Rosen, M.A., Kishawy, H.A. (2012). Sustainable manufacturing and design: Concepts, practices and needs. *Sustainability*, 4, 154–174.

Różański, P., Borecki, M., Niesler, M., Stecko, J., Szulc, W., Zdonek, B. (2022). Decarbonisation pathways of the steel industry. *Journal of Metallic Materials*, 74(3–4), 47–60. https://doi.org/10.32730/imz.2657-747.22.3-4.6.

Rüßmann, M., Lorenz, M., Gerbert, P., Waldner, M., Justus, J., Engel, P., Harnisch, M. (2015). Industry 4.0: The future of productivity and growth in manufacturing industries. *Boston Consulting Group*, 9(1), 54–89.

Ruppert, T., Jaskó, Sz., Holczinger, T., Abonyi, J. (2018). Enabling technologies for operator 4.0: A survey. *Apply Science*, 8, 1650; MDPI, https://doi.org/10.3390/app8091650; [online:] https://www.mdpi.com/2076-3417/8/9/1650, [access data: 20.01.2021].

Salam, M.A., Shaikh, M.A.A., Ahmed, K. (2023). Green hydrogen based power generation prospect for sustainable development of Bangladesh using PEMFC and hydrogen gas turbine. *Energy Reports*, 9, 3406–3416.

SALCOS: Argenta P. Sustenovability. SALCOS: Hydrogen for Steel Making. Tenova, S.p.A., Castellanza, Italy. https://sustenovability.tenova.com/Tenova-Salcos-Hydrogen-for-Steel-Making.php, [access data: 10.03.2023).

SALCOS: Salzgitter. https://salcos.salzgitter-ag.com/en/index.html, [access data: 10.03.2023).

Saldivar, A.A.F., Li, Y., Chen, W.N., Zhan, Z.H., Zhang, J., Chen, L.Y. (2015). Industry 4.0 with cyber-physical integration: A design and manufacture perspective. In: 21st International Conference on Automation and Computing (ICAC). https://doi.org/10.1109/IConAC.2015.7313954.

Saniuk, S., Grabowska, S., Gajdzik, B. (2020a). Social expectations and market changes in the context of developing the Industry 4.0 concept. *Sustainability*, 12, 1362. https://doi.org/10.3390/su12041362.

Saniuk, S., Grabowska, S., Gajdzik, B. (2020b). Personalization of products in the Industry 4.0 concept and its impact on achieving a higher level of sustainable consumption. *Energies*, 13, 5895. https://doi.org/10.3390/en13225895.

Santos, C., Mehrsai, A., Barros, A.C., Araújo, M., Ares, E. (2017). Towards Industry 4.0: An overview of European strategic roadmaps. In: Manufacturing Engineering Society International Conference, MESIC 2017, 28–30 June 2017. Vigo (Pontevedra), Spain.

Santos, C.A., Spim, Jr, J.A., Ierardi, M.C., Garcia, A. (2002). The use of artificial intelligence technique for the optimisation of process parameters used in the continuous casting of steel. *Applied Mathematical Modelling*, 26(11), 1077–1092.

Schlaepfer, R.C., Koc, M. (2015). Deloitte AG, Industry 4.0: Challenges and Solutions for the Digital Transformation and Use of Exponential Technologies, Audit, Tax, Consulting, Corporate Finance. https://www2.deloitte.com/content/dam/Deloitte/ch/Documents/manufacturing/ch-en-manufacturing-industry-4-0-24102014.pdf

Schmidt, B., Rutkowsky, S., Petersen, I., Klotzke, F. (2015). Digital supply chains-Increasingly critical for competitive edge, European A.T. Kearney, www.atkearney.com, [access data: 27.10.2023].

SEforALL, Sustainable Energy or All Strategic Direction (Detailed) (un.org). https://www.un.org/millenniumgoals/pdf/SEFA.pdf, (access data: 15.03.2023).

Senn, C. (2019). The nine pillars of Industry 4.0. https://www.idashboards.com/blog/2019/07/31/the-pillars-of-industry-4-0/, [access data: 27.10.2023].

Shafiq, S.I., Sanin, C., Toro, C., Szczerbicki, E. (2016). Virtual engineering object (VEO): Toward experience-based design and manufacturing for Industry 4.0. *Cybernetics and Systems*, 46(1–2). https://doi.org/10.1080/01969722.2015.1007734.

Shahabuddin, M., Brooks, G., Rhamdhani, M.A. (2023). Decarbonisation and hydrogen integration of steel industries: Recent development, challenges and technoeconomic analysis. *Journal of Cleaner Production*, 395, 136391. https://doi.org/10.1016/J.JCLEPRO.2023.136391, [access data: 27.10.2023].

Shmeleva, I.A., Shmelev, S.E. (2019). How sustainable is smart and how smart is sustainable? *Sustainable Cities Reimagined*, pp. 316–328, Routledge. https://doi.org/10.4324/9780429287725-11.

Shrouf, F., Ordieres, J., Miragliotta, G. (2014). Smart factories in Industry 4.0: A review of the concept and of energy management approached in p\Production based on the internet of things paradigm. In: Proceedings of the IEEE International Conference on Industrial Engineering and Engineering Management. Bandar Sunway. Malaysia; pp. 9–12.

SIDERWIN. (2019). H. Lavelaine, ArcelorMittal Maizières, France, ΣIDERWIN partners, https://www.siderwin-spire.eu/, [access data: 10.03.2023).

Singh, A., Shivapuji, A.M., Dasappa, S. (2023). VPSA process characterization for ISO quality green hydrogen generation using two practical multi-component biomass gasification feeds. *Separation and Purification Technology*, 315, 123667.

Sniderman, B., Mahto, M., Cotteleer, M.J. (2016). Industry 4.0 and manufacturing ecosystems Exploring the world of connected enterprises, Deloitte Development LLC, pp. 1–24. https://www2.deloitte.com/content/dam/insights/us/articles/manufacturing-ecosystems-exploring-world-connected-enterprises/DUP_2898_Industry4.0ManufacturingEcosystems.pdf, [access data: 27.10.2023].

Sobaszek, L., Gola, A., Swic, A. (2017). Predictive scheduling as a part of intelligent job scheduling system. In: Intelligent Systems in Production Engineering and Maintenance—ISPEM 2017: Proceedings of the First International Conference on Intelligent Systems in Production Engineering and Maintenance. Springer. Berlin, Germany; pp. 358–367.

Sohn, H.Y., Mohassab, Y. (July 2016). Greenhouse Gas Emissions and Energy Consumption of Ironmaking Processes Chapter. https://doi.org/10.1007/978-3-319-39529-6. https://www.researchgate.net/publication/305764142, [access data: 27.10.2023].

Somers, J. (2022). Technologies to decarbonise the EU steel industry, EUR 30982 EN, Publications Office of the European Union, Luxembourg. Luxembourg. https://doi.org/10.2760/069150.

Sreedharan, V.R., Unnikrishnan, A. (2017). Moving towards industry 4.0: A systematic review. *International Journal of Pure and Applied Mathematics*, 117(20), 17–28.

Steelonthenet.com. Steel Industry Emissions of CO_2. https://www.steelonthenet.com/kb/CO2-emissions.html, [access data 10.03.2023].

Stock, T., Obenaus, M., Kunz, S., Kohl, H. (2018). Industry 4.0 as enabler for a sustainable development: A qualitative assessment of its ecological and social potential. *Process Safety and Environmental*, 118, 254–267. https://doi.org/10.1016/j.psep.2018.06.026

Stock, T., Seliger, G. (2016). Opportunities of sustainable manufacturing in Industry 4.0. *Procedia CIRP*, 40, 536–541.

Strange, R., Zucchella, A. (2017). Industry 4.0, global value chains and international business. *Multinational Business Review*, 25(3), 174–184.

Strassburger, J.H., Brown, D.C., Dancy, T.E., Stephenson, R.L. (1969). *Blast Furnace-Theory and Practice*. Gordon and Breach Science, London.

SuSteel (Project). 01.09.2016 – 29.02.2020. https://www.k1-met.com/non_comet/susteel, [access data: 10.03.2023].

Tata Steel. (2020). HIsarna: Building a Sustainable Steel Industry. Steel for Sustainable Future. https://www.Tatasteeleurope.com/en/sustainability/steel-for-a-sustainable-future/the-life-cycle-of-steel, [access data: 10.03.2023].

The Boston Consulting Group. (June, 2016). Przemysł 4.0 Szansa czy zagrożenie dla rozwoju innowacyjnej gospodarki? pp. 7–17 [online].https://przemysl-40.pl/wp-content/uploads/2017-Gospodarka-4.0.pdf, [access data: 27.10.2023].

Tuttokmaği, Ö., Kaygusuz, A. (2018). *Smart Grids and Industry 4.0*. IEEE: Turkey, Malatya. https://doi.org/10.1109/IDAP.2018.8620887.

ULCOS: TataSteel. (2013). Development of ULCOS—Blast Furnace. 2013. https://ieaghg.org/docs/General_Docs/Iron%20and%20Steel%202%20Secured%20presentations/1050%20Jan%20van%20der%20Stel.pdf, [access data: 10.03.2023].

UN (United Nations). (1987). *Our Common Future. Report of the World Commission on Environment and Development*. UN: New York.

Vogl, V., Åhman, M., Nilsson, L.J. (2018). Assessment of hydrogen direct reduction for fossil-free steelmaking. *Journal of Cleaner Production*, 203, 736–745.

Wang, Y., Ma, H.-S., Yang, J.-H., Wang, K.-S. (2017). Industry 4.0: A way from mass customization to mass personalization production. *Advances in Manufacturing*, 5(4), 311–320. https://doi.org/10.1007/s40436-017-0204-7.

Whicher, A., Harris, C., Beverley, K., Swiatek, P. (2018). Design for circular economy: Developing an action plan for Scotland. *Journal of Cleaner Production*, 172, 3237–3248.

Wiesmüller, M. (2014). Industrie 4.0: surfing the wave? E&I *Elektrotechnik und Informationstechnik*, 1, 15–28.

World Steel Association Report. (2022). World Steel Association (abbreviation: WorldSteel). World Steel in Figures 2022. https://worldsteel.org/steel-topics/statistics/world-steel-in-figures-2022/, [access data: 27.10.2023]

Worrell, E., Price, L., Neelis, M., Galitsky, C., Nan, Z. (2008). *World Best Practice Energy Intensity Values for Selected Industrial Sectors*. Lawrence Berkeley National Laboratory, Berkeley, CA. LBNL-62806.

Wyns, T., Khandekar, G., Robson, I. (2018). Industrial Value Chains – A Bridge Towards a Carbon Neutral Europe. https://ec.europa.eu/info/funding-tenders/opportunities/portal/screen/opportunities/topic-details/lc-gd-3-1-2020, [access data: 27.10.2023].

Xylia, M., Silveira, S., Duerinck, J., Meinke-Hubeny, F. (2018). Weighing regional scrap availability in global pathways for steel production processes. *Energy Efficiency*, 11, 1135–1159.

Zaini, I.N., Nurdiawati, A., Gustavsson, J., Wei, W., Thunman, H., Gyllenram, R., Samuelsson, P., Yang, E. (2023). Decarbonising the iron and steel industries: Production of carbon-negative direct reduced iron by using biosyngas. *Energy Conversion and Management*. https://doi.org/10.1016/j.enconman.2023.116806.

Zawadzki, P., Zywicki, K. (2016). Smart product design and production control for effective mass customization in the Industry 4.0 concept. *Management and Production Engineering Review*, 7, 105–112.

Zhou, K., Liu, T., Zhou, L. (2015). Industry 4.0: Towards future industrial opportunities and challenges. In: 12th International Conference on Fuzzy Systems and Knowledge Discovery (FSKD); pp. 2147–2152.

Zucchella, A., Strange, R., Mascherpa, S. (2019). Which organizational capabilities matter for international performance? An analysis of entrepreneurial firms. *European Journal of International Management*, 13(4), 454–478.

2 The analysis of steel industry development in policies and numbers

2.1 The essence of steel industry development in governmental policies

The development of the steel industry is often heavily influenced by governmental policies, as this industry plays a vital role in a country's economic growth and infrastructure development. Government policies can affect various aspects of the steel industry, including production, trade, environmental regulations, and research and development.

Governments often impose tariffs and trade policies that can either protect domestic steel producers or promote international trade. Tariffs can make imported steel more expensive, thereby protecting domestic steel manufacturers from foreign competition. Conversely, the reduction of trade barriers can open up new markets for steel exports. Governments can provide financial incentives, such as tax breaks or subsidies, to encourage investment in steel production and technology. These incentives can stimulate the development of modern and efficient steel manufacturing facilities (Pourmehdi et al., 2022).

Infrastructure development projects, such as the construction of highways, bridges, and buildings, can significantly boost steel demand. Government policies that allocate funds for infrastructure projects can have a direct impact on the steel industry. Environmental policies can impact the steel industry in multiple ways. Governments may impose regulations to reduce emissions and promote cleaner production methods. This can lead to investments in technologies that improve the environmental performance of steel manufacturing processes.

Government regulations related to labour conditions and safety standards can affect the steel industry's operation. Compliance with these regulations can lead to changes in work practices and investments in safety measures. Government funding for research and development in the steel industry can lead to innovations in production methods and materials, making the industry more competitive and sustainable.

Governments can impose restrictions on the import and export of steel products for various reasons, including national security, trade balance, and anti-dumping measures. These controls can influence the global market dynamics of the steel industry. The energy consumption of the steel industry is substantial. Government

DOI: 10.4324/9781032697611-2

policies related to energy sources, pricing, and efficiency can impact the steel industry's operating costs and environmental performance (Yu et al., 2015).

Participation in international agreements and organizations can also shape a country's steel industry policies. For example, commitments made under global trade agreements or environmental treaties can influence a nation's approach to steel production. Governments may implement policies to address overcapacity in the steel industry, such as encouraging mergers, closures, or capacity reduction initiatives to balance supply and demand.

Global overproduction of steel and the aggressive pro-export policies of third-party countries, with insufficient protection of the EU market against cheap and often unfair imports of steel products, have caused a decline in the competitiveness of European steel producers. Competitiveness has also decreased due to the high costs of the ambitious climate policy pursued by the European Commission, costs that third-party countries do not bear. For steel producers in Poland, an additional factor reducing competitiveness is the higher prices of electricity and gas compared to other EU countries.

Similar to other industrial sectors in EU countries, particularly in energy-intensive sectors, there is a competitiveness threat due to anticipated unfavourable changes in the legal environment, particularly related to EU climate policy, and rising energy costs (Polish Steel Industry, 2017).

For example, in India The National Steel Policy, as of March 15, 2021, reflects the long-term vision of the government to stimulate the growth of the steel sector. The policy's objective is to establish a technologically advanced and globally competitive steel industry that fosters self-sufficiency in steel production and contributes to economic growth. In the context of a deregulated steel sector, the government serves as a facilitator by creating an enabling environment for the sector's development.

Key initiatives implemented by the government in pursuit of these goals include (National Steel Policy, 2021):

- Domestically Manufactured Iron & Steel Products (DMI&SP) Policy: This policy encourages the production and consumption of domestically produced steel.
- Steel Scrap Policy: Aimed at increasing the availability of domestically generated scrap for steel production.
- Issuance of Steel Quality Control Orders: These orders prevent the manufacturing and import of non-standardized steel, ensuring quality standards are met.
- Steel Import Monitoring System (SIMS): An advanced registration system for steel imports to track and manage steel trade.
- Engagement with Industry Stakeholders: The government collaborates with industry associations and domestic steel industry leaders to identify and address issues that require the intervention of relevant central and state government ministries and departments.
- Expanding Steel Demand: Collaboration with stakeholders from various sectors, including Railways, Defence, Petroleum and Natural Gas, Housing, Civil

Aviation, Road Transport and Highways, Agriculture, and Rural Development, to enhance the overall demand for steel in the country.

- Inclusion of 'Specialty Steel' in the Production Linked Incentive (PLI) Scheme: A recent government initiative to promote speciality steel production.
- Tax and Duty Schemes: Implementation of various schemes like the Duty Drawback Scheme and Advanced Authorization Scheme, aimed at refunding or exempting taxes and duties on inputs used in the export production process, to improve the cost competitiveness of exported items.

Poland's metals and steel industry is currently displaying financial resilience in 2023, with positive forecasts for subsectors, including basic metals, non-ferrous metals, and castings of metals. However, there are looming downside risks that could impact the sector's performance. Atradius maintains a neutral underwriting stance across major subsectors, considering the industry's strengths in terms of business financials and weaknesses such as decreasing demand and high-energy prices.

Several potential risks could lead to higher insolvency rates than currently expected. These include a severe deterioration in the German buyer segment, significant monetary tightening by the Polish Central Bank to combat inflation, and delays in payments from EU recovery funds due to disputes between the European Commission and the Polish government over rule-of-law issues. Such delays could affect economic recovery and infrastructure construction, a significant buyer of steel in the Polish market.

Overall, while the industry shows financial resilience, it faces potential challenges that may impact its credit risk assessment, including profit margin trends, dependence on bank financing, non-payment expectations, willingness of banks to provide credit, and insolvency rates (Industry Trends, 2022).

2.2 Determinants for the smart steel manufacturing

Manufacturing is evolving and taking different forms. The Fourth Industrial Revolution introduces the integration of physical production resources with cyberspace to create cyber-physical systems (Chen, 2017). Industry 4.0 is revolutionizing the way companies manufacture, improve, and distribute their products. Manufacturers are integrating new technologies, including Internet of Things (IoT), cloud computing and analytics, and AI and machine learning into their production facilities and throughout their operations. Smart machines, smart robots, predictive maintenance systems, autonomous process optimization systems, and mobile and IoT devices are just some of the solutions that are needed to be smart manufacturing (SM). Industry 4.0 as a development concept based on the Fourth Revolution technologies is a broader and more general concept than smart manufacturing. This concept and its key technologies play an important (fundamental) role in making industrial systems autonomous and thus enabling the automated collection of data from industrial machines/components. Based on the collected data type, machine-learning algorithms can be applied for automated fault detection and diagnosis

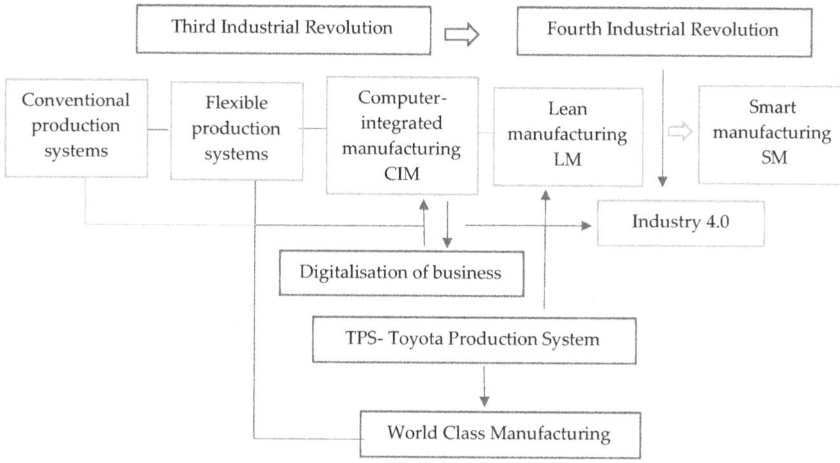

Figure 2.1 Evolution of production systems.

Source: This figure was prepared by B. Gajdzik and was published in Organization and Management (2023) based on: (Von CIM über Lean Produktion zu Industrie 4.0", by J. Soder, 2017 In T. Bauernhansl, B. ten Hompel, B. Vogel-Heuser (Eds), *Handbuch Industrie 4.0*, Band 1: Produktion, Springer, Wiesbaden).

(Çınar et al., 2020). A new form of evolution of the concept of Industry 4.0 is Industry 5.0 (Xu et al., 2022). Steel mills are more in line with Industry 5.0 than Industry 4.0 because they are strongly focused on sustainable steel production. In both concepts, the strategic direction is smart manufacturing, in the case of the steel mills it is smart steel manufacturing (Gajdzik, 2022b, 2022c; Gajdzik and Wolniak, 2022a).

Smart manufacturing is built on the pillars of the Industry 4.0 concept, which are the results of the Fourth Industrial Revolution. According to Soder (2017), smart manufacturing is another form of manufacturing. Soder outlined that the manufacturing is changing from conventional systems through flexible and computer-integrated systems, Lean Manufacturing, to Industry 4.0 (Figure 2.1).

There is no generally accepted definition of smart manufacturing. According to the National Institute of Standards and Technology (NIST), smart manufacturing is a fully integrated, collaborative manufacturing system that responds in real time to meet changing demands and conditions in the factory, supply network, and customer needs. Kusiak (2017) said that:

> smart manufacturing integrated manufacturing assets of today and tomorrow with sensors, computing platforms, communication technology, data intensive modelling, control, simulation and predictive engineering. Smart manufacturing utilises the concepts of the Cyber-Physical Systems (CPSs), Internet of Things (IoT) or Internet of Everything (IoE), cloud computing, service-oriented computing, artificial intelligence (AI) and data science.
>
> (p. 509)

These technologies are also mentioned in the smart manufacturing definitions of the following authors Wang et al. (2021), Hobbs (2004), as well as in the RAMI4.0 (March 2017) and in Japanese SMKL (2020).

Smart manufacturing can be considered to be a new version of intelligent manufacturing that highlights the use of advanced information and communication technology and advanced data analytics (Tao, 2019; Zhong et al., 2017, Thoben et al., 2017). Smart manufacturing is based on data and information, largely the term 'smart' refers to the creation and use of data (Zhong et al., 2017). Technologies are equipped with advanced sensors, embedded software, and robotics to collect and analyse data and enable better decision-making. Even greater value is gained when data from manufacturing operations is combined with operational data from ERP, supply chain, customer service, and other enterprise systems to create a whole new level of visibility and insight from previously collected data. Transmission and analysis of data take place in real time throughout the product life cycle with model-based simulation and process optimization, creating "smart" to bring a positive impact on all aspects of production (Tao et al., 2018, 2019; O'Donovan et al., 2015).

Smart manufacturing means manufacturing that improves its performance aspects with integrated and intelligent use of processes and resources in cyber, physical, and human spheres to create and deliver products and services, which also collaborates with other domains within enterprises' value chains (Winter, 2022). Smart manufacturing promises improved performance through the digital transformation of manual and mechanical systems, and the further integration of automated systems with business systems and advanced technologies. The performance aspects include productivity, agility, efficiency, safety, security, sustainability, rapidity, quality, waste zero, or any other performance indicators identified by the enterprise (KPIs – Key Performance Indicators). In addition to manufacturing, other enterprise domains can be included into smart solutions, e.g. engineering, logistics, marketing, procurement, distributions, sales, or any other domains identified by the enterprise (Winter, 2022).

A key determinant for smart manufacturing is cyber-physical integration. The stronger the integration of information technology (IT) and physical objects (OT), the stronger the core of smart manufacturing. The word "core" for cyber–physical integration was used by Tao et al. (2019). In general, smart manufacturing is a result of a "marriage" of the physical object and virtual object. It is previewed that for each physical object or asset, a corresponding virtual object (sometimes called a Digital Twin) exists. The virtual object can be a placeholder (directly or indirectly) for data and information related to the physical object, and it exists throughout its full life or possibly longer. On the level of factory, this "marriage" of physical objects and virtual objects are manifested in Cyber-Physical Production System (CPPS). The structure of CPPS is multidimensional and consist of complex systems that integrate the cyber world and the dynamic physical world (He, 2010; Rajkumar et al., 2010). In this structure, collaboration of computing, communication, and control, known as the "3C", is needed (Tao et al., 2019). CPS provide real-time sensing, information feedback, dynamic control, and other services (Hu et al., 2012; Liu et al., 2017).

Table 2.1 Framework of smart manufacturing

Pillar	*Description*
Intelligent (smart) products	A product manufactured using the latest technology and very often with the latest materials, with operational features built in, as well as product history charts throughout its life cycle. Built-in functions (applications) to enhance its usability, and the consumer can configure the product according to his or her needs.
Smart production processes	Smart production focuses on intelligent processes with the various steps in the product lifecycle (from design phase to retirement phase). Computer systems autonomously control the capacity of production processes (KPIs are the control tools) and intelligent robots and machines learn from historical data to meet new challenges.
Vertical integration	Vertically integrated manufacturing systems consist of systems involved in the business value chain (from strategic management level to operational plant floor level), particular systems are integrated.
Horizontal integration	Horizontally integrated manufacturing systems implies that the systems involved in the supply chain (from procurement to shipping) are integrated.

Source: Own elaboration based on Johsson and Brandl (2018).

Modern technologies and digital solutions allow production of personalized (customized) goods according to customers' wishes. Modern technologies help to make customer needs more realistic. Ahelroff et al. (2019) emphasizes that in personalization, the needs of customers meet the possibilities of manufacturing processes. The basis of personalization is dialogue. Therefore, personalization involves internal (what a person needs) and external (environmental) data collection (Aheleroff et al., 2019). Customers are the beginning of smart manufacturing. The customer is the centre of smart manufacturing, the realization of customer integration, and the starting point of smart manufacturing, and the organic integration of customer needs through some smart technology will certainly double the value of manufacturing.

Smart manufacturing has key pillars that define its framework. One of these is the levels of integration and technologies that enable the development of smart products and smart processes. According to Johsson and Brandl (Feb., 2018), smart manufacturing focuses on the establishment of intelligent products and smart production processes, as well as on vertically and horizontally integrated manufacturing systems. These four integration perspectives describe smart manufacturing (Table 2.1).

According to Kusiak (2018), there are six pillars of smart manufacturing: (1) manufacturing technology and processes, (2) materials, (3) data, (4) predictive engineering, (5) sustainability, and (6) resource sharing and networking. Table 2.2 presents these pillars of smart manufacturing.

A smart factory needs smart manufacturing, smart machines, smart processes, smart logistics, smart engineering, smart products, and, of course, IoT intelligent devices (Ryalat, 2023) (Table 2.3). Everything is integrated in the smart factory. Smart factory is vertically integrated, horizontally integrated, and value chain integrated.

According to the international model, the vertical factory system consists of a three-layer structure: a Shop Floor Control system (SFC), a Manufacturing

Table 2.2 Six pillars of smart manufacturing based on Kusiak (2018)

Pillar	*Description*
Manufacturing technology and processes	An example of a new technology is additive manufacturing which encourages the development of new materials, influences the design and manufacture of products and their application. Manufacturing tools are designed to integrate different operations, e.g. machines capable of horizontal and vertical milling and drilling (machining centre). Traditional technologies are merging with additive ones. A new generation of low-cost robots improves plant automation. Sensors and software capabilities are making new manufacturing equipment smarter and more factory and supply chain friendly.
Materials	Products are made from new organic materials, biomaterials, new mixes and forms of materials, such as metal powders. In smart manufacturing, the recovery of materials from products at the end of their life cycle is growing in importance.
Data	Data from sensors is sent in real time to process control systems (advances in data analytics have improved decision-making processes). New technologies have greater capacity to collect data from different sources. Data is used to feed any system related to production and related processes.
Predictive engineering	Predictive engineering leads to an anticipatory rather than reactive enterprise. Predictive engineering offers a new paradigm of constructing high-fidelity models (digital representations) of the phenomena of interest. Such models allow exploring spaces, some within the realm of the existing technology and others that have not been seen previously.
Sustainability	Smart manufacturing saves materials and energy and reduces pollution associated with production. Manufacturing is to be waste-free. In the process optimization, technologies use the algorithms of circular economy. Sustainability starts with product design, sustainable production processes, sustainable materials and sustainable products and services. The boundaries between production and service are blurring, e.g. remanufacturing a used product.
Resource sharing and networking	Smart manufacturing enables the sharing of resources between companies, including competing companies, e.g. the sharing of production equipment, software, knowledge, and, most importantly, collaborative modelling and space for creativity. Networking is changing supply chains, making them more flexible and surrounding them with digital spaces. Networks are the result of integration around value. Networks add value through nodes and connections.

Source: Own elaboration based on: (Kusiak, 2018).

Execution System (MES), and an Enterprise Resources Planning system (ERP). A smart factory is three layers up and down, each layer is modularized to form an intelligent platform; at the same time, a production data centre is created. In this way, the data flow between the product's intelligent nuclear smarts can be realized, thus realizing automatic data collection, automatic data transmission, automatic decision-making, automatic operation and handling, and automatic error handling. This vertical integration represents an interconnected production

Table 2.3 Pillars of smart factory

Pillar	*Description*
Smart manufacturing	Smart manufacturing integrates various technologies related to manufacturing, computing, virtualization, connectivity, data handling etc. Manufacturing is a basic process, it is here that added value is created, and modern technologies help to create a "new" face of added value. Smart manufacturing is a broad production concept aimed at optimization of production transactions and products through full use of advanced technologies information and production. Intelligent technologies greatly improve the design, production, management, and integration of the entire lifecycle of a typical product. The whole product life cycle can be monitored by various smart sensors, adaptive models decision-making, advanced materials, smart devices, and data analytics (Li et al. 2017; Jeschke et al., 2017; Bahrin et al., 2016; Lopez Research, 2014)
Smart machines	Smart machines are devices equipped with machine-to-machine (M2M) and/or cognitive computing technologies, such as artificial intelligence (AI), characterized by rapid learning. Machine learning is used for reasoning, problem-solving, decision-making, and action. Intelligent machines include robots and other cognitive processing systems (cognitive computing) that perform tasks, often without human intervention (Jiafu et al., 2014).
Smart processes	Intelligent production processes are dynamic, efficient, and automated. Communication is realized in real time in order to manage and control the highly dynamic production environment implemented through the Internet of Things. Intelligent devices (Internet of Things) enables communication of devices and interactions between them and, if required, with the more centralized controller. This also decentralizes analyses and decision-making, allowing for responding in real time. IoT is also created by sensors and their readers in industry, transport, or trade (Lee et al., 2015).
Smart logistics	Smart logistics includes smart logistics tools and processes. Self-organizing logistics is an example of intelligent internal logistics, responding to unexpected changes in production, such as bottlenecks and material shortages (Douaioui et al., 2018).
Smart engineering	Smart engineering is mostly the product design and development, product engineering, production as well as after-sales service (Trappey et al., 2015; Kinsy et al., 2011).
Smart devices	A smart device is a context-aware electronic device capable of performing autonomous calculations and connecting to other devices wired or wirelessly for data exchange (Silverio-Fernández et al., 2018).
Smart product	Smart products have abilities to track (e.g. RFID tags) throughout their lifecycle – from production, through transport, servicing, to recycling.

Source: Own elaboration based on Łukasik and Stachowiak (2020). More in: Li et al. (2017), Lee et al. (2015), Jiafu et al. (2014), Jeschke et al. (2017), Trappey et al. (2015), Kinsy et al. (2011), Bahrin et al. (2016), Lopez Research (2014), Douaioui et al. (2018).

system in the factory. This network production system consists of many modules, including models, data, communication, algorithms, and so on. In the process of producing different products, the modular network production system can reorganize the module topology as necessary to meet the needs of personalized product production. This integrated networked production system can be seen as a huge intelligent machine system; the module can be seen as its software unit, and the process of changing the topology is a reprogramming process, but all activities are automatically performed. According to the instructions given by the various products, the networked production system can organize production according to the customer's needs (Pérez-Lara et al., 2020; Werr, 2014).

Horizontal integration encompasses the integration of intelligent systems across various stages of production, spanning the configuration of materials, energy, and information within a company (such as raw materials, production processes, product materials, marketing, etc.), as well as the establishment of value networks between different companies. Horizontal integration, vertical integration, and value chain integration form an intelligent production network. Thanks to new technologies such as the Internet, IoT, cloud computing, big data, mobile communication, etc., distributed smart manufacturing resources are highly integrated, thus building the integration of network-based smart factory (Pérez-Lara et al., 2020; Werr, 2014; Ryalat, 2023; Wang et al., 2016). Horizontal integration is also the basis of value chain integration. Horizontal and vertical integrations build the value chain integration.

The process of producing a product may involve multiple links in the value chain, such as determining product demand, product design, product planning, product engineering, production, sales support, etc. Each link may have different companies. So-called value chain integration is the integration of products in one company or multiple companies from demand analysis to the full sales service value chain to ensure the realization of personalized products. Value chain integration is a way of achieving customer value, horizontal integration, and vertical integration to ensure maximum realization of this value. Two forms of integrations create an intelligent production system.

In traditional product manufacturing, end-to-end value chain integration is generally achieved through CAX data interfaces, SFCMESERP, and other systems. In an intelligent manufacturing system, this will be realized through seamless base layer integration via the CPS, and data interaction is realized through vertical integration between the CPS and SFCMESERP. Value chain integration links horizontal and vertical integration to maximize final value and maximize customer satisfaction.

Smart Manufacturing (SM) consists of many projects including production technology modification projects and new machine investments, IT projects, operation visualization projects, process monitoring projects, activity automation projects, machine data collection projects, etc. (IEC PAS 63088:2017). Each company chooses its own pathway (pathway) of smart manufacturing. There are many IT projects on the market that can be adapted to a company's needs. To build smart manufacturing you need to analyse, understand, organize, plan, do, and act (Siemens, 2017). These management functions (Table 2.4) ultimately enable process, product, and supply chain improvements.

Table 2.4 The path to smart manufacturing

Function	*Questions/actions*
Analyse/ diagnosis	Analyse other companies • What digital technologies have been adopted by others? • What business benefits have been achieved? • Would this approach be successful in my organization? • Could my company achieve similar benefits? Track information on new technologies related to Industry 4.0 • Can these technologies be applied in my facility? • What benefits would they achieve?
Understand	• Constant monitoring of literature and publications on digital solutions to keep up to date on new technologies and digital solutions and their application in the industry. • Participation in training courses, business meetings. • Exchange of knowledge at different levels of the organization. • Cooperation with external IT companies (consultancy).
Organize	• Establish a unit within the organization responsible for the adaptation of new technologies and digital solutions. • The department (position) should be interdepartmental in scope, avoiding the pitfalls of a "silo" approach to digital strategies. • Collaboration on SM at the level of capital-linked companies (alliances with partners, customers, research centres and universities, and even some competitors). • Selection of an external co-operator: ICTs provider, sensor assembler, etc.
Plan	• Chief Digital Officer (CDO) or Chief Digital Information Officer (CDIO) is responsible for planning and coordinating activities across the organization. • Strategic plans need to be broken down into projects.
Do	• Launching pilot projects and subsequent projects transforming manufacturing into smart manufacturing. • Staff training on the possibilities of new technologies and popularizing them within the organization. • Development of smart technologies at shop-floor level. • Creating virtual models and achieving feedback between shop-floor and virtual model/IT-OT integration. • Embedded sensors and interconnected machinery produce a significant amount of big data for manufacturing companies. • Building a hybrid multicloud IT infrastructure i innych rozwiązań optymalizacji obciążeń transferu danych. • Custom manufacturing: advanced simulation software applications, new materials, and technologies such as 3-D printing, etc. • Supply chain: sharing some production data with suppliers, predictive shipping, improving networking, building blockchain for transparency of cooperation (blocks are chronological data about products and processes connected with them/circular information life cycles).
Act	Analysis of the results of implementing smart projects. • Feedback loop: verification of assumptions made in the strategy and changes to the strategy 'on the fly'. Changes to the smart manufacturing roadmap.

Source: Own elaboration based on Siemens (2017). More in: Gajdzik, Monograph (2022a) and Gajdzik et al. (2021).

Table 2.5 Benefits of implementing smart manufacturing (examples)

Production	• Increased productivity – opportunities better use of assets and minimizing downtime. • Development of planning and monitoring processes • Manufacturing. • Optimization of processes – identification of losses and cost monitoring. • High visibility of production information at different organizational levels of companies. • Ability to track the current working status machinery and handling failures. • Ability to implement a predictive strategy maintenance. • Improving the quality of planning through the availability of data. • Manufacturing "smart" products with abilities to track (e.g. RFID tags) throughout their lifecycle – from production, through transport, servicing, to recycling. • Greater scalability of production – use of cloud platforms. • Ability to use platforms more easily crowd-sourcing. • Ability to use hybrid multi-cloud (two or more public and private clouds to manage their computing workloads). This cloud gives companies the ability to optimize their workloads across all their clouds, as some environments are better suited to or more cost-effective for certain workloads.
Company	• Increasing the competitiveness of the company – new market offers. • Conditions for manufacturing products personalized, produced in accordance with customer preferences while at the same time minimization of marginal production costs. • Transformation of the offer for consumers, building closer relationships with customers, creation of customer-centric organization. • Better matching of offer to market requirements, faster reacting to changes. • Reduced design and implementation times products to market (time-to-market). • Integration of production processes, warehousing, and logistics. • Ability to create new streams revenue and new business models. • Easier manufacturing management for geographically distributed production departments. • Ability to offer the use of data from smart products and systems as a service. • Ability to use 3D printing (machine parts) for your own needs and for sale. • Better control over the full life cycle of the product, including its use phase, thanks to the ability to transmit data to the customer to monitor the product parameters and diagnose the technical condition.
Supply chain	• Increasing the flexibility of supply chains. • Intelligent supply and logistics systems. • Tracking the flow of raw materials and products throughout the chain. • Integration of production processes, warehousing and logistics. • Managing materials, products, and information throughout the chain to optimize logistics and production processes. • Digital and "visibility" production allows for easier sharing of information between the organization and its contractors and suppliers, on the one hand, and customers and companies in the distribution network, on the other. • Sharing materials and building a common transport space – spatial logistics. • Transparency in supply chain – blockchain. • LCA and material management build green supply chain

Source: Lines 1 and 2 in this table was prepared based on Siemiens (2018) From Industry 4.0 to smart factory. Available online: https://przemysl-40.pl/index.php/2018/01/25/od-industry-4-0-do-smart-factory-czesc-1/.

Results of the smart manufacturing are more rapid product development, facilitated customized production, improved handling of complex production and testing environments, more efficient supply chains, better use of production resources, and more holistic life-cycle management (Johsson and Brandl, 2018). Table 2.5 presents the benefits of implementing smart manufacturing. The benefits are organized into three segments: production, company, and supply chain. The segment typology stems from the essence of the development of smart technology, i.e. from the basic process, which is manufacturing, through other processes within the company, to supply chains.

The birth of Industry 4.0 is giving way to growth and change, asking us to help move our companies towards smart manufacturing. Companies are investing and governments around the world are pouring a lot of money into this idea as the way of the future. Traditionally, the manufacturing industry has focused on using data for analysis, monitoring, and control, e.g. productivity analysis, process monitoring, and quality control. Traditional efforts have emphasized the past over the future states of manufacturing processes and systems. Smart manufacturing changes the situation.

Today's models are enriched with multiple systems (e.g., models integrating efficiency, product quality, energy, and transport) to support decisions about current and future production and market conditions. Smart manufacturing is a new form of manufacturing with technologies including the Internet of Things (IoT), cyber-physical system (CPS), cloud computing, artificial intelligence (AI), etc., that integrate manufacturing assets with sensors, cloud computing, communication technology, control, simulation, data-intensive modelling, and predictive engineering (more about the future of SM in: Kang et al., 2016, Kusiak, 2018, Lee, 2015, Zhou et al., 2018). Smart manufacturing has become an inevitable trend, achieving cyber-physical interaction, and integration in manufacturing is an important prerequisite of smart manufacturing. CPS and Data Technologies (DTs) are the preferred means to this end (Tao et al., 2019). However, not all companies are able to build smart manufacturing. Some invest more in new technologies, others invest less. On the market, there are companies that have modern production lines, e.g., in the automotive industry or in the food industry, as well as companies that have created only islands of modern technologies in their enterprises. On the market, part of the production will become highly distributed and part can be centralized. For example, products that are sensitive to transport costs, time to market, and customization could be produced at locations close to customers (Kuo and Kusiak, 2019).

The numbers connected with European steel industry are in Table 2.6.

2.3 Problems and challenges for the smart steel manufacturing

Improving steel manufacturing towards a "smart" and technologically advanced process is essential for the steel industry to remain competitive, sustainable, and environmentally responsible. However, this transformation is not without its share of problems and challenges.

Table 2.6 World and European Union steel industry in numbers: compilation every last three decades

World	*in*	*2000*	*2010*	*2020*
Crude steel production (total)	Million tonnes	849	1,435	1,881
Crude steel production by regions • Asia	Million tonnes	333 (39.2)	920 (64.1)	1,392.4 (73.9)
• of which China • of which India • of which Japan	Million tonnes (%)	128.5 (15.1) 26.9 (3.2) 106.4 (12.5)	638.7 (44.5) 69.0 (4.8) 109.6 (7.6)	1,064.7 (57.7) 100.3 (5.5) 83.2 (4.6)
• Europe & CIS • of which European Union • of which CIS	Million tonnes (%)	308.9 (36.4) 163.4 (19.3) 98.5 (11.6)	314.8 (21.9) 172.9 (12.1) 108.2 (7.5)	279.5 (15.2) 139.3 (7.6) 100 (5.2)
• North America • of which United States	Million tonnes (%)	135.4 (16.0) 101.8 (12.0)	111.6 (7.8) 80.5 (5.6)	101 (5.5) 72.7 (4.0)
• South America	Million tonnes (%)	39.1 (4.6)	43.9 (3.1)	38.7 (2.1)
• Middle East	Million tonnes (%)	10.8 (1.3)	20.0 (1.4)	45.7 (2.2)
• Africa	Million tonnes (%)	13.8 (1.6)	16.6 (1.2)	18.1 (0.7)
• Australia/ New Zealand	Million tonnes (%)	7.8 (0.9)	8.1 (0.6)	6.1 (0.3)
World Crude steel production by process				
• Oxygen	%	61.6	69.2	73.3
• Electric	%	33.9	29.5	26.3
• Open hearth	%	4.3	1.1	0.7
Continuously cast steel output	Million tonnes	726.6	1,332.2	1,818.3
Crude steel output	%	86.0	94.7	96.9
European (UE)	In	2000 (15)	2010 (27)	2020 (28)
Crude steel production	Million tonnes	158.9	172.6	139.295
Crude steel production by process				
• Oxygen	%	58.9	57.7	57.4

(*Continued*)

Table 2.6 (Continued)

World	*in*	*2000*	*2010*	*2020*
• Electric	%	37.1	41.1	43.7
• Open hearth	%	0.5	0.4	0
Continuously cast steel output	Million tonnes	157.2	167.1	134.7
Crude steel output	%	144.9	98.4	96.8
World apparent steel use	Million metric tons finished steel products	758.9	1,318	1,788
Apparent steel use per capita	Kilograms finished steel products	134.6	189	227.5
European Union Apparent steel use	Million metric tons finished steel products	147.7	147.8	140.6
Apparent steel use per capita	Kilograms finished steel products	389.2	294.0	273.9
World steel trade in products	Million tonnes	783.6	1,337.6	1,751.4
• Export	Million tonnes	307.5	392.7	405.6
• Export share	%	39.2	29.4	22.9
• Import	Million tonnes	299.4	386.7	398.7
• Import share	%	38.19	29.0	22.7
Indirect trade in steel	Million tonnes	172.1	285.4	–
European Union steel trade	Million tonnes	110.2	134.7	118.5
• Export				
• Import		106.8	125.8	127.7
Indirect trade in steel exports	Million tonnes	180.1 (2001 r.)	285.4	358.9 (2019 r.)
World employment	Number	–	–	6,100,000 (2017 r.)
EU employment	Number	–	369,267	326,000

Source: Own elaboration based on: World Steel in Figures; Steel Statistical Yearbook from World Steel Association. Available online: https://worldsteel.org/steel-topics/statistics; Reports: European Steel in Figures from Eurofer. Available online: https://www.eurofer.eu.

In Table 2.7, there is a description of selected problems and challenges of improving the steel manufacturing towards being smart. Enhancing energy efficiency in steel manufacturing is a paramount challenge. Traditional steel production methods are energy-intensive, and reducing this energy consumption is critical to lower production costs and minimize the industry's environmental footprint. Implementing technologies like heat recovery systems and energy-efficient furnaces is essential.

In the era of Industry 4.0, steel manufacturers are inundated with vast amounts of data. Harnessing this data for process optimization and predictive maintenance

Table 2.7 Main challenges of improving the steel manufacturing towards smart

Challenge	*Description*
Energy efficiency	Achieving higher energy efficiency is essential to reduce greenhouse gas emissions and production costs. Technologies like heat recovery, more efficient furnaces, and process optimization are key to addressing this challenge.
Data integration and analytics	Effective data integration and analytics can help identify process inefficiencies, track equipment health, and make data-driven decisions. Big data tools, AI, and machine learning are essential for this task.
Automation and workforce transition	The transition to smart manufacturing requires training and upskilling of the workforce to manage advanced automation, robotics, and AI. Retraining and ensuring a smooth workforce transition are critical.
Sustainability and environmental impact	Reducing the environmental impact of steel manufacturing involves adopting cleaner technologies, recycling, and carbon capture. Meeting sustainability targets and regulatory requirements is essential.
Supply chain integration	Integrating the steel supply chain involves real-time communication with suppliers, distributors, and customers for better coordination, reducing lead times, and minimizing inventory.
Cybersecurity	Cybersecurity is crucial to protect sensitive data, control systems, and prevent potential threats like ransomware attacks that can disrupt the manufacturing process and compromise safety.
Sensor and IoT technology	Sensors and IoT devices are used to collect real-time data from various stages of production. They must be rugged, reliable, and capable of withstanding harsh conditions to ensure data accuracy.
Materials innovation	Research and development in materials science is crucial for creating materials that can withstand extreme temperatures, corrosion, and wear in the harsh steel manufacturing environment.
Maintenance and reliability	Predictive maintenance relies on data analytics and sensors to monitor equipment health and detect potential failures before they occur, reducing downtime and maintenance costs.
Regulatory compliance	The steel industry faces complex and evolving regulations related to emissions, waste management, labour practices, and safety standards. Compliance is vital for avoiding legal and financial consequences.

Source: Own elaboration on basis: (Wanag et al., 2021; Zheng et al., 2022; Yin, 2017; Fan et al., 2023; Ometto et al., 2023; Mishra et al., 2023).

necessitates advanced data integration and analytics capabilities. Big data tools, artificial intelligence, and machine learning are instrumental for identifying inefficiencies and enhancing production (Ometto et al., 2023). As smart manufacturing technologies are adopted, there is a need for a workforce that is proficient in operating and maintaining automated systems, robotics, and AI-driven machinery. Workforce transition, including training and upskilling, is crucial to ensure a seamless shift towards smart manufacturing (Hajoary, 2022).

The steel industry has long been associated with significant environmental impact. Meeting stringent environmental regulations and reducing carbon emissions in steel production is a pressing challenge. The adoption of cleaner technologies, recycling, and carbon capture are vital steps towards a more sustainable future (Zheng et al., 2023). Effective integration of the steel supply chain, from raw material suppliers to distribution networks, is essential for streamlined operations and improved demand forecasting. Real-time communication and data sharing with all stakeholders is key to achieving this (Pourmehdi et al., 2022).

As steel manufacturing becomes more reliant on digital systems, ensuring robust cybersecurity is imperative. Protecting sensitive data, control systems, and critical infrastructure from cyber threats such as hacking and ransomware attacks is of utmost importance to maintain the integrity of the manufacturing process (Govender et al., 2019). Sensors and Internet of Things (IoT) devices play a pivotal role in collecting real-time data from different stages of production. These devices need to be durable and reliable, capable of withstanding the harsh conditions within steel mills to ensure data accuracy and integrity (Miśkiewicz and Wolniak, 2020).

To withstand the extreme temperatures, corrosive atmospheres, and wear and tear within steel manufacturing, continuous research and development in materials science is vital. Innovations in materials are essential for improving the longevity and performance of equipment. Predictive maintenance, driven by data analytics and sensors, is integral to monitor equipment health and detect potential failures before they occur. This approach reduces downtime and maintenance costs, but implementing it effectively can be a challenge (Dai and Zuo, 2020).

Also, the steel industry is subject to a complex web of regulations, including those related to emissions, waste management, labour practices, and safety standards. Adhering to these evolving regulations is crucial to avoid legal and financial repercussions (Tolettini and Lehmann, 2020).

In Table 2.8, we put the potential solutions to overcome most important challenges in the way towards smart steel manufacturing. The path towards smarter steel manufacturing is full of challenges, but it's also rich in opportunities for innovation and improvement. Overcoming these challenges requires a coordinated effort involving technological advancements, workforce development, adherence to best practices, and a commitment to sustainability and regulatory compliance. With these solutions in place, the steel industry can progress towards a more competitive, environmentally responsible, and technologically advanced future.

2.4 Steelworkers 4.0/5.0 skill models in government policy

The steel industry is characterized by its significant diversity and complexity, which necessitates a workforce with a wide range of skills and a variety of scientific backgrounds. This diversity is essential to meet the demands and challenges posed by the steel production processes. Metallurgists play a crucial role in the steel industry, as they specialize in the study of metals and their properties. They are responsible for ensuring the quality and integrity of steel products through the control of alloy compositions and production processes (Biały et al., 2019; Gajdzik and Wolniak, 2022c; Szczepańska-Woszczyna and Gajdzik, 2016).

Table 2.8 Approaches to overcome challenges in the way towards smart steel

Challenge	*Approach*
Energy efficiency	• Implement energy-efficient technologies like heat recovery systems and more efficient furnaces. • Optimize processes to reduce energy consumption. • Invest in renewable energy sources such as solar or wind power for a greener energy supply.
Data integration and analytics	• Develop a comprehensive data integration strategy. • Implement advanced analytics, artificial intelligence, and machine learning tools. • Train staff in data analysis and interpretation.
Automation and workforce transition	• Provide extensive training programmes for the workforce to adapt to automation. • Foster a culture of continuous learning and upskilling. • Collaborate with educational institutions to develop relevant skill sets.
Sustainability and environmental impact	• Invest in cleaner technologies like electric arc furnaces and hydrogen-based reduction. • Implement carbon capture and utilization techniques. • Promote recycling and circular economy practices. • Monitor emissions and work towards compliance with environmental regulations.
Supply chain integration	• Implement an integrated supply chain management system. • Employ real-time communication and data-sharing platforms. • Collaborate closely with suppliers and customers for better coordination.
Cybersecurity	• Implement robust cybersecurity protocols and practices. • Regularly update and patch software and systems. • Educate employees on cybersecurity best practices. • Conduct regular security audits.
Sensor and IoT technology	• Use rugged and reliable sensors designed for the steel manufacturing environment. • Regularly calibrate and maintain sensors. • Implement redundancy in sensor networks for data accuracy and reliability.
Materials innovation	• Invest in research and development of advanced materials. • Collaborate with material scientists and universities. • Conduct rigorous testing of materials under real-world conditions.
Maintenance and reliability	• Implement a predictive maintenance strategy. • Invest in condition monitoring systems and sensors. • Develop maintenance schedules based on data-driven insights. • Train maintenance personnel in data analysis and equipment diagnostics.
Regulatory compliance	• Stay informed about changing regulations. • Allocate resources for compliance initiatives. • Collaborate with regulatory agencies for guidance. • Conduct regular audits to ensure adherence to standards.

Source: Own elaboration on basis: (Wanag et al., 2021; Zheng et al., 2022, Yin, 2017; Fan et al., 2023; Ometto et al., 2023; Mishra et al., 2023).

Material scientists focus on the structure, properties, and applications of materials, including metals. In the steel industry, their expertise is essential for developing new materials, improving existing ones, and addressing issues related to material performance and durability. A sound understanding of chemistry is fundamental in the steel industry. Chemists are involved in various aspects, such as analysing chemical compositions, controlling reactions during steelmaking, and addressing corrosion-related challenges. Physics plays a vital role in understanding the behaviour of materials, heat transfer, and fluid dynamics within the steel manufacturing process. Physicists contribute to optimizing manufacturing techniques and solving complex engineering problems.

The integration of information technology and computer science is indispensable in modern steel production. These professionals work on developing and implementing sophisticated software and systems for process control, data analysis, and automation, which enhance efficiency and quality. The steel industry is not solely reliant on scientific and technical skills. Business and accounting professionals are essential for managing the financial aspects, logistics, supply chain, and overall operations of steel companies. They ensure that the industry remains economically sustainable and competitive (Gajdzik and Wolniak, 2022b).

Employment in the steel industry requires extensive specialized training. Many steel companies are international companies and provide international opportunities for the workforce. The scope of employment for steelworkers is very broad. Steelworkers are often employed in the construction industry as well as building and installing steel components (Liao et al., 2017). The scope of their work includes bridges, commercial buildings, and infrastructure projects. Often riveting, bolting, and welding technologies are used to join the structural components. Some of the steelworkers are also employed by steel mills and metal fabrication companies. Steel workers either work in the manufacturing of steel or the process of shaping steel into components used in construction. Steelworkers are also called *ironworkers* or *iron and steel workers*. Employment projections indicate that employment of steelworkers will increase by 5% by 2030 (Schwab and Zahide, 2020).

A steelworkers career typically requires a vocational high school degree. There are many vocational programmes focusing on welding and metal fabrication. There are also apprenticeships providing paid hands-on experience combined with classroom instruction. An apprenticeship programme requires a high school equivalency diploma and may take three-to-four years to complete. This is a very intensive programme. Participants complete annually 150 hours of classroom instruction and 2,000 hours of hands-on training.

Apprenticeship programmes are offered through vocational technical schools, community colleges, or contractors' associations. Iron and steel workers usually get a different type of certification based on their practical experience and theoretical knowledge. The most popular certifications include the following:

- Welding Certification from the American Welding Society
- Crane Operator Certification from the National Center for Construction Education and Research

In addition to technical skills, the certificate training programmes are also developing communication and leadership skills. Those soft skills are very important for promotions to supervisory or management positions. The most important skills of iron and steel workers are listed as follows (Schwab and Zahidi, 2020):

- being a team player,
- having good communication skills,
- reading blueprints and technical drawings,
- paying attention to details,
- having the ability to do analytical thinking,
- understanding and following safety procedures,
- knowing how to operate overhead cranes, and
- having physical stamina.

Even though most positions in the iron and steel industry do not require a university degree, there are many positions in managerial and technical fields requiring advanced degrees in Material Sciences and Metallurgy, Civil Engineering, Management, Accounting, etc.

Advancements in computer technology (Internet of Things and artificial intelligence) revolutionized different industries (Germany, 2017). Operationally intensive companies with labour consuming repetitive tasks are the primary candidates for digitization and automation (Dorst, 2016). The manufacturing industry contains the largest number of tasks (58%) that are technically easy to automate. Therefore, the manufacturing industry is the one benefiting the most from smart automated manufacturing. The second job sector to benefit the most from automated Industry 4.0 technology is the food industry with 53% of the tasks which can be automated (Kim and Park, 2020).

The construction industry is harder to automate with approximately 46% of the tasks which can be performed by robotics 4.0 technology. Repetitive and predicable tasks are the easiest to automate. In United States and Europe, the repetitive predictable jobs are expected to decline by 30% over the next ten years. At the same time, the number of jobs in the technology sector is expected to increase by 50% (The White House, 2011). Industry 4.0 technologies are being applied in many steel companies. New technologies and automation increase the efficiency of the supply chain as well as the efficiency of production (Pfohl et al., 2015). Smart technology helps with inventory management, quality control as well as production planning and customer service. During the COVID-19 pandemics, the steel industry was affected negatively by logistic problems as well as the labour shortage. Smart Industry 4.0 technology allowed the steel industry to recover and grow (Sigov et al., 2022). Smart technology and automated logistics allowed for real-time coordination of production, pricing, and sales. Reliance on manual labour has significantly decreased (Zhong et al., 2017).

Automated production processes as well as logistics are more energy efficient and environmentally sustainable. Ongoing innovations and continuous quality improvement constantly improve the efficiency and sustainability of the processes (Xu et al., 2014).

Reskilling of the workforce can be accomplished in three different ways.

1 Hiring new workers with the desired skills. In this approach, organizations bring in new employees who already possess the skills and qualifications needed for the jobs that require reskilling. This strategy provides an immediate solution by adding individuals with the required expertise to the workforce.
2 Retraining the existing workers for the new positions. Existing employees are given the opportunity to acquire the necessary skills and knowledge to transition into new responsibilities within the organization. This approach is cost-effective and promotes the retention of experienced staff while adapting to evolving job requirements.
3 Using the hybrid approach combines aspects of the first two methods. Initially, external workers with the desired skills are hired to meet immediate staffing needs. Simultaneously, the organization invests in retraining its current employees to develop the required skills internally. This strategy strikes a balance between immediate skill acquisition and long-term workforce development, optimizing the organization's ability to adapt to changing demands.

The most popular approach is the hybrid approach. Companies are trying to retain their existing workers and retrain them for the new positions. Existing employees are already familiar with the company's products and structure. Many of them are long-term loyal employees. Modern proactive companies are presently investing in retraining their existing workforce in automated technology and Industry 4.0. Reskilling the workforce is a very significant investment that will pay back by increasing the profit through automated manufacturing.

Digital transformation is a very complex process requiring collaboration by all employees. The plans for reskilling the workforce usually contain the following steps (Adepoju and Aigbayboa, 2021):

- Identifying all the skills needed to implement and operate automated 4.0 technology.
- Conducting an inventory of the knowledge and skills of the current workforce.
- Identifying the skill gap that must be filled by an employee retraining programme.

Skills inventory also allows the company to plan reassignment of staff to new positions. Even though digital skills are the highest priority, the range of skills is very broad (Gray, 2016). The skills which are in great demand are emotional intelligence, creativity, and enterprise initiative taking as well as leadership and entrepreneurship. A measurable pattern of knowledge, skills, and behaviours determines employee competence for a specific position. Competencies are used for the following:

- selecting the right person for the position,
- workforce distribution, and
- planning of in-service training and professional development.

Steel companies traditionally offered many in-service training programmes in the areas of production, manufacturing, engineering, technology development, marketing, logistics, etc. (Gajdzik and Wolniak, 2022b). Many steel companies are cooperating with local universities and have a tuition reimbursement programme.

Employees training and education enhance their work performance as well as limit the workforce turnover. As technology advances, in-service education is more important than ever before (Kim and Park, 2020). Steel companies are in the process of implementing the next generation of steelmaking processes. This next generation of steelmaking practices is more environmentally friendly and sustainable. These new technologies significantly lower the emissions of carbon dioxide. The demand for trained engineers, technicians, and technology experts is higher than ever before. The steel industry seeks graduates from many different majors including computer science, computer engineering as well as material sciences, metallurgical engineering, and even mathematics. The steel industry is always searching for talented individuals who will help to further develop the new technologies and innovations.

The changing technologies in the steel industry are also oriented towards occupational safety. Safety requirements need to be enforced from the top down and cannot be compromised. The steel industry is becoming one of the safest work environments.

The World Economic Forum estimates that within the next five years 50% of the employees will need to develop additional skills to keep up with technology. Lifelong learning has become a necessity. The top skills listed by the World Economic Forum are as follows (Whiting, 2020):

- analytical thinking and innovation,
- complex problem-solving,
- technology-related skills, and
- emotional intelligence.

There is also a demand for many skills related to the use of smart technology. Effectively preparing society for the challenges of Industry 4.0 necessitates close cooperation among key stakeholders in the education sector.

Business leaders play a vital role in this collaboration by supplying valuable data regarding the industry's expectations and workforce skill requirements. Their insights contribute to the alignment of educational programmes with industry needs. Both secondary and post-secondary educational institutions are responsible for developing curricula that serve a dual purpose: educating the next generation of the workforce and facilitating the reskilling of current employees. Their role is pivotal in ensuring that educational offerings remain relevant and adaptable to the demands of Industry 4.0. Governments, at both the national, state, and local levels, play a critical role by providing the necessary funding and support for training the future workforce and simultaneously reskilling the existing workforce. Their financial backing is instrumental in the creation and implementation of effective educational initiatives.

To cater to the diverse needs and skill development required for Industry 4.0, the education and retraining efforts must be carried out at various educational levels. Secondary schools as well as Career and Technology Centers offer daytime programmes for traditional high school students and evening programmes tailored to adult and displaced workers, ensuring accessibility to education and skills development for a broad demographic. In the United States, community colleges were established with the specific mission of training and retraining the workforce for new high-technology positions. They serve as crucial hubs for hands-on education and skill enhancement. Higher education institutions play a significant role by offering internship programmes and continuing education courses. These programmes ensure that students and professionals remain adaptable and well-prepared for the evolving demands of Industry 4.0/5.0.

Professional societies and certificate programmes offer specialized training and certifications that enhance the skill sets of individuals by, providing industry-specific expertise. Employers play a pivotal role in retraining the workforce through on-the-job training programmes, where employees acquire new skills and knowledge while continuing to work at their present jobs.

Bibliography

Adepoju, O.O., Aigbavboa, C.O. (2021). Assessing knowledge and skills gap for construction 4.0 in a developing economy. *Journal of Public Affairs*, 21(3), e2264.n.

Aheleroff, S., Ross, P., Zhong, R.Y., Xu, X. (2019). The degree of mass personalization under Industry 4.0. *Procedia CIRP*, 81, 1394–1399. In 52nd CIRP Conference on Manufacturing Systems.

Bahrin, K.M.A., Othman, M.F., Nor Azli, N.H., Talib, M.F. (2016). Industry 4.0: A review on industrial automation and robotic. *Jurnal Teknologi*, 78(6–13), 137–143.

Biały, W., Gajdzik, B., Jimeno, C.L., Romanyshyn, L. (2019). Engineer 4.0 in a metallurgical enterprise. *Multidisciplinary Aspects of Production Engineering*, 2(1), 172–182.

Chen, H. (2017). Applications of cyber physical systems—A literature review. *Journal of Industrial Integration and Management*, 2(3), 17–192.

Çınar, Z.M., Nuhu, A.A., Zeeshan, O., Korhan, O., Asmael, M., Safaei, B. (2020). Machine learning in predictive maintenance towards sustainable smart manufacturing in Industry 4.0. *Sustainability*, 12, 8211. https://doi.org/10.3390/su12198211.

Dai, H., Zuo, X. (2020). Industry 4.0 boosts the steel industry into a new era of digitalization and smart technology. In: AISTech – Iron and Steel Technology Conference Proceedings, 3, pp. 1829–1841.

Digital Report. (2020). Reuters Institute Digital News Report 2020. Reuters Institute for the Study of Journalism. (Newman N. with Fletcher, R., Schulz, A., Andı, S. and Rasmus Kleis Nielsen). https://reutersinstitute.politics.ox.ac.uk/sites/default/files/2020-06/DNR_2020_FINAL.pdf, [access data: 27.10.2023].

Dorst, W., Ed. (2016). Implementation Strategy Plattform Industrie 4.0: Result Report. zvei.org/filesadmin/user_upload/Pressse_und_Medien/Publikationen/2016/januar/.g, [access data: 27.10.2023].

Douaioui, K., Fri, M., Mabroukki, C., Semma El, A. (2018). The interaction between Industry 4.0 and smart logistics: Concepts and perspectives. In: 11th International Colloquium of Logistics and Supply Chain Management Logistiqua, April 2018, 26–27 FST, Tangier, Morocco IEEE; pp. 128–132.

Fan, L., Wang, X., Chen, Y., Wang, W.Y., Li, J. (2023). Smart design and manufacturing the Welded Q350 steel frames via lifecycle management strategy of digital twin. *Journal of Beijing Institute of Technology* (English Edition), 32(4), 385–395.

Gajdzik, B. (2022a). Diagnoza kierunków transformacji przemysłu stalowego w Przemyśle 4.0, Title in English: Diagnosis of the steel Industry transformation direction in the Industry 4.0. Silesian University of Technology, Gliwice, Poland 2022, Monography no. 945.

Gajdzik, B. (2022b). Frameworks of the maturity model for Industry 4.0 with assessment of maturity levels on the example of the segment of steel enterprises in Poland. *Journal of Open Innovation: Technology, Market, and Complexity*, 8, 77. https://doi.org/10.3390/joitmc8020077.

Gajdzik, B. (2022c). Steel company in industry 4.0: Diagnosis of changes in direction to smart manufacturing based on case study. Scientific papers of Silesian University of Technology, Gliwice. *Organization and Management* Series no. 160, 193–211.

Gajdzik, B. (2023). Kaizen in smart manufacturing (SM) projects: Framework and examples of improvement areas. *Scientific Papers of Silesian University of Technology – Organization and Management Series*, vol. 169, s. 281–299. http://dx.doi.org/10.29119/1641-3466.2023.169.16.

Gajdzik, B., Wolniak, R. (2022a). Influence of Industry 4.0 projects on business operations: Literature and empirical pilot studies based on case studies in Poland. *Journal of Open Innovation: Technology, Market, and Complexity*, 8, 44. https://doi.org/10.3390/ joitmc8010044.

Gajdzik, B., Wolniak R. (2022b). Smart production workers in terms of creativity and innovation: The implication for open innovation. *Journal of Open Innovation: Technology, Market, and Complexity*, 8, 68. https://doi.org/10.3390/joitmc8020068.

Gajdzik, B., Grabowska, S., Saniuk, S. (2021). A theoretical framework for Industry 4.0 and its implementation with selected practical schedules. *Energies*, 14(4), 940. https://doi.org/10.3390/en14040940.

Gajdzik, B., Jaciow, M., Wolniak, R., Wolny, R., Grebski, W.W. (2023). Energy behaviors of Prosumers in example of Polish households. *Energies*, 16(7), 3186. https://doi.org/10.3390/en16073186

Germany: Industrie 4.0. (2017). *Digital Transformation Monitor.* ati.ec.europa.eu/sites/default/files/2020–06/DTM_industrie%204.0_DE.pdf, [access data: 27.10.2023].

Govender, E., Telukdarie, A., Sishi, M.N. (2019). Approach for implementing Industry 4.0 framework in the steel industry. In: IEEE International Conference on Industrial Engineering and Engineering Management, pp. 1314–1318, 8978492.

Gray, A. (2016). The 10 skills you need to thrive in the fourth industrial revolution. *World Economic Forum.* Annual Meeting: Davos 2016. https://www.weforum.org/agenda/2016/01/the-10-skills-you-need-to-thrive-in-the-fourth-industrial-revolution/ [access data: 27.10.2023].

Hajoary, P.K. (2022). Industry 4.0 maturity and readiness – A case of a steel manufacturing organization. *Procedia Computer Science*, 217, 614–619.

He, J. (2016). Cyber–physical systems. *Commun CCF*, 6(1), 25–29. Chinese.

Hobbs, D.P. (2004). Lean manufacturing implementation, pp. 1–5. https://books.google.pl/books?hl=pl&lr=&id=pJa0rwBt74wC&oi=fnd&pg=PR7&dq=Hobbs,+D.+P.+(2004).+Lean+Manufacturing+Implementation,+pp.+1%E2%80%935&ots=xSLbrPo7DE&sig=zL4nXe1xL8XmVGtO0mwH6XBFX-s&redir_esc=y#v=onepage&q&f=false.

Hu, L., Xie, N., Kuang, Z., Zhao, K. (2012). Review of cyber–physical system architecture. In: Proceedings of the IEEE 15th International Symposium on Object/Component/

Service-Oriented Real-Time Distributed Computing Workshops (ISORCW); 11 April 2012; Shenzhen, China. IEEE. Washington, DC; pp. 25–30.

IEC PAS 63088:2017. (2017). *Smart Manufacturing – Reference Architecture Model Industry 4.0 (RAMI4.0)*, March 2017.

Industry Trends. Metals and Steel Industry. (2022). Atradius N.V. Netherlands. https://atradiuscollections.com/global/reports/metals-steel-industry-trends-germany-2022.html (access data: 27.10.2023).

Jeschke, S., Brecher, C., Meisen, T., Özdemir, D., Eschert, T. (2017). Industrial internet of things and cyber manufacturing systems. In Sabina Jeschke, Christian Brecher, Houbing Song, Danda B. Rawat (Eds.) *Industrial Internet of Things*. Springer, 3–19.

Jiafu, W., Zou, C., Zhou, K., Lu, R., Li, D. (2014). IoT sensing framework with inter-cloud computing capability in vehicular networking. *Electronic Commerce Research*, 14(3), 389–416.

Johnsson, Ch., Brandl, B. (Febr. 2018) Introduction to smart manufacturing. White paper. https://www.researchgate.net/publication/323226474, [access data: 27.10.2023].

Kagermann, H., Helbig, J., Hellinger, A., Helbig, J. (2013). Recommendations for implementing the strategic initiative INDUSTRIE 4.0: Securing the future of German manufacturing industry; final report of the Industrie 4.0 Working Group. Forschungsunion.

Kang, H.S., Lee, J.Y., Choi, S., Kim, H., Park, J.H., Son, J.Y., Kim, B.H., Noh, S.D. (2016). Smart manufacturing: Past research, present findings, and future directions. *International Journal of Precision Engineering and Manufacturing-Green Technology*, 3(1), 111–128.

Kim, J., Park. C.Y. (2020). Education, skill training, and lifelong learning in the era of technological revolution: A review. *Asian-Pacific Economic Literature*, 34(2), 3–19.

Kinsy, M., Khan, O., Ivan, C., Majstorovic, D., Celanovic, N., Devadas, S. (2011). Time-predictable computer architecture for cyber-physical systems: Digital emulation of power electronics systems. In: Proceedings of the IEEE Thirty-Second Real-Time Systems Symposium (RTSS); pp. 305–316.

Kusiak, A. (2018). Smart manufacturing. *International Journal of Production Research*, 56(1–2), 508–517. https://doi.org/10.1080/00207543.2017.1351644.

Lee, E.A. (2015). The past, present and future of cyber–physical systems: A focus on models. *Sensors* (Basel), 15(3), 4837–4869.

Lee, J., Bagheri, B., Kao, H.A. (2015). A cyber-physical systems architecture for industry 4.0-based manufacturing systems. *Manufacturing Letters*, 3, 18–23.

Li, B., Hou, B., Yu, W., Lu, X., Yang, C. (2017), Alications of artificial intelligence in intelligent manufacturing: A review. *Frontiers of Information Technology & Electronic Engineering*, 18(1), 86–96.

Li, L., Lu, Y. (2021). Status, opportunities and barriers in implementing Industry 4.0 in the US (dCh. 16). In Muller, J., Kazantsev, N. (Eds), *Industry 4.0 in SMEs across the Globe: Drivers, Barriers, and Opportunities*. (1st Ed.). CRC Press: Boca Raton, FL.

Liao, Y., Deschamps, F., Loures, E.F.R., Ramos, L.F.P. (2017). Past, present and future of Industry 4.0—A systematic literature review and research agenda proposal. *International Journal of Production Research*, 55(12), 3609–3629.

Liu, C., Jiang, P. (2016). A cyber-physical system architecture in shop floor for intelligent manufacturing. *Procedia CIRP*, 56, 372–377.

Liu, Y., Peng, Y., Wang, B., Yao, S., Liu, Z. (2017). Review on cyber–physical systems. *IEEE/CAA Journal of Automatica Sinica*, 4(1), 27–40.

Lopez Research, Building smarter manufacturing with the Internet of Things (IoT). (2014). https://www.manufacturing.net/home/whitepaper/13222234/building-smarter-manufacturing-with-theinternet-of-things-part-2, [access data: 27.11.2019].

Łukasik, K., Stachowiak, T. (2020). Intelligent management in the age of industry 4.0 – An example of a polymer processing company. *Management and Production Engineering Review*, 11(2), June, 38–49. https://doi.org/10.24425/mper.2020.133727.

Mishra, R., Singh, R.K., Gunasekaran, A. (2023). Adoption of industry 4.0 technologies for decarbonisation in the steel industry: Self-assessment framework with case illustration. *Annals of Operations Research*, 7(4), 15–34.

Miśkiewicz, R., Wolniak, R. (2020). Practical application of the industry 4.0 concept in a steel company. *Sustainability* (Switzerland), 12(14), 1–21, 5776.

National Steel Policy. (2021). Ministry of Steel. https://www.pib.gov.in/PressReleasePage.aspx?PRID=1704809, [access data: 27.10.2023].

O'Donovan, P., Leahy, K., Bruton, K., O'Sullivan, D.T.J. (2015). An industrial big data pipeline for data-driven analytics maintenance applications in large-scale smart manufacturing facilities. *Journal of Big Data*, 2(25), 1–26.

Ometto, M., Polo, A., Pietrosanty, C. (2023). Towards smarter steel manufacturing. *Steel Times International*, 40(4), 34–36.

Pérez-Lara, M., Saucedo-Martinez, J.A., Marmolejo-Saucedo, J.A., Salais-Fierro, T.E., Vasant P. (2020). Vertical and horizontal integration systems in Industry 4.0. October *Wireless Networks*, 26(1). https://doi.org/10.1007/s11276-018-1873-2.

Pfohl, H.C., Yahsi, B., Kurnaz, T. (2015). The impact of Industry 4.0 on the supply chain. In: Innovations and Strategies for Logistics and Supply Chains: Technologies, Business Models and Risk Management. Proceedings of the Hamburg International Conference of Logistics (HICL), 20, epubli GmbH: Berlin, Germany; pp. 31–58.

Polish Steel Industry. (2017). Polish Steel Association. https://www.hiph.org/ANALIZY_RAPORTY/pliki/PPS-2017.pdf, (access data: 27.10.2023.

Pourmehdi, M., Paydar, M.M., Ghadimi, P., Azadnia, A.H. (2022). Analysis and evaluation of challenges in the integration of Industry 4.0 and sustainable steel reverse logistics network. *Computers and Industrial Engineering*, 163, 107808.

Rajkumar, R.R., Lee, I., Sha, L., Stankovic, J. (2010). Cyber–physical systems: The next computing revolution. In: Proceedings of the 47th Design Automation Conference; 13–18 July; Anaheim, CA. ACM: New York.

Reports: European Steel in Figures from Eurofer. https://www.eurofer.eu, [access data: 14.11.2023].

Ryalat, M., ElMoaqet, H., AlFaouri, M. (2023). Design of a smart factory based on cyber-physical systems and internet of things towards Industry 4.0. *Applied Science*, 13, 2156. https://doi.org/10.3390/app13042156.

Schwab, K., Zahidi, S. (2020). The future of jobs report 2020. *World Economic Forum*. https://www.weforum.org/docs/WEF_Future_of_Jobs_2020.pdf, [access data: 27.10.2023].

Siemens. (2017), authors: Mychlewicz C., Piatek Z. (2017). Od Industry 4.0 do smart manufacturing. Warsow, Nov. 2017. https://przemysl-40.pl/index.php/2018/01/25/od-industry-4-0-do-smart-factory-czesc-1/, [access data: 27.10.2023].

Sigov, A., Ratkin, L., Ivanov, L., Xu, L.D. (2022). Emerging enabling technologies for Industry 4.0 and beyond. *Information Systems Frontiers*. https://doi.org/10.1007/s10796-021-10213-w.

Silverio-Fernández, M., Renukappa, S., Suresh, S. (2018). What is a smart device? - A conceptualisation within the paradigm of the internet of things. *Visualization in Engineering*, 6(3). https://doi.org/10.1186/s40327-018-0063-8.

Soder, J. (2017). Von CIM über Lean Produktion zu Industrie 4.0. In Bauernhansl, T., ten Hompel, B., Vogel-Heuser, B. (Eds), *Handbuch Industrie 4.0, Band 1: Produktion*. Springer: Wiesbaden.

Stawiarska, E., Szwajca, D., Matusek, M., Wolniak, R. (2020). Wdrażanie rozwiązań Przemysłu 4.0w wybranych funkcjonalnych obszarach zarządzania przedsiębiorstw branży motoryzacyjne. Gliwice: CeDeWu.

Szczepańka-Woszczyna, K., Gajdzik, B. (2016). Competencies of engineering staff in steelworks after their restructuring. *Metalurgija*, 55(2), 271–274.

Tao, F., Qi, Q., Liu, A., Kusiak, A. (2018). Data-driven smart manufacturing. *Journal of Manufacturing Systems*, 48(Part C), 157–169.

Tao, F., Qu, Q., Wang, L., Nee, A.Y.C. (2019). Digital twins and cyber–physical systems toward smart manufacturing. *Engineering*, 5, 653–661. https://doi.org/10.1016/j.eng.2019.01.014.

The-White-House. (2011). President Obama launches advanced manufacturing partnership: Technical Report. *Office of the Press Secretary*. https://obamawhitehouse.archives.gov/the-press-office/2011/06/24/president-obama-launches-advanced-manufacturing-partnership, [access data: 27.10.2023].

Thoben, K., Wiesner, S., Wuest, T. (2017). "Industrie 4.0" and smart manufacturing–A review of research issues and application examples. *International Journal of Automotive Technology*, 11(1), 4–19.

Tolettini, L., Lehmann, C. (2020). Industry 4.0: New paradigms of value creation for the steel sector. *Knowledge Management and Organizational Learning*, 9, 179–206.

Trappey, A.J.C., Trappe, C.V., Ma, L., Chang, J.C.M. (2015). Intelligent engineering asset management system for power transformer maintenance decision supports under various operating conditions. *Computers & Industrial Engineering*, 84, 3–11. https://www.sciencedirect.com/science/article/abs/pii/S0360835214004628, [access data: 10.10.2023].

Wang, B., Tao, F., Fang, X., Liu, C., Liu, Y., Freiheit, T. (2021). Smart manufacturing and intelligent manufacturing: A comparative review. *Engineering*, 7, 738–757. https://doi.org/10.1016/j.eng.2020.07.017.

Wang, J.-Q., Li, W., Ma, Z.-C., Sun, L., Zhang, C.-Y. (2021). 5G industrial Internet empowers smart steel. *Kang T'ieh/Iron and Steel*, 56(9), 56–61.

Wang, S., Wan, J., Li, D., Zhang, S. (2016). Implementing smart factory of Industry 4.0: An outlook. *International Journal of Distributed Sensor Networks*, 12, 3159805.

Werr, P. (2014). Horizontal and vertical integration with Zenon. Spotlight smart factory. *The Copa Data Magazine* No. 26 (26 Nov.). https://www.copadata.com/download/0/436/4095e614-edde-4537-a6af-b87b68d5aa85, [access data: 27.10.2023].

White Paper SMKL. (2020). *(Smart Manufacturing Kaizen Level) Approach to Smart Manufacturing*. IAF Shinbashi: Minato-ku, Tokyo, 4/1, p. 62.

Whiting, K. (2020). These are the top 10 job skills of tomorrow and how long it takes to learn them: Education, skills and learning. *World Economic Form: The Jobs Reset Summit*. https://www.weforum.org/agenda/2020/10/top-10-work-skills-of-tomorrow-how-long-it-takes-to-learn-them/, [access data: 27.10.2023].

Winter, J. (2022). Smart Manufacturing (Industry 4.0) in: ISA's Flagship Publications August 2022 Introduction: The Birth of Industry 4.0 and Smart Manufacturing, inTech Logo Introduction: The Birth of Industry 4.0 and Smart Manufacturing. Available online: https://www.isa.org/intech-home/2022/august-2022/features/introduction-the-birth-of-industry-4-0-and-smart-m [access data: 27.10.2023].

World Steel in Figures; Steel Statistical Yearbook from World Steel Association. https://worldsteel.org/steel-topics/statistics, [access data: 14.11.2023].

Xu, L., He, W., Li, S. (2014). Internet of things in Industries: A survey. *IEEE Transactions on Industrial Informatics*, 10(4), 2233–2243.

Xu, X., Lu, Y., Vogel-Heuser, B., Wang, L. (2022). Industry 4.0 and Industry 5.0—Inception, conception and perception. *Journal of Manufacturing Systems*, 61, 530–535.

Yin, R.-Y. (2017). A discussion on smart steel plant-view from physical system side. *Kang T'ieh/Iron and Steel*, 52(6), 1–12.

Yong-Hong Kuo, A.K. (2019). From data to big data in production research: The past and future trends. *International Journal of Production Research*, 57(15–16), 4828–4853, August. https://doi.org/10.1080/00207543.2018.1443230.

Yu, B., Li, X., Qiao, Y., Shi, L. (2015). Low-carbon transition of iron and steel industry in China: Carbon intensity, economic growth and policy intervention. *Journal of Environmental Sciences (China)*, 28, 137–147.

Zeng, P., Wang, H., Sang, Z., Zhong, R.Y., Liu, Y., Liu, Ch., Mubarok, K., Yu, S. Xu, X. (2018). Smart manufacturing systems for Industry 4.0. *Frontiers of Mechanical Engineering*, 13(2), 137–150. https://doi.org/10.1007/s11465-018-0499-5.

Zheng, Z., Zhang, K.T., Gao, X.Q. (2022). Human-cyber-physical system for production and operation decision optimization in smart steel plants. *Science China Technological Sciences*, 65(2), 247–260.

Zhong, R.Y., Xu, X., Klotz, E., Newman, S.T. (2017). Intelligent manufacturing in the context of Industry 4.0: A review. *Engineering*, 3, 616–630.

Zhou, J., Li, P., Zhou, Y., Wang, B., Zang, J., Meng, L. (2018). Toward new-generation intelligent manufacturing. *Engineering*, 4(1), 11–20.

3 Smart steel manufacturing

3.1 The literature background about smart steel manufacturing

Technological development in a dynamic environment forces companies to invest quickly (immediately) in new technologies. The production hall must be digitally operated and integrated into the supply chain in order to be able to adapt quickly to the dynamic market situation. By combining leading intellectual property (IP) practices and proven digital methods for data loss detection and analytics, as well as new manufacturing technologies, businesses are better able to achieve operational excellence than they did two decades ago. Continuous improvement of production efficiency (elimination of bottlenecks) is a prerequisite for business development. New technologies with enormous potential are able to correct operations according to the "predict and prevent" algorithm, which replaces the "detect and repair" algorithms. A huge opportunity for operational improvement is machine learning, which will be able to solve problems that human-designed programs can't cope with. But in order for technology to learn, it needs data. Just as long ago the foundation of the revolution was the pair, so today the foundation of modern industry is data. Machines and devices equipped with sensors enable production and logistics processes based on collected data and their analysis in real time. The whole spectrum of technologies used in smart manufacturing, such as the Internet of Things (IoT), artificial intelligence (AI), big data analytics, edge computing, digital twin, augmented reality, cloud computing, 5G, exists for and thanks to data. The industrial revolution started in Europe, and today Europe is also imposing the transformation of Industry 4.0. Directions such as automation, robotization, and AI implementation are strategic for business development. Companies take a pragmatic and evolutionary approach to change with small steps, which allows them to scale solutions until the implementation of a holistic strategy. New technological solutions are tested in companies, and after confirmation of their effectiveness they are extended to other positions in production halls (Gajdzik et al., 2021).

Strongly popularized in Europe, the Industry 4.0 concept is an opportunity for the development of many industries, including the steel industry. New (high) technologies will change the way steel is produced and entire supply chains function. Chain changes are important for the steel sector as steel producers are strongly linked to producers of steel user markets. As a rule, the situation on the market of

DOI: 10.4324/9781032697611-3

steel producers (e.g. a decline in steel production, an increase in steel prices) affects the situation on dependent markets (automotive, machinery, household appliances, construction, etc.). Steel is an essential material at the beginning of the value chain and is constantly being developed. Stringent customer demands, coupled with a framework for sustainable development and evolving social conditions such as societal mobility and demographic shifts, drive a profound innovation dynamic. High customer requirements, but also a sustainable development framework, social conditions: the mobility of society and demographic developments lead to an intensive innovation dynamic. Intelligent manufacturing, as a new generation of information and communication technology and advanced manufacturing technology, can quickly respond to internal and external changes in enterprises and establish a new model of personalized customization and resource optimization configuration centred on customer needs by improving the manufacturing industry's intelligence level (Zhou et al., 2022).

For steel, the term 'driving force', 'motor' is used for other industrial sectors. The demand for steel increases with the activity of the steel-consuming sectors and this translates into an increase in the share of steel production in total industrial production. Industry 4.0 offers metallurgical companies a wide range of opportunities for operational improvement at the various stages of steel and steel products production. Changing market mechanisms is a strong driving force which will require flexibility of operations and mass-customization of products with a small batch-size and short lead-time. Surfing the waves of this change will require the steel industry to have a sharp awareness of customer dynamics and expertise on the implementation of tools and strategies offered through Industry 4.0. In the transformation to Industry 4.0 steelworks are not alone because government institutions encourage steelworks to introduce technological changes, and funds from European programmes flow to steelworks (Branca et al., 2020).

European industry is deeply committed to integrating the concept of digitization into its production and organization in order to be more competitive in the context of globalization. The use of digital technologies enables the implementation of new processes throughout the value chain through production and sales for services. In this theme, digitalization is a holistic approach that encompasses all areas and functions of a company to harness the digital potential and analyse every step of its value chain. For this reason, it should be stressed that digitization is not a simple transfer from "analogue" to digital data and documents. It is more about networking between business processes, creating efficient interfaces and integrated data exchange and management (Branca et al., 2020; Bogner et al., 2016).

The steel industry accounted for 3.8% of annual global GDP in 2017 and contributed to the employment of more than 6 million people. The European steel industry has an annual turnover of EUR 166 billion and contributes 1.3% to the EU's GDP. In terms of workforce, the European steel industry provided 328,000 direct jobs (COM, 2016). Currently, the European steel industry is facing important challenges due to cost pressures, regulatory requirements (deep decarbonization), as well as product and service requirements (new materials, additive manufacturing). The steel industry is involved in several policy actions, R&D projects, and patents in the field of digitalization and carbon reduction (Naujok and Stamm, 2018).

The steel industry is undergoing a huge digital transformation (see, for example, Cheng and Westman, 2020). Initiatives related to the steel industry in Europe include the Smart Factory working group of the ESTEP platform, founded in 2008 under the former name 'Intelligent Integrated Manufacturing', which published the first edition of the roadmap for European steel production in 2009 with a vision until 2020. Further visions have been developed at European level up to 2025 and beyond. The ESTEP working group includes a wide range of stakeholders and consists of plant manufacturers and several European universities and R&D institutions (https://www.estep.eu/).

European Research Programmes contribute to the development of smart steel manufacturing. From the early 1990s, when projects appeared, dealing with different aspects of the digitization of the steel industry, until today, steel groups, and organizations are using them (see, for example, Branca et al., 2020; Arens et al., 2018). The source of funding is EUREKA, which is a pan-European research and market development network. Table 3.1 summarizes the projects involving the digitization of the steel sector carried out in recent years (last two decades). The most active players among research institutions and steel companies in these projects were: VDEh Betriebsforinstitut BFI, Swerea MEFOS/KIMAB, RINA Consulting-Centro Sviluppo Materiali, Scuola Superiore Sant'Anna, Centre de Recherches Metallurgiques, ArcelorMittal, ThyssenKrupp, as well as Tata Steel and, to some extent, Gerdau and Voestalpine (Branca et al., 2020; Arens et al., 2018).

The steel sector, like other European industries, is implementing digital technologies in its steelmaking processes. In the digital transformation taking place, the levers important for the successful implementation of the digitalization process are digital data, automation, connectivity, digital customer access, smart machines and additive manufacturing, cyber-physical systems, and the supply chain with blockchain. Industry 4.0 is a fully flexible concept with evolving technologies. Therefore, it is difficult to identify a complete set of solutions that the steel industry can adapt and integrate. Many authors and researchers claim that the transformation of the steel industry towards Industry 4.0 is already underway (Gajdzik, 2021, 2022a, 2022b, 2022c; Gajdzik and Wolniak, 2021; Miśkiewicz and Wolniak, 2020; Herzog et al., 2017; Zeman, 2017; Neef et al., 2018). Particular authors study the level of maturity of changes in the steel sector using the pillars of Industry 4.0 as reference criteria (Gajdzik, 2022c). According to Zeman (2017) and Gajdzik (2022a) the steelworks are halfway to level 4.0 (Zeman, 2017). Their current transformation is estimated at 3.5 (Gajdzik, 2022a).

The strategic direction of the steel industry is to build steel smart manufacturing or smart mills or steelworks 4.0. In this strategy, there are the steel producers' requirements and key technologies (pillars) of Industry 4.0. Following Herzog et al. (2017), the requirements are end-customer integration, lot-size 1, new business models, knowledge management, supplier integration, new steel graders (e.g. high-quality automotive exposed steel grades), availability of information, and ergonomic operator support. In economies with a strong focus on ESG (environmental, social, and

Table 3.1 Projects involving the digitization aspect of the steel sector

RFCS (Research Fund for Coal and Steel)

AdaptEAF	DroMoSPlan	I2MSteel	Plant Temp	Telerescuer
AUTOADAPT	DYNERGYSteel	IConSys	PRESED	TRACKOPT
CYBERMAN4.0	ENCOP	INFOMAP	ROBOHARSH	
Cyber-POS	EvalHD	NEWTECH4STEEL	QUALITY4.0	
DESDEMONA	GASNET	OptiScrapManage	SoProd	

Steel industry digitalization

EUREKA	**H2020**	**SPIRE**	**FP7**
BRICK	WATERWATT	DISIRE	AREUS
OREXPRESS	FACTS4WORKERS	COPRO	
TAM		FUDIPO	
H2PREDICTOR		MORSE	
		RECOBA	
		COCOP	

Low carbon future technologies

CDA	**PI**	**CCU**
HYBRIT	IDEOGAS	Biocon-co2
GrInHy	OSMet S2	CarbonNext
H2FUTURE	HISARNA B, C &D	I3UPGRADE
IERO	ACASOS	FresMe
SALCOS	CO2RED	M4CO2
	REGTGF	Carbon4PUR
	RenewableSteelGases	Steelanol
	SHOCOM	
	Torero	
	GREENEAF	
	GREENEAF2	
	ENCOP	
	IDEOGAS	
	LoCO2Fe	
	STEPWISE	

Source: Branca et al. (2020).

governance) reporting, as well as in the light of the radicalness of environmental law, environmental aspects, including priority aspects such as energy efficiency, carbon reduction (Tolettini and Di, 2023), and social aspects (human factor in industrial transformation) should be added to this strategy. Requirements meet key technologies, Herzog et al. (2017) listed: communication technologies, computational power, Internet technologies, cloud computing, Big Data and analytics, self-learning systems, mobile devices, augmenter reality. New technologies are used to achieve better productivity, quality, and flexibility. Smart manufacturing integrates various technologies related to manufacturing, computing, virtualization, connectivity, data handling, etc. According to Phuyal et al. (2020) the scope of smart manufacturing technologies has become broader due to the inter-operation of various technologies resulting in cost-effectiveness, time-saving, easy configuration, better understanding, quick response to market demand, flexibility, and remote monitoring (see, for

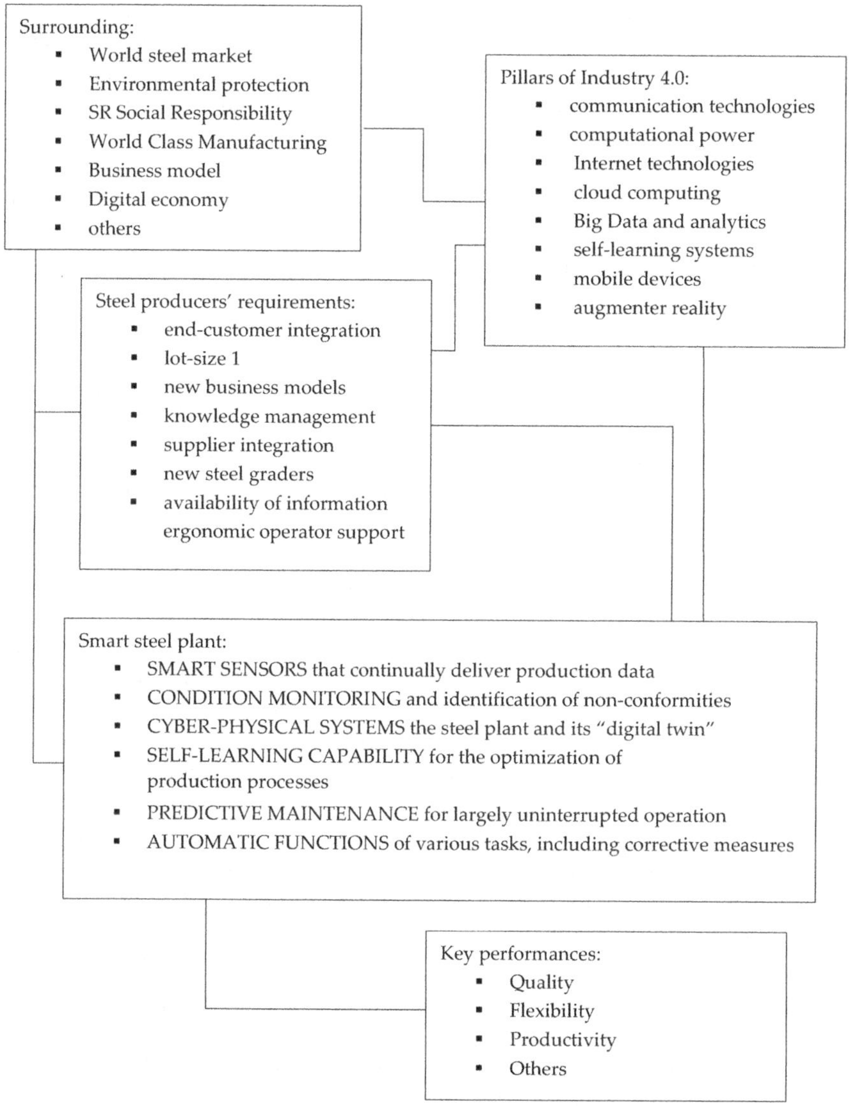

Figure 3.1 Pathways of steel mills to smart manufacturing.

Source: Own elaboration B. Gajdzik based on: (Herzog et al., 2017; Metals Magazine, 2018).

example: Govender et al., 2019). Smart manufacturing is challenges for world steel market. Figure 3.1 presents the place of smart manufacturing in industrial transformation of the steel industry.

The steel industry, as a typical process industry, has many production procedures, a large number of pieces of equipment, a large amount of energy consumption, a large number of operators, and a large number of complex reactions, including chemical reactions during the smelting procedure and physical changes during the rolling procedure. The interweaving of various influencing elements is the specific of intelligent manufacturing in steel mills, and may even be a barrier to smart steelmaking (Zhou et al., 2022). Throughout the entire steel production process, factors such as quality control, energy management, and product management procedures must be carefully considered, as they can potentially act as barriers to the implementation of smart steelmaking practices.

Smart steel manufacturing is rooted in the digitalization of the steel mills. There is no one "ready-made" solution for all areas of digitization applications in the steel industry. The changes are aimed at creating an architecture of Cyber-Physical Steel Production Systems (CPSPS) (see, for example, Iannino et al., 2019). Steel plants gradually implement modular digital solutions that are currently available on the market (see, for example, Gajdzik and Wolniak, 2021; Miśkiewicz and Wolniak, 2020). Steel mills take advantage of available modular systems (market offers of computer system providers). IT players help companies to introduce technology and generate benefits from digital solutions. Depending on the market situation, production processes can be optimized towards set targets, e.g. productivity, reliability, and quality. Digital technologies offer the possibility of high accuracy in the manufacture of products with established tolerance bands and guarantee a high degree of reproducibility of operations. Steel mills use statistical control systems (SPC) for the parameters of steel products to improve quality. Quality at each stage of the use of digital technologies grows faster than with classic technologies. Production lines with digital solutions are more flexible than traditional ones. Steel mills with digital technologies and automated production lines gain the ability to produce a wide range of steel products, even in very small batches. IT and computer solutions target interoperability and process optimization (Mori et al., 2018). The purchase of automation systems and information technology accounts for 20–40% of the total investment, the remaining 60–80% are additional costs resulting from the maintenance and adaptation of systems to the specifics of the company's operation, the so-called modernization services (Tihinen et al., 2017). According to J. Cheng and J. Westman (2020), based on research by other authors, it is possible to distinguish several levels of process savings due to the use of digital technology and process solutions in the steel industry. The authors present such benefits:

- a decrease in production costs by 10–30% (Bauernhansl et al., 2016);
- a decrease in maintenance costs by o 10–40% using predictive maintenance (Cheng and Westman, 2020), planned machine downtime is optimized and accounts for 2–10% of maintenance costs (McKinsey, 2016);
- a waste reduction by 10–20% using process optimization systems (McKinsey, 2016);
- a decrease in operating costs of 2–10% (McKinsey, 2016);
- an increase in production efficiency by 20–30% (Boston Consulting Group, 2015);
- a decrease in overhead costs in the process of converting raw material into finished products by 15–20% (Boston Consulting Group, 2015); and
- a decrease in labour costs together with operating costs and overheads by 30% over a period of five to ten years from the introduction of ICTs (Rüßmann et al., 2015).

Other authors (Zhou et al., 2022) add that during smart transformation, the steel sector can expect:

- a shorter research and product development cycles of a typical steel industry by 30%,
- a decrease in the product defect rate by 10–20%,
- a decrease in energy consumption per one tonne of steel by 10%, and
- a decrease in production costs by 10% and an increase in production efficiency by 10–25%.

A smart steel plant works towards one common goal, namely to ensure flexible production of consistent-quality steels at the highest-possible productivity levels.

To achieve this goal, three dimensions of integration are needed:

- the first dimension is horizontal transparency and interconnectedness,
- the second is process optimization, and
- the third is time and predictive maintenance.

Smart manufacturing means a steel-producing smart factory and smart steel value chain. It is a significant transformation in the way we source raw materials, manufacture, and market our products through horizontal and vertical supply chain integration – and it is profoundly customer-focused. This change is not a one-step process as there are obvious challenges of trust and data security to overcome between diverse parties in the supply chain. There are a number of examples of early adopters within the steel industry; especially in vertical integration within business segments where building blocks of smart factories are being put together. Table 3.2 presents a few examples.

In steelworks integrated with BF+BOF technology, where the complete steel production process is carried out (Figure 3.2), smart manufacturing models are offered. The first model relates to the rolling process and the second model is a combination of the complete production cycle in these mills. Zhou et al. (2022) calls the first model "Rolling Process Intelligent Manufacturing Model" and the second "Steelmaking and Rolling Process Intelligent Manufacturing Model". These authors describe both models on the example of the Chinese steel industry and point to the justified use of the full model (i.e. the other model). In the first model, the rolling process of steel semi-finished products is fully automatic (unmanned plate storage, quality monitoring of the whole process, intelligent control, robots, and other intelligent applications are used). Intelligent robots and modern generation roll-forming machine use important technologies such as industrial Internet data integration, hybrid model and data analysis, and multi-objective interaction optimization. Computer systems control the process towards optimizing energy synergy, rolling accuracy, and improving work efficiency. State-of-the-art rolling solutions enable intelligent control, prediction, and early warning of the future and a multi-objective level of optimization of business cooperation, as well as ultimately improving production stability and flexibility of the hot-rolled production line and reducing production costs.

Table 3.2 Smart manufacturing in steel plants: examples

Field of change	*Used solutions*
Logistics	• Real-time tracking of supplies and orders assisted through GPS, RFID, WiFi (indoor & outdoor accurate positioning); • Dynamic management of in-process inventory, consumables and spares.
Product quality systems	• Modelling of material and surface characteristics for local process control resulting in optimum quality; • Computer Aided Quality Control (CAQC) with 100% testing, inspection and storage of data related to hot-rolled coils minimizing claims and cost of potential quality issues; • Intelligent grading of coils and rerouting of coils within production lines to find best match with customer orders reducing rejects and optimizing yield; • Operational research (Big Data analytics) of process data related to coil segments for fault tracking and process efficiency; • Real-time dynamic line scheduling and adjustment of process parameters with Artificial Intelligence (BIOMIMIC + Parallel Computing) in rolling and finishing.
Predictive maintenance	• Predictive asset maintenance increasing up-time assisted by advance warnings of failures. • Remote assistance of maintenance teams with smart glasses.
Process control and safety	• Dynamic real-time analysis and control of blast furnace process parameters using sonic, laser and radar visualization; • Sensors detect harmful stray gases, noises and temperatures, and notify operators of threats; • Advanced fully automated BOF from charging to tapping; • Networked platforms of assets such as blast furnaces where process experts can see every operation in real-time and collaborate with each other; • Use of drone technology for inspection of areas that are difficult to reach in the plant and surveying and planning of mining operations.

Source: Own elaboration based on WorldSteel Association (2023), R. Janjua.

The second model – Steelmaking and Rolling Process Intelligent Manufacturing – involves the integration of the technology of two processes, i.e. steelmaking and rolling. This model includes a number of process interfaces such as steel smelting and refining, continuous casting and rolling process. There is still a lot to be done on this model. The main goal in the process of steel production and rolling intelligent production model is to establish a horizontal and seamless integration of the whole industrial chain system of R&D, procurement, production, marketing, and service. The second goal is to achieve vertical and seamless integration between the IT system and the automation system. The third goal is to achieve a smooth, comprehensive integration of IT systems at the workshop and enterprise level. The fourth goal is to achieve information exchange between companies operating upstream and downstream in the supply chain (Zhou et al., 2022). This model requires the realization of a deep integration of computerization and

Table 3.3 Technologies and solutions in the model "steelmaking and rolling process intelligent manufacturing": examples

Tech/solutions	*Goals/projects*	*Results*
Intelligent sensing system	• Monitoring systems of important process parameters such as steelmaking converters, refining furnaces, continuous casting ladles, and continuous casting machines. • Control model optimization systems (sensors, intelligent cameras, radio-frequency identification, gateways, technologies image recognition and voice recognition). • Big Data: equipment data, product identification data and factory environmental data. • High-performance network equipment with large system capacity, high transmission rate, multiple fault-tolerant mechanisms and low latency. • Distributed industrial control networks. • Software-defined agile networks. • Network resource allocation optimization system.	• Optimize control and increase the degree of process intelligence • Meet the demand for real-time knowledge of the production process (operational data and status of important equipment) • Improve real-time transmission of sensor data • Optimize decision-making.
Centralized monitoring and controlling system	• Integrated control systems of major steelmaking and continuous casting processes, such as the converter area, refining area, continuous casting area, heating furnace area, and rolling area. • Configured production line monitoring system based on data collection • Decision-making centre.	• Real-time monitoring of the production process, • Remote centralized control of devices • Reminders of abnormal alarms • Minimum number of operators on site and inspection staff • Less labor-intensive • Product safety
Production management and intelligent scheduling system	• Production organization and intelligent planning system built on the basis of raw material and fuel conditions, equipment condition and field requirements with plan execution, resource utilization, statistical analysis of productivity and quality, optimal planning of stable working conditions, dynamic planning of abnormal working conditions, as well as auxiliary production planning and decision-making functions.	• Real-time production monitoring • Production balance coordination, • Real-time decision making • Production without production delays • Production without production losses

(*Continued*)

Table 3.3 (Continued)

Tech/solutions	*Goals/projects*	*Results*
Intelligent device administration system	• Systems for monitoring equipment lifecycle status, tracking and maintenance of information throughout the planning, design, production, procurement, installation, operation, maintenance, upgrading and transformation and scrapping of equipment. • Database on the state of equipment and processes. • Analytics of big data, artificial intelligence, virtual reality and other technologies. • Simulation models of equipment failure early warning, alarming and diagnosis • Standardized systems for the collection and control of information. • Automatic diagnostic systems • Fault prediction models based on expert system and fault rate knowledge base. • Unmanned remote control systems, early warning of hazardous working environment, operational status monitoring, fault diagnosis and self-repair.	• Autonomous smart equipment, • Machine learning, • Process optimization • Continuity of production, • Predictive maintenance, • Reduction of maintenance costs • Reduction of production costs (reduction of resources, energy, etc.)
Quality controlling system	• Quality management system with maintenance of quality standards, quality monitoring, inspection and laboratory testing, statistical analysis and quality optimization. • Integrated management system of product quality and performance parameters of the whole product manufacturing process • Quality analysis system: big data sets and machine learning methods that can assess product quality online and analyse the quality traceability of the whole process • System of control of important quality characteristics in steel production and rolling processes. • Quality control system – finished product quality can be obtained through online statistics, diagnostics, forecasting, analysis and optimization to improve the stability of product quality.	• Ensuring product quality, • Decrease in cost of defective production, • Elimination of defective products, • Product development

(*Continued*)

Table 3.3 (Continued)

Tech/solutions	*Goals/projects*	*Results*
Process simulation and prediction system	• Improvement of metallurgical process model determined by statistical analysis, machine learning, big data analysis and other technical means. • Development of model generalization capacity through model training, production experience, mathematical modeling, etc. • Embed the AI components of the decision optimization system into the process model to achieve operational guidance and predict the actual production process. • Complex process simulation calculations. • Procedures and virtual system of processes.	• The equipment interacts in real time, which can optimize production operating parameters during steelmaking and rolling processes.
An early warning system for employee safety	• Personnel management system using satellite location, Wi-Fi, 5G and other communication technologies. • Working conditions monitoring system. • Safety management system with employee training using virtual reality. • Early warning system for employees with smart analytics.	• Automatic perception and acquisition of basic information about: number of staff, location of staff, security status, process of operation of the surrounding environment, • Statistical analysis of the trajectory of staff location and the status of staff posts (workplaces), • Automatic display of alarm information (appropriate process monitoring screens) • Sending reminders to appropriate stations or personnel when entering the danger zone; or when critical equipment malfunctions, serious hazards or other situations occur, • Online monitoring (smart analytics to maintain employee safety).

Source: Own elaboration based on Zhou et al. (2022) (see also: Rudy et al. (2018), World Steel Association. The White Book of Steel, 2013; Yao and Wang, 2020; Liu, 2020; Lin and Zeng, 2021).

industrialization to solve the problem of data islands between different procedures, improve the level of globalization of quality control and production control, and finally realize the deep integration of computerization and industrialization. Within this model, the technologies and solutions shown in Table 3.3 can be applied.

3.2 Smart steel manufacturing – selected case studies

A case study is a detailed description of the activities of enterprises or changes in their processes. A case study is carried out to identify the detections of development under specific business conditions. In this chapter, used case studies are a description of steel mills activities in steel manufacturing in the condition of transformation to Industry 4.0. The purpose of the case studies are to outline the scope of steel manufacturing transformations in the described enterprises that produce steel under specific business conditions in the global steel market. Information about changes comes from the enterprises themselves (steel mills, steel producers). In this chapter, examples of changes implemented at steel mills operating in the global steel market and belonging to international capital groups are included. The sources of the case studies were open information – available on the websites of the analysed steel capital groups. In the description were used three steel capital groups: ArcelorMittal, ThyssenKrupp, and Tata Steel. For each of steel producers was used the same structure for presenting changes.

The analysis conducted enables us to paint a comprehensive picture of the industrial transformation towards smart steel manufacturing. Modern steelmaking technologies are enriched with IT solutions that merge two areas of business activity: physical and digital. The end result is the integration of technologies, processes, and products into cyber-physical production systems that are strongly oriented to personalized customer needs.

An additional argument in favor of these groups was the enhanced accessibility to information available on their websites.

The study included changes made at three capital groups: ArcelorMittal, ThyssenKrupp, and Tata Steel. The choice of these capital groups was determined by their strong transformation activities in the European steel market. These steel producers were participants in European development programmes and members of working teams in the key European projects. Moreover, the capital groups used for the analysis are among the world's top steel producers – the Top 50 list compiled by the World Steel Association. A strong argument for choosing these groups for the case studies is their significant impact on the development of the European steel industry. Two of the analysed groups, namely ArcelorMittal and ThyssenKrupp, are headquartered in Europe. Third group – Tata Steel – is based in India but also operates, under a common name: Tata Steel Europe, in the European market. An additional argument in favour of the aforementioned groups was the easy accessibility to needed information on their websites.

Reasons for selection of these companies/capital groups/steel producers for case studies:

- **Reason 1**: activities of the analysed capital groups in the European programmes: RFCS(2003–2014), RFCS (2015–2017) FP7 (2007–2013), FP7 (2014–2020), EUREKA (1989–2018), EUREKA (2018), CORDIS (2018), workshops on concept and operational benefits of digital twins in the steel sector in Charleroi in 2018 (see ESTEP, 2019; Branca et al., 2020) and working groups: (1) Industrie 4.0, (2) Steelinstitute VDEh, (3) Integrated Intelligent Manufacturing, (4) Development of an European roadmap, (5) other projects: Flag Ship Projects.

- **Reason 2**: ArcelorMittal, thyssenkrupp, and Tata Steel are in the Top 50 ranking of the world's steel producers. Being in the Top 50 list obliges capital groups (steel producers) to take on new development challenges for the purpose of maintaining a leadership position in the world steel market. Until 2019 (in rankings compiled by the World Steel Association), the leading position with annual production of more than 100 million tonnes of crude steel was held by ArcelorMittal. In 2020, the group was in second place. The surveyed Tata Steel was in 12th position, and ThyssenKrupp was 43rd (2020).
- **Reason 3**: location of important plants (steel mills) in the European steel market. The analysed groups have steel mills in the European steel market, which affects their participation in the development of the European steel industry. ThyssenKrupp (headquartered in Essen) is the largest steel group operating in Germany (the group is ranked second in Europe) with annual production of more than 10 million tons of steel. ArcelorMittal (headquartered in Luxembourg) operates in many European countries, including: Belgium, the Czech Republic, Romania, Italy, France and Ukraine. Tata Steel is one of Europe's leading steelmakers, with steel plants in the Netherlands and the United Kingdom. Production plants are also in Germany, France, Belgium, Sweden, Norway, Finland, Spain, and Turkey. This steel producer employs 20,000 people in Europe.
- **Reason 4**: Availability of information on the implementation of the Industry 4.0 strategies in steel mills. The capital groups used for the case studies provide information on ongoing investments under the Industry 4.0 concept on their own websites.

The list of sources used for the research was as follows:

- Case study 1: ArcelorMittal (AM): Source: https://corporate.arcelormittal.com/media/case-studies/industry-4-0 (2021-03-14)
- Case study 2: ThyssenKrupp: Source: https://www.thyssenkrupp.com/en/company/innovation/industry-4-0 (2021-02-04).
- Case study 3: Tata Steel: Source: https://www.tatasteeleurope.com/ts/automotive/industry-themes/digitalization (2021-02-04).

The listed sources were used at the beginning of 2021. Thus, the activities of the groups selected for the study presented were current as of the end of the first quarter of 2021. Presented case studies were a part of own research realized by PhD (hab.) Eng. Bożena Gajdzik, assoc. Professor of Silesian University of Technology (see more: Monography no. 945, 2022, Silesian University of Technology).

Case study 1 ArcelorMittal (AM). In the industrial transformation, the analysed steel producer focuses on achieving technological progress in three key areas of its activity: (1) steel products, (2) steel manufacturing, (3) steel consumers. In product development strategy, this steel mill is focusing on lightweight sheets for modern and agile car producers, unique products for the construction industry – modern skyscraper-type buildings, railroad rails for high-speed trains, steel sheets for equipment, and facilities designed for extreme weather conditions. The product strategy is strongly linked to the process strategy. This steel mill is focused on process improvement – process improvement is handled by process research teams, which work closely with individual units across the company to improve process reliability and efficiency. In addition, products and processes are strongly linked to customer service. This steel producer has launched applications: S-in motion® and Steligence® (catalogues of steel products) for automotive and construction consumers. Consumers through these applications receive information about steel products and realized processes. These applications show the benefits of using advanced steels and manufacturing processes. One of the benefit is environmental aspects of using advanced technologies and steel products with high utility quality. Other benefits are the safety of use of steel products, modern forms, lightweight products, etc.

The strategy of AM is based on a holistic vision of digitization that includes the Internet of Things (IoT), big data, and artificial intelligence (AI). The choice of these three segments (the pillars of Industry 4.0) was dictated by the fact that IoT enables all data to be collected and made available to the big data platform. (ArcelorMittal's IoT platform allows the group to manage all devices and processes, make corrections, and develop machine learning algorithms by accessing metadata, etc.) Big data stores huge amounts of data, consolidates sources, centralizes information, and exposes a managed interface to access and use the data to solve process problems that the company was previously unable to solve due to limited device memory capacity and long analysis execution time. AI explores data, identifies patterns, and discovers insights, models device behaviour, and uses optimization algorithms to turn it into recommendations for better machine operations.

ArcelorMittal investments and key projects:

1 Centres of Digitalization – they are created near AM Group's manufacturing facilities around the world, enable the development of new technologies from prototype to maturity faster than ever before. The scope of activities of the centres includes acquiring new technologies, testing the usability of technological solutions in metallurgical processes, evaluating the results of introduced changes, and expanding the scope of application of technologies to expanding the scope of application of new technologies to achieve smart steel manufacturing.
2 Big data and platforms – data is collected from tens of thousands of devices that analyse processes for their optimization and improvement

of the delivery performance (on-time and completeness of deliveries) in conjunction with resource capacity (production resource intensity analysis). To optimize the supply chain, a set of supplier evaluation indicators was selected and entered into process algorithms. Supply control is implemented using information-computer technology on the basis of integrated supply indicators that measure the performance of deliveries to customers. Data in the system is enhanced with customer metrics and delivery methods. The system enables individualized delivery of steel products to multiple locations on different continents. Information from the integrated delivery system is virtually accessible from anywhere. Such investment was fully implemented at ArcelorMittal, the United States.

3 Production scheduling using the Ant Colony Optimization (ACO) algorithm. Device operators and researchers have built a digital landscape that maps sequences of actions according to an assumed performance criterion for a specific problem. The structure of the algorithm is based on an ant colony behaviour simulation system and involves finding paths to reach a destination. The adaptation of the ACO optimization algorithm, which was developed by the Université Libre de Bruxelles (ULB) in an academic environment to industrial applications, enables ArcelorMittal to optimize production scheduling (the process is implemented in just a few minutes).

4 Drones are used to improve operational safety, as well as to control performance and measure the accuracy of equipment operations. Examples of drone applications:

- checking the maintenance needs of objects, technologies, machines, and transport networks in enterprises;
- minimizing risks to workers who would have to work on high structures to inspect the condition of facilities (buildings, steel constructions); and
- tracking energy consumption – drones with infrared cameras moving at a fixed altitude measure the energy intensity of objects and technologies.

5 ELIOS technical and structural engineering control and inspection system for machinery, equipment, and facilities – the system works with drones, operating in enclosed or confined spaces in the cold rolling mill at AM Poland, and monitors places where workers cannot enter or where staying is associated with danger. LED lighting installed in the drones allows the devices to work even in the dark.

6 Automation of delivery to increase productivity of processes and quality of products. In the analysed group, investments began with the automation of metallurgical product stockpiles in conjunction with the scheduling of production lines and access to transportation equipment, such as autonomous cranes and overhead cranes with functions for

identifying and selecting products delivered to customers. Technologies allow scaling of products according to multiple technical parameters and quality assessment criteria, as well as the requirements of key customers. Applied solutions, equipped with information and computer systems, in the process of storing steel products, are expected to reduce inventory levels and shorten delivery times. Investments are made at ArcelorMittal in Canada, the United States, Mexico, among others.

7 Genesis system to help locate stored steel products. The system quickly and accurately locates each product in stock. The process of identifying products is done remotely, without the need for employees to move around the shop floor. The system tracks the entire path of the coils from the hot rolling mill to shipment to the customer. The solution has streamlined the process of storing steel products, as well as increased work safety. The system is used, among others, in AM Poland.

8 STRIP registration and transport information platform, thanks to which cars can transport materials and steel products more smoothly.

9 Artificial intelligence (AI) is being introduced into steel manufacturing processes among the projects are image recognition and computer models of processes and products. Artificial intelligence saves time and leads to increased productivity in manufacturing processes, and contributes to improving the accuracy of features (quality assessment parameters) of manufactured products. Examples of solutions: (1) production decision to release a weld in a hot rolling mill (plant in Canada) based on image recognition of the width of a cold coil, (2) environmental decision to classify emissions into the environment (plant in Brazil).

10 Digital twinning – a set of models used to optimize physical assets and manufacturing processes using data collected from device sensors (objects). The sensors create a digital imprint of the product that can be delivered to the next process. Quality features are tagged with a barcode and linked to a digital twin in the cloud. Customers scan the barcode and get access to complete quality data about the steel product.

11 Computer vision (CV) algorithm is used to build pictures of the production environment. Example of projects: (1) recognizing the numbers of cars (vehicles) entering a steel mill, (2) recognizing the type of material moved by overhead cranes or recognizing the level of filling a vat with liquid metal.

12 IT-computer system for tracking rail production allowing for precise identification and tracking of products in the rolling mill (AM Poland). The solution allows operators to preview the current state of production, increase the throughput of the production line, accelerate the quality acceptance of products, and reduce the risk of human errors.

13 The COKLEVFIL radar measurement system, which is designed to determine the filling level of a coke chamber after backfilling with coal mixture and levelling. Based on the data obtained, chamber backfilling

operations can be better carried out while reducing emissions to the environment (ArcelorMittal plants in Europe and the United States).

14 Steel product defect detection system – POMINI INSPEKTOR CUBE roll defect detection system was installed in the grinding room of the hot rolling mill at AM Poland. The latest generation of measuring systems used in the system contributes to the effective detection of surface cracks and defects hidden deep below the surface, including cracks covered by other metal.

15 Additive manufacturing: 3D printing of machine spare parts in both metal (metal powders) and plastic (masses, powders); precision laser cutting technologies; technologies that increase the precision of steel products, e.g. four pairs of sensors enhance strip alignment on disc shears within the cold rolling mill and etching mill, enabling precision cutting of etched sheet metal edges and reducing instances of jams.

16 Professional Maintenance (PM) and Autonomous Maintenance (AM) system development – operators through an application installed on their phone scan QR codes, and after completing the inspection, confirm the task. Data from the mobile devices of operators of individual machines and technological installations is sent directly to the ERP-SAP information system.

17 Virtual Training (VT) – virtual training technology is used during instruction in occupational safety – simulating hazards or accidents at work. Training using virtual reality (VR) is implemented at ArcelorMittal plants in Brazil and the United States, among others.

Case study 2 ThyssenKrupp

The ThyssenKrupp Group is carrying out investments worth EUR 40 billion. The investments are mainly carried out in steelworks in Germany.

Key investments:

1 Connected (interactive) value chain – using the latest communication and digital technologies are built interactive producer-customer relationships in cyberspace. An example: one of the group's plants (a steel plant) has implemented Industry 4.0 solutions that go far beyond the boundaries of individual companies, and are characterized by:

- A sequence of innovations throughout the supply chain: advanced technologies applied to chain participants' collaboration, intelligent process collaboration systems, compatible information systems, modern communication devices, platforms, LCA systems, solutions for steel blockchain, etc.

- Integrating cooperation processes into a common digital network in the full life cycle of the product, i.e. from the raw material to the finished product and its use and recycling.
- The system of Quick response to customer requirements regarding deadlines, even with regard to the raw material already at the stage of production of semi-finished products (input) thanks to automatic communication and production process tracking systems. Using the system, customers can influence the production of products and place orders directly in the IT system of the plant, specifying the date of completion of the order (processing), as well as make changes to the specifications in terms of width and thickness of the product until the start of production to its completion. Interactive chain of links between manufacturer and customer saves space and reduces storage costs for materials and products, freeing up capital that can be used for other purposes.

2 Cyber-physical dialogue between product and production. This dialogue is based on interfaces to the Internet. In this project, the physical world of things merges with data networks. Each product has its own unique identifier and goes through the entire production process, carrying a large amount of data. In the codes are written data about the customer for whom the product is produced, the current state of processing and the state of the product as it left the previous stage of the process. The project is realized in Ilsenburg plant.

Continuous investments:

3 Cyber-Physical Systems of Production (CPS) – an intelligent production tracking system with products and machines with memories and record paths of production of a specific type of product for each of customers. The system tracks all operations and elements of the production process. Each element of the process (product) has its own name, history, and interface on the Web. The final goal of building cyber-physical production systems is to create an intelligent factory, capable of managing itself, learning, and operating flexibly.

4 Plant design in 3W (three-dimensional) layouts – the system is based on the solutions of the digital factory. The system is designed for the production line of products for the automotive industry for the production lines of car bodies, engine assembly, and gearboxes. This system can design entire car production lines on computers, along with the machines, robots, and equipment needed to operate and perform the work.

5 Full robotization of production lines – lines of robots – hundreds of robots are engaged in assembling complete BIW (Body-In-White) from individual parts into whole components. Production lines are completed in handling and storage equipment, as well as connectivity technologies,

such as welding pliers, to join individual parts from sheet metal. All robots, machine islands, and controls are being assembled and tested using three-dimensional simulation (3D). The created image of the production line automatically appears to the customer, who participates in monitoring the progress of the work and influences the shape of the production line structure of the custom product. The validated virtual production line significantly reduces the start-up time of the actual production line.

6 New business models with smart products in the digital ecosystem. The group has initiated the development of new customer-centric business models featuring smart products and services. Retailers and logistics service providers are creating a digital ecosystem within which all participants are constantly informed about the product location and its status. In the new business model, demand of goods is compared with customer needs.

7 Security in the industrial data space: security passwords and other solutions to ensure the rapid and secure transfer of large amounts of data, both internally and externally between plants and cooperators. The industrial data space aims to eliminate potential uncertainties during data collection, processing, and transfer. In the systems of communication, users retain full control over their data.

Case study 3 Tata Steel

Tata Steel, in its business strategy, joins individual customer service with the creativity of its employees (the group focuses on new ideas). The group works closely with customers and is committed to long-term business relationships focused on developing new products and technologies. Social trust and the development of local communities are part of the group's strategy. Business activity of the group is based on the principle: *Our actions should always benefit the public.*

The key digital components of Tata Steel's strategy are:

- smarter technologies,
- smarter connections, and
- smarter services.

These three transformational pillars—(1) next-generation technologies, (2) Industrial Internet of Things (IIOT), and (3) cloud-based services—are present within each value chain in the steel market. These three pillars of transformation (1) next generation of technologies; (2) Industrial Internet of Things (IIOT); (3) services based on cloud, there are in each of the value chains in the steel market.

Key investments/projects:

1 **Digitization in the automotive value chain.** The project is based on the CASE (or ACES) principles, meaning connected, autonomous, share, and electrified. Digitization of manufacturing processes is one of the key factors enabling cost savings while improving overall machine efficiency (OEE). The system cooperates with the ERP system. Processes are improved based on end-user experience or by purchasing new programs (applications) from the system provider.
2 **Increasing value through digital innovation** – the production based on requirements of the automotive consumers (customized production with personalized steel products).
3 **Smarter technologies** are created in the Digital Innovation Centre belonging to the Producer. The centre is constantly experimenting with the latest technologies, such as digital twins, artificial intelligence, augmented, virtual and mixed reality, blockchain, drones, and digital services with new added value.
4 **Smarter connections** – plants use the Internet of Things (IoT) and advanced communication systems. The group works with third parties to develop and shape future ways of sharing data across the value chain. The vision of the group is a fully integrated ecosystem that is nurtured by the flow of information between all stakeholders. The group cooperates with leading institutions to develop and standardize key cyber-physical systems.
3 **Smarter services** – the projects of smarter steel product by accessing the Steel Data Package (services help steel products to be more smart). The steel data package is based on material data, computer models, and intelligent algorithms. The group is constantly working on the development of new digital services for smart factories. Quality management, dynamic process control, and predictive maintenance are just some of the key areas of change within the Group.

Summary of these case studies:

- Each groups implement strategies based on the technologies of smart future that are implemented in steel manufacturing. In the strategies of the surveyed capital groups, the image of Industry 4.0 appears as smart manufacturing and smart steel. A cyber-physical dialogue is realized between product and production. In addition, interactive producer-customer relationships are built. The end result of the changes will be digital ecosystems that wrap around steel mills, customer markets, and third parties. The world's steel producers are interested in building the sustainable and responsible business. In the organizational structures of each company, there are departments responsible for development of smart steel manufacturing (digitization centres, innovation centres,

Research and Development (R & D) departments with their own research laboratories).

- Key investments are connected with process digitization, automation, and robotization as well as the integration of the physical and digital world into the common steel production system (Cyber-Physical Steel Production System). The steel mills create cyber-physical systems by using intelligent technologies (handling and transportation robots, artificial intelligence solutions at levels: M2M and I2M, autonomous control systems, product lifecycle tracking), intelligent connections (Industrial Internet of Things, platforms), and intelligent services (cloud computing, e-commerce, e-business). The process of collecting and processing data – big data – is facilitated by thousands of smart sensors and sensors. Data is analysed in real time, and the main purpose of analysis and control systems is to optimize processes.
- In the area of data processing and process control, the steel mills surveyed applied the principle of integrating information and communication systems according to three functions: computing, communication, and control, or 3C: Computing, Communication, Control. Steel mills are developing information (communications) and information and communication systems to support technological processes, which, in conjunction with technological installations and physical facilities, give rise to cyber-physical production systems (CPS).
- Sources of market advantage are high-quality products tailored to the needs of customer markets (key consumer sectors are automotive and construction) with the possibility for customers to participate in the co-creation of the product, as well as in the package of services carried out to the customer's order using the latest solutions. Augmented, virtual, and mixed reality is built by using 3D image presentation, control of devices by voice or motion, remote information transfer, codes of product identification, computer modelling, 3D design, and computer process simulation.
- Changes in technologies are compatible with the customer needs. The studied steel mills develop cyberspace with products and machines with memories and record paths of the production run of a specific type of product for a specific customer, with interconnected cooperative processes and shared digital services across entire supply chains.
- The scopes of change presented in the case studies can be grouped into several areas: digitalization of plants, differentiation of production, full automation and robotization of activities, artificial intelligence, custom manufacturing, customization, optimization of processes, full communication, and rapid access to data.
- New technologies and systems create a new image of steel market. Changes can be called "smarter" (but not yet "smart") because this is only the beginning of changes in new industrial transformation called Industry 4.0.

3.3 Smart steel manufacturing – the results of field research

The research was carried out in the period from 2020 to 2023 in Poland. The objective of the research was to determine (establish) the scope of changes in the surveyed companies from the perspective of the development of Industry 4.0. The research topic was as follows: The concept of Industry 4.0 in the Polish steel industry and in the market of steel product users (consumers) and distributors. Moreover, steel market researchers in Poland were invited to participate in the study. Respondents were divided into four segments: producer P, distributor D, consumer C, and researcher R (Producer; Distributor; Consumer; Researcher).

The research was realized by PhD (hab.) Eng. Bożena Gajdzik, assoc. Professor at the Silesian University of Technology in Poland. The author formulated the following research hypothesis: in the Fourth Industrial Revolution, the accession of companies in the steel section to Industry 4.0 is necessary to be in the market and execute business smartly. The first part of her research was published in her monograph, no. 945, Gliwice, 2023 (Gajdzik, 2022a). That research was a form of pilot research, and this research are realized based on that research structure. After the publication of research results in her scientific monograph, the author (B. Gajdzik) continued her research. The old segment consisted of 79 people, the new segment has 253 people. The qualification of people for the study was carried out in compliance with the requirements of the postulates of randomness and representativeness of the sample. The selection of the sample was confirmed by statistical tools (test in the computer program MEDCALC) in accordance with the methodology of sampling (Machin et al., 2009). The obtained test result of 245, after comparing with the number of respondents (research participants), which were 253 was obtained 253>245, so it was confirmed that the research sample was sufficient (the requirements of the postulates of randomness and representativeness of the sample were maintained).

The research was conducted using survey and interview methods. This chapter presents the results of the survey. Respondents chose answers, using a scale from 1 to 5, where 1 being the lowest, and 5 being the highest. In questions with a quasi-ranging scale, respondents had an one choice – 5 possibilities – from 1 to 5. The survey consisted of 10 specific questions on the topic of implementing Industry 4.0 technologies into steel companies. The last three questions were not with scales, but were cafeteria and multiple choice.

In the first stage of the research, 289 completed surveys (questionnaires) were obtained but 267 were correctly completed. The statistical evaluation of the surveyed questionnaire (questionnaire) thus included a total of 267 correctly completed surveys (questionnaires) out of the original 289 analysed. After applying the expert evaluation, 253 respondents were obtained who were considered experts, which were people with knowledge of Industry 4.0 and metallurgical technologies. At this second stage of the research, the expert competence factor (coefficient/index) was applied K_k (formula 1). The key to selecting the expert (respondent) was his self-assessment of his knowledge of Industry 4.0.

$$K_k = \frac{k_z + k_a}{2} \tag{1}$$

where:

K_k – respondent competence coefficient,

k_z – coefficient of the degree of knowledge of the expert about the problem (research topic),

k_a – argumentation coefficient.

Coefficients k_z and k_a take values in the range <0;1>, so the expert competence coefficient K_k can take a minimum value of zero and a maximum value of unity. This paper uses a modified expert method, based on direct determination of the expert competence coefficient K_k. To determine the value of this coefficient based on the analysis of the evaluation of answers to the questions: What do you know about Industry 4.0? (Q1_1). Do you know an idea of changes in the steel sector? (Q1_2) What is your activity in developing knowledge about the steel industry transformation? (Q1_3). At this stage of the research, formula (2) was applied:

$$K_k = \frac{\text{Analysis\_Q1\_1(points)} + \text{Analysis\_Q1\_2(points)} + \text{Analysis\_Q1\_3(points)}}{3} \tag{2}$$

Based on the resulting evaluation based on the modified expert method, a total of 14 respondents were rejected, with 5 respondents rejected from the Producers segment, 3 respondents rejected from the Distributors segment, 4 respondents rejected from the Consumers segment, and 2 respondents rejected from the Researchers segment. Producers were the best experts, so only the results of this group are shown in this book (Figure 3.2). In addition, the survey results obtained in the Steelmakers segment relate to the topic of the book and the title of this chapter.

The producer segment was made up of employees of steel mills and steel product companies. In total, this segment consisted of 62 people (Figure 3.3). Respondents

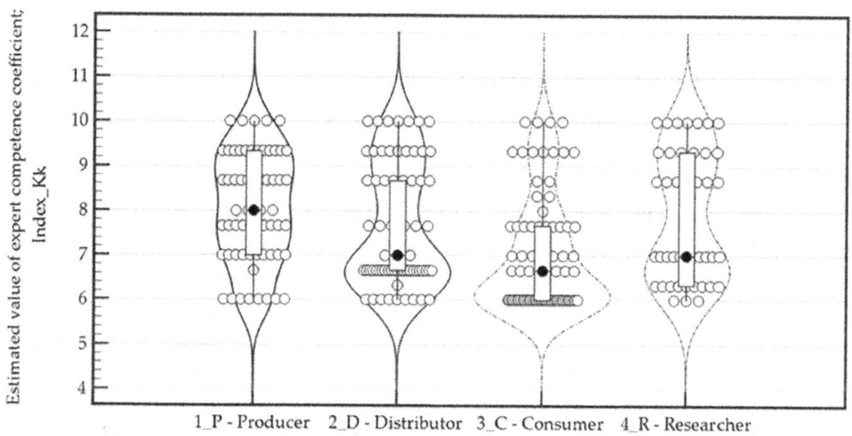

Figure 3.2 Values of the expert competence coefficient K_k in all study groups (median and quartiles of 25% and 75%).

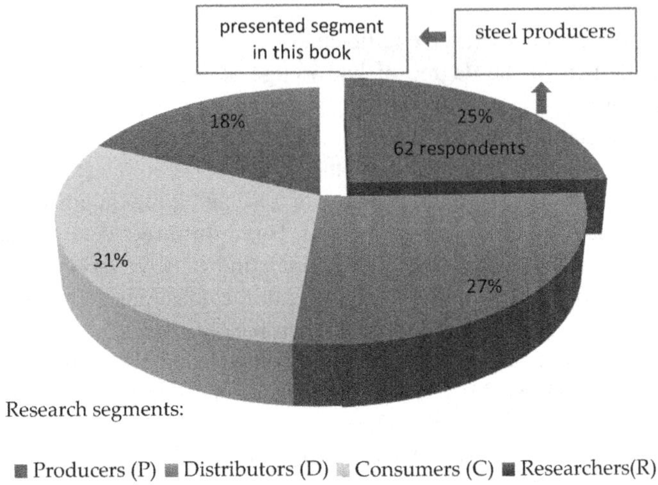

Figure 3.3 Research segments.

of the segment P (Producers) were operational managers at companies – production line managers – and therefore people directly involved in the implementation of Industry 4.0 technologies.

The presented research results are a pilot study for all Polish steel sector, which consist of 2 converter steel mills and 7 electric steel mills, 5 rolling mills for the production of flat products, 12 rolling mills for the production of long products, and 10 rolling mills for the production of tubes and z/closed sections. The listed process plants belong to nine steel mills (Polish Steel Association, Report, Katowice). The largest steel mills in Poland are owned by foreign capital. The strategic transformation to Industry 4.0 at steel mills in Poland is in line with the policy of headquarters, which are located outside Poland. Strong equity groups in the Polish steel sector are leading the digital transformation. A strong benchmark in the market is ArcelorMittal Poland. Small and medium-sized enterprises (manufacturers of metal products) are constrained by capital and market barriers in the ongoing transformation to Industry 4.0. The surveyed group of 62 respondents, representatives of enterprises in the manufacturer sector, was diverse structure business profile of the companies was presented in Figure 3.4. In Table 3.4 was presented the structure of steel sector in Poland (data from Central Statistical Office in Poland).

In this chapter, the key results of the research for segment 1_P are presented. Professor of statistics and mathematics, J. Szymszal, co-author of the book, was responsible for statistical supervision of the research. The database was created in a Microsoft Excel spreadsheet. After checking the consistency of the answers given by the respondents consisting of assessing the completeness, completeness and completeness of the statistical material – the database was implemented into licensed statistical packages: Statitistica v.7.1. PL firmy StatSoft, MedCalc Statistical Software v.19.4.1 (MedCalc Software bvba, Ostend, Belgium, PQStat Software v. 1.6.8).

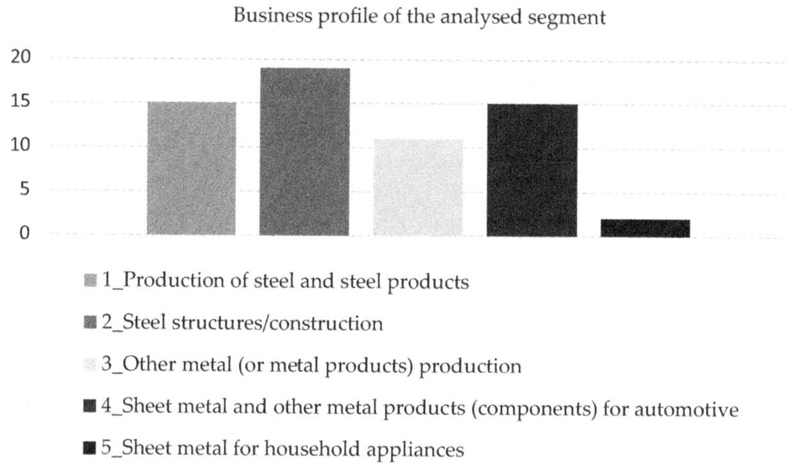

Figure 3.4 Business profile of the companies in the segment: Producer (1_P).

Table 3.4 Number of business entities in the steel sector in Poland

Sector	*Number*
Production of pig iron, steel and products	16
Manufacture of pipes and profiles	24
Production of other pre-treated products	27

Source: Statistical Yearbook of Industry – Poland (https://stat.gov.pl/)' Polish Steel Association, Katowice, Poland.

Presentation of survey results: Analysis of responses from a selected segment: Producer (1_P)

After question Q1: Do you have knowledge of the Industry 4.0 concept? that was used to select the expert was question Q2: Do you know the pillars of Industry 4.0? for all pillars (Q2_1…Q2_9). The results were presented in Table 3.5. On the other hand, Figure 3.5 shows the distribution of knowledge about these pillars in the segment Producer (1_P). Moreover, the results were ordered from largest to smallest in Figure 3.6.

Third question (Q3) was about the impact of the Industry 4.0 pillars on the company development. Research results were presented in Table 3.6, Figures 3.7 and 3.8.

Respondents in the analysed segment are aware of the impact of Industry 4.0 technologies on the development of their companies. Of the nine evaluated pillars of Industry 4.0, they said, additive manufacturing is the most useful at this stage of change. In the future, Industry 4.0 technologies will contribute to the development of cyber-physical steel production systems (CPSPS), but in order for this strategic goal to be achieved it is necessary to gradually (in stages, segments, processes) invest in all pillars of Industry 4.0.

Table 3.5 The response structure for question Q2: Do you know the pillars of Industry 4.0? for all pillars (Q2_1 .... Q2_9) in the segment: Producers (1_P)

Pillars of Industry 4.0	*Segment 1_P – Producer (N=62)*				
Q2. Knowledge about the pillars of Industry 4.0	Q2=1	Q2=2	Q2=3	Q2=4	Q2=5
Q2_1. Big data & analytics – *n* (% of row)	3 (4.84%)	10 (16.13%)	27 (44.55%)	15 (24.19%)	7 (11.29%)
Q2_2. Autonomous robots and AI - *n* (% of row)	2 (4.23%)	9 (14.52%)	25 (40.32%)	18 (29.03%)	8 (12.9%)
Q2_3. Systems integration towards CPS – *n* (% of row)	5 (8.06%)	19 (30.65%)	19 (30.65%)	12 (19.35%)	7 (11.29%)
Q2_4. Horizontal and vertical system integration – *n* (% of row)	1 (1.61%)	5 (8.06%)	7 (11.29%)	27 (44.55%)	22 (35.48%)
Q2_5. IoT /IIoT – *n* (% of row)	5 (8.06%)	33 (54.23%)	9 (14.52%)	11 (17.74%)	4 (6.45%)
Q2_6. Cyber-Physical Systems (CPSs) and cybersecurity – *n* (% of row)	7 (11.29%)	37 (59.68%)	12 (19.35%)	4 (6.45%)	2 (4.23%)
Q2_7. Cloud computing – *n* (% of row)	1 (1.61%)	6 (9.68%)	10 (16.13%)	30 (48.39%)	15 (24.19%)
Q2_8. Additive manufacturing – *n* (% of row)	1 (1.61%)	9 (14.52%)	18 (29.03%)	21 (34.87%)	13 (20.97%)
Q2_9. Virtual and augmented reality – *n* (% of row)	9 (14.52%)	39 (62.9%)	10 (16.13%)	3 (4.84%)	1 (1.61%)
Kruskal-Wallis test: $H=166.01$; $p<0.001$.					

Source: Own research.

The next question – question four (Q4) – was a refinement of the question Q3, and addressed the scope of the results of the impact of Industry 4.0 technologies on improving steel production. Respondents most often pointed to the increasing automation of production processes, with automation being implemented in stages, first they will put up islands of the latest generation of technologies, then there is a merging of technologies, and almost fully automated production lines are created, autonomous robots and AI solutions with

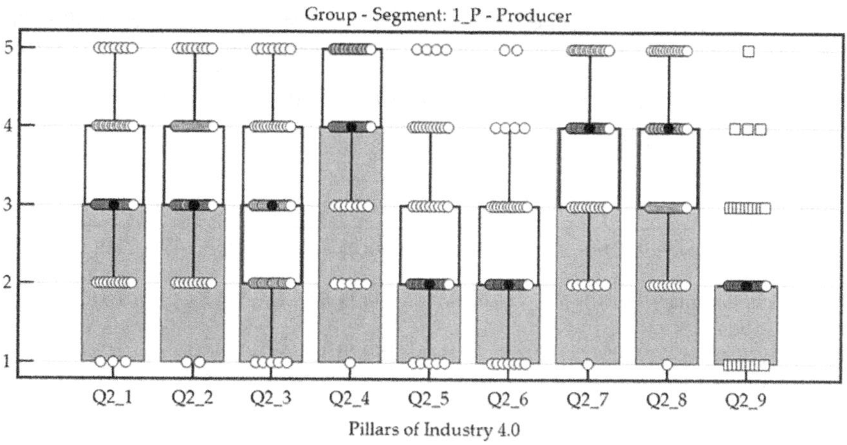

Figure 3.5 The response structure for question Q2: Do you know the pillars of Industry 4.0? for all pillars (Q2_1 .... Q2_9) in the segment: Producers (1_P).

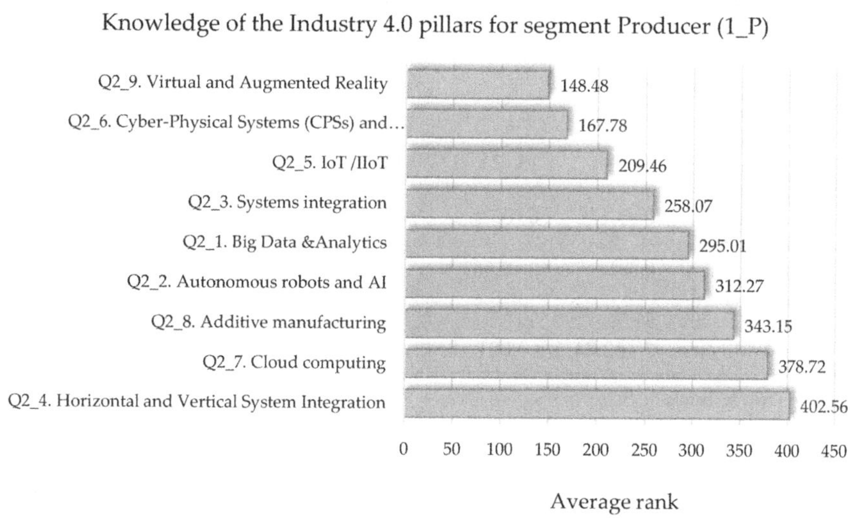

Figure 3.6 Detailed results of Kruskal-Wallis ANOVA test for Q2 in the segment: Producers (1_P).

machine learning (ML) algorithms are added to the resulting lines over time. In parallel with the progress (development) of automation of technological sequences, investments are being made in information and computer systems for process support. The development and integration of technology-based systems (ICTs) are being carried out within companies and supply chains.

Digitalization supported by modern technologies of Industry 4.0 generates huge amounts of data (Big Data), which are increasingly stored in computer clouds. New technologies in the steel sector need platforms and IoT to be more independent

Table 3.6 The response structure for question Q3 for assessing the impact of all pillars (Q3_1…Q3_9) on the company development in the segment: Producers (1_P)

Q3: the impact of the Industry 4.0 pillars on the company development	*Segment: Producer (1_P) – n (% of row)*				
	Q3 = 1	*Q3 = 2*	*Q3 = 3*	*Q3 = 4*	*Q3 = 5*
Q3_1: Big data & analytics	0 (0%)	2 (3.39%)	14 (23.73%)	32 (54.24%)	11 (18.64%)
Q3_2: Autonomous robots and AI	0 (0%)	1 (1.67%)	13 (21.67%)	30 (50%)	16 (26.67%)
Q3_3: Systems integration (…)	0 (0%)	0 (0%)	15 (26.32%)	32 (56.14%)	10 (17.54%)
Q3_4: Horizontal and vertical system Integration (in company and in supply chain)	0 (0%)	1 (1.64%)	4 (6.56%)	32 (52.46%)	24 (39.34%)
Q3_5: IoT / IIoT	0 (0%)	2 (3.51%)	13 (22.81%)	33 (57.89%)	9 (15.79%)
Q3_6: Cyber-Physical Systems (CPSs) and cybersecurity	1 (1.82%)	0 (0%)	5 (9.09%)	28 (50.91%)	21 (38.18%)
Q3_7: Cloud computing	0 (0%)	13 (21.31%)	19 (31.15%)	21 (34.43%)	8 (13.11%)
Q3_8: Additive manufacturing	0 (0%)	0 (0%)	4 (6.56%)	28 (45.9%)	29 (47.54%)
Q3_9: Simulation and augmented reality	0 (0%)	3 (5.66%)	9 (16.98%)	22 (41.51%)	19 (35.85%)
Kruskal-Wallis test: $H = 62.81$; $p < 0.001$.					

Source: Own research.

from human activities. Moreover, respondents from the steelmaking sector also noted the need to develop blockchain technology, which can improve transparency in the *steel industry* by enabling the industry to become more transparent and traceable. Blockchain technology can help the industry save money through digitization initiatives, in a sector that still uses millions of paper documents, faxes, and emails. The digital revolution is expected to transform the steel industry by improving operational efficiency, customer service, inventory levels, and profit margin. Block chain in steel sector is connected with development of new technologies like predictive analytics and data lakes, agile computer technologies and systems etc. The blockchain technology must be combined with the Internet of Things (IoT) and analytics (see: Jenabi, 2023).

The next question was about changes in your company (Q5). Results are presented in a proper table and figures.

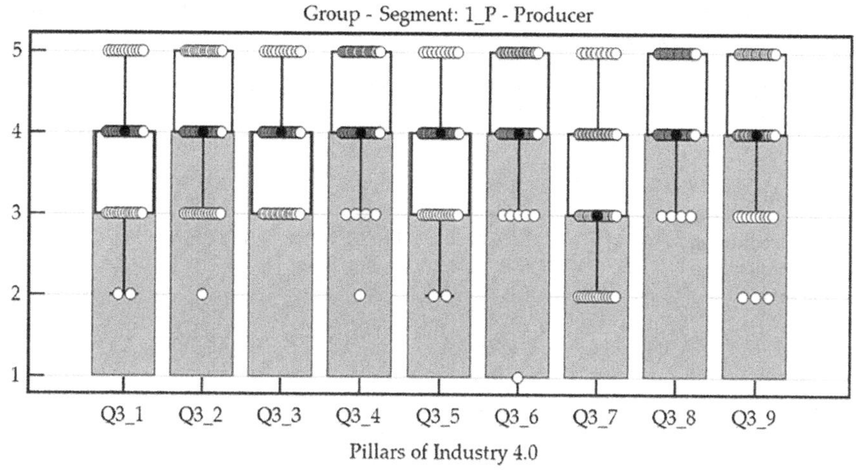

Figure 3.7 The response structure for question Q3 for assessing the impact of all pillars (Q3_1...Q3_9) on the company development in the segment: Producers (1_P).

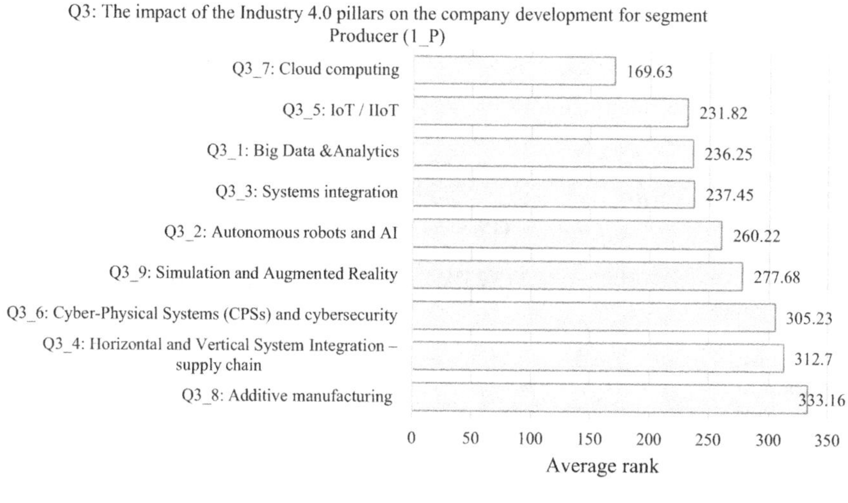

Figure 3.8 Detailed results of Kruskal-Wallis ANOVA test for Q3 in the segment: Producers (1_P).

The question 6 (Q6: Impact of Industry 4.0 technologies or pillars on the business operations) was with the following responses:

- Q6_1: Better productivity
- Q6_2: Real-time analysis of the production and other processes
- Q6_3: Increasing process execution capacity/optimizing processes
- Q6_4: More flexibility in process operations
- Q6_5: Reduction in labour costs

Table 3.7 The response structure for question: Q4 for the range of influence of all pillars (Q4_1…Q4_9) in the segment: Producers (1_P)

Q4: Identify the impact of technologies on the company development	*Segment: Producer (1_P) – n (% of row)*				
	Q4 = 1	*Q4 = 2*	*Q4 = 3*	*Q4 = 4*	*Q4 = 5*
Q4_1: Production automation / machine island	0 (0%)	0 (0%)	11 (17.74%)	20 (32.26%)	31 (50%)
Q4_2: Full production automation	0 (0%)	2 (3.23%)	8 (12.9%)	30 (48.39%)	22 (35.48%)
Q4_3: Autonomous robots and AI	0 (0%)	0 (0%)	8 (12.9%)	26 (41.94%)	28 (45.16%)
Q4_4: Full automation warehouse	0 (0%)	1 (1.61%)	11 (17.74%)	29 (46.77%)	21 (33.87%)
Q4_5: Multitasking automatically controlled production lines with machine learning (ML)	0 (0%)	1 (1.61%)	10 (16.13%)	28 (45.16%)	23 (37.1%)
Q4_6: Electronic customer service	0 (0%)	12 (19.35%)	18 (29.03%)	21 (33.87%)	11 (17.74%)
Q4_7: Autonomous system of decisions, predictive maintenance (PM)	0 (0%)	2 (3.23%)	10 (16.13%)	33 (53.23%)	17 (27.42%)
Q4_8: IC systems (Cax, MES, ERP etc.).	0 (0%)	0 (0%)	14 (22.58%)	33 (53.23%)	15 (24.19%)
Q4_9: Intelligent value chain/ smart manufacturing/ CPSs	0 (0%)	2 (3.23%)	5 (8.06%)	34 (54.84%)	21 (33.87%)
Q4_10: Big data	0 (0%)	4 (6.45%)	16 (25.81%)	32 (51.61%)	10 (16.13%)
Q4_11: Cloud computing and IoT	0 (0%)	13 (20.97%)	17 (27.42%)	22 (35.48%)	10 (16.13%)
Q4_12: Blockchain	0 (0%)	3 (4.84%)	10 (16.13%)	26 (41.94%)	23 (37.1%)

Kruskal-Wallis test: $H = 67.65$; $p < 0.001$.

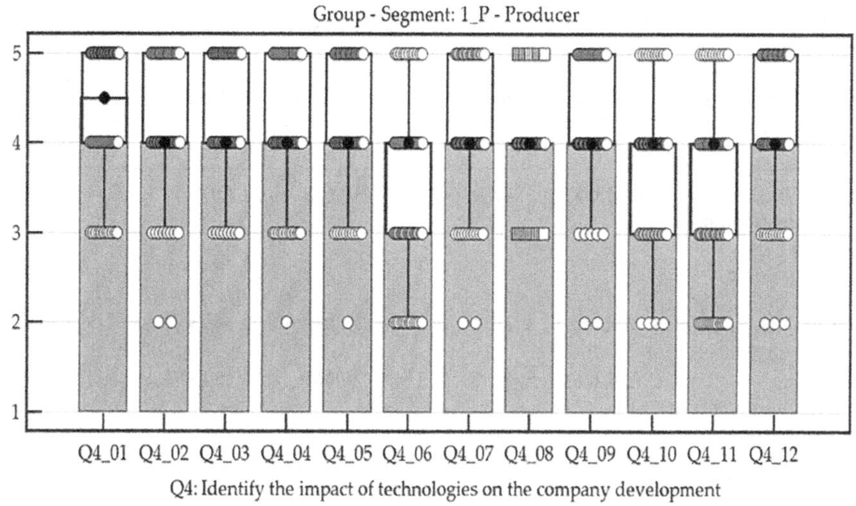

Figure 3.9 The response structure for question Q4 for the range of influence of all pillars (Q4_1.... Q4_9) in the segment: Producers (1_P)

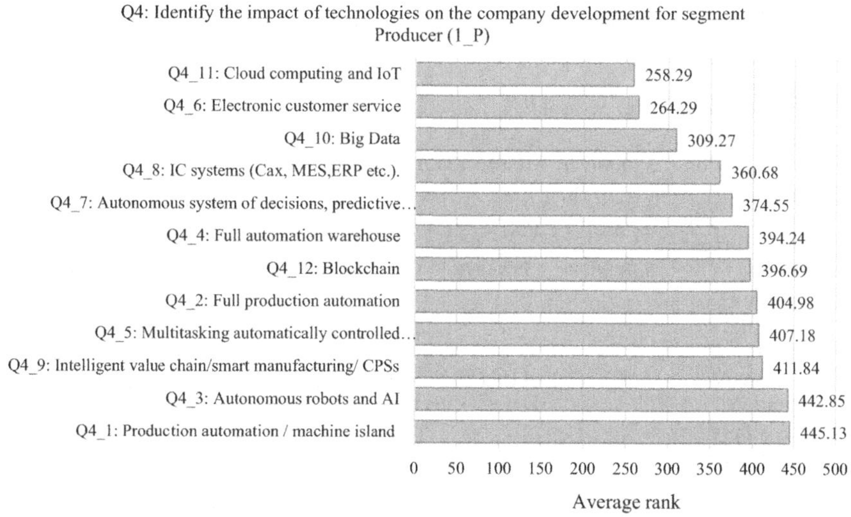

Figure 3.10 Detailed results of Kruskal-Wallis ANOVA test for Q4 in the segment: Producers (1_P).

- Q6_6: Better product quality, product accuracy, repeatability, etc.
- Q6_7: Reduction of operating costs through production flexibility
- Q6_8: Profits from the sale of personalized products
- Q6_9: Increase in the market value of the company by automation and robotics
- Q6_10: Flexible distribution systems/speed and quality of supply
- Q6_11: Increased involvement in supply chain management

Table 3.8 The response structure for question: Q5 about changes.... (Q5_1...Q5_12) in the segment: Producers (1_P)

Q5. Changes are in your company:	*Segment: Producer (1_P) – n (% of row)*				
	Q5 = 1	*Q5 = 2*	*Q5 = 3*	*Q5 = 4*	*Q5 = 5*
Q5_1. Production automation and new technologies (ICTs)	2 (3.23%)	3 (4.84%)	19 (30.65%)	31 (50%)	7 (11.29%)
Q5_2. Automation with M2M	3 (4.84%)	4 (6.45%)	16 (25.81%)	34 (54.84%)	5 (8.06%)
Q5_3. Autonomous robots/robot assembly in production	2 (3.23%)	5 (8.06%)	8 (12.9%)	37 (59.68%)	10 (16.13%)
Q5_4. Warehouses automation	1 (1.61%)	6 (9.68%)	10 (16.13%)	34 (54.84%)	11 (17.74%)
Q5_5. Production automation with multitasking systems	3 (4.84%)	6 (9.68%)	14 (22.58%)	27 (43.55%)	12 (19.35%)
Q5_6. Development of electronic customer service process	8 (12.9%)	13 (20.97%)	12 (19.35%)	22 (35.48%)	7 (11.29%)
Q5_7. Installation of sensors generating data from machines	3 (4.84%)	10 (16.13%)	13 (20.97%)	30 (48.39%)	6 (9.68%)
Q5_8. Systems integration (CAx, ERP, MES, etc.)	5 (8.06%)	5 (8.06%)	14 (22.58%)	29 (46.77%)	9 (14.52%)
Q5_9. Systems integration in the supply chain (intra-and extra-group)	7 (11.29%)	4 (6.45%)	10 (16.13%)	30 (48.39%)	11 (17.74%)
Q5_10. Big data & analytics with intelligent decision-making	6 (9.68%)	9 (14.52%)	13 (20.97%)	28 (45.16%)	6 (9.68%)
Q5_11. Cloud computing and IoT/IIoT	3 (4.84%)	16 (25.81%)	16 (25.81%)	19 (30.65%)	8 (12.9%)
Q5_12. Blockchain	4 (6.45%)	12 (19.35%)	16 (25.81%)	17 (27.42%)	13 (20.97%)

Kruskal-Wallis test: $H = 24.44$; $p < 0.001$.

Source: Own research.

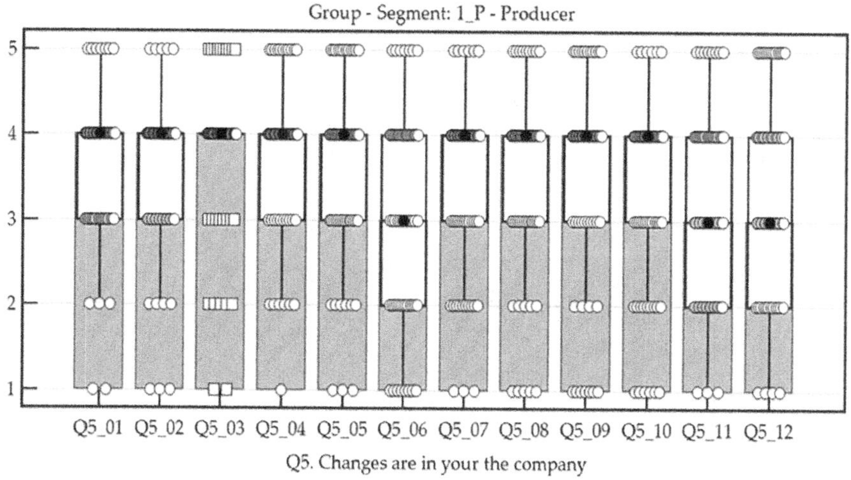

Figure 3.11 The response structure for question Q5 for the range of changes (Q5_1… Q5_12) in the segment: Producers (1_P).

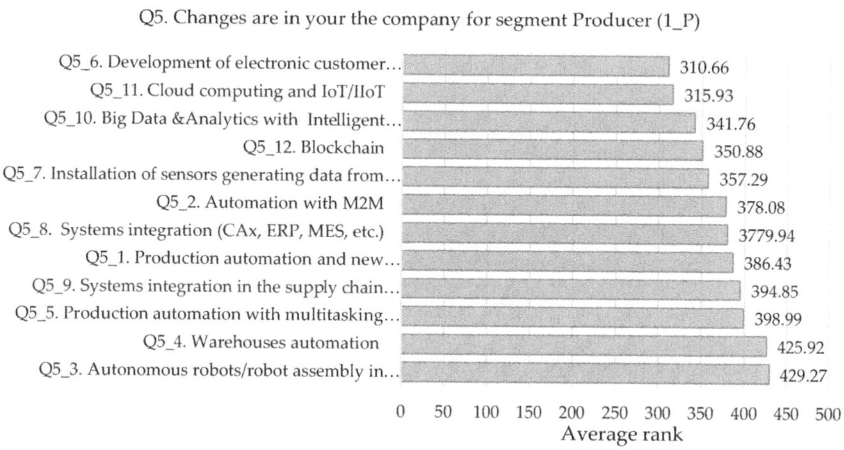

Figure 3.12 Detailed results of Kruskal-Wallis ANOVA test for Q5 in the segment: Producers (1_P).

Respondents in the Producer (1_P) segment stated that all technologies or pillars of Industry 4.0 have a significant impact on the business operations but high noted was answer Q6_5 in the form of result called "reduction of labor costs". The average wages in the manufacturing sector in Poland are rising year by year (the average monthly salary in the industrial sector in 2023 was more than PLN 7,000 gross, or about €1,500). Replacing human labour with machine labour is

Table 3.9 The response structure for question Q6 about impact (Q6_1…Q6_11) on the company in the segment: Producers (1_P)

Q6. Impact of Industry 4.0 technologies/pillars on the company operations:	*Segment: Producer (1_P) – n (% of row)*				
	Q6=1	*Q6=2*	*Q6=3*	*Q6=4*	*Q6=5*
Q6_1: Better productivity	0 (0%)	2 (3.23%)	7 (11.29%)	22 (35.48%)	31 (50%)
Q6_2: Real-time analysis of the production and other processes	0 (0%)	2 (3.23%)	8 (12.9%)	20 (32.26%)	32 (51.61%)
Q6_3: Increasing process execution capacity/ optimizing processes	0 (0%)	1 (1.61%)	9 (14.52%)	20 (32.26%)	32 (51.61%)
Q6_4: More flexibility in process operations	0 (0%)	2 (3.23%)	10 (16.13%)	15 (24.19%)	35 (56.45%)
Q6_5: Reduction in labour costs	0 (0%)	0 (0%)	6 (9.68%)	17 (27.42%)	39 (62.9%)
Q6_6: Better product quality, product accuracy, repeatability, etc.	0 (0%)	3 (4.84%)	7 (11.29%)	28 (45.16%)	24 (38.71%)
Q6_7: Reduction of operating costs through production flexibility	0 (0%)	0 (0%)	11 (17.74%)	31 (50%)	20 (32.26%)
Q6_8: Profits from the sale of personalized products	0 (0%)	0 (0%)	10 (16.13%)	32 (51.61%)	20 (32.26%)
Q6_9: Increase in the market value of the company by automation and robotics	0 (0%)	0 (0%)	11 (17.74%)	33 (53.23%)	18 (29.03%)
Q6_10: Flexible distribution systems/speed and quality of supply	0 (0%)	1 (1.61%)	8 (12.9%)	33 (53.23%)	20 (32.26%)
Q6_11: Increased involvement in supply chain management	0 (0%)	0 (0%)	9 (14.52%)	33 (53.23%)	20 (32.26%)
Kruskal-Wallis test: $H=24.73$; $p=0.006$					

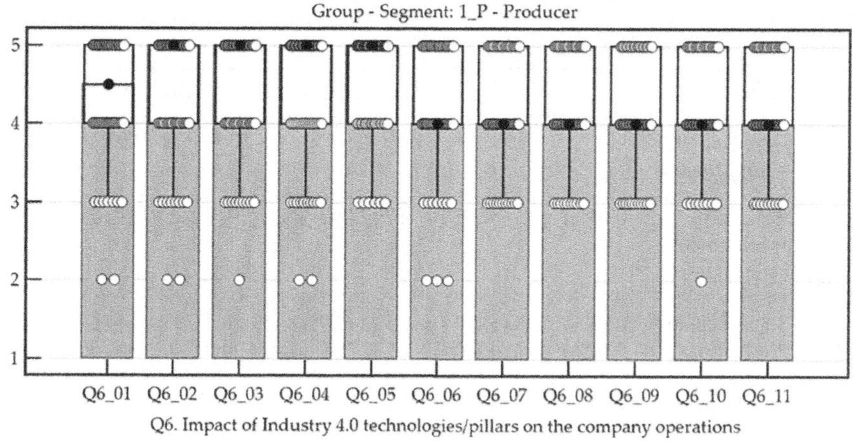

Figure 3.13 The response structure for question Q6 about impact (Q6_1…Q6_11) on the company in the segment: Producers (1_P).

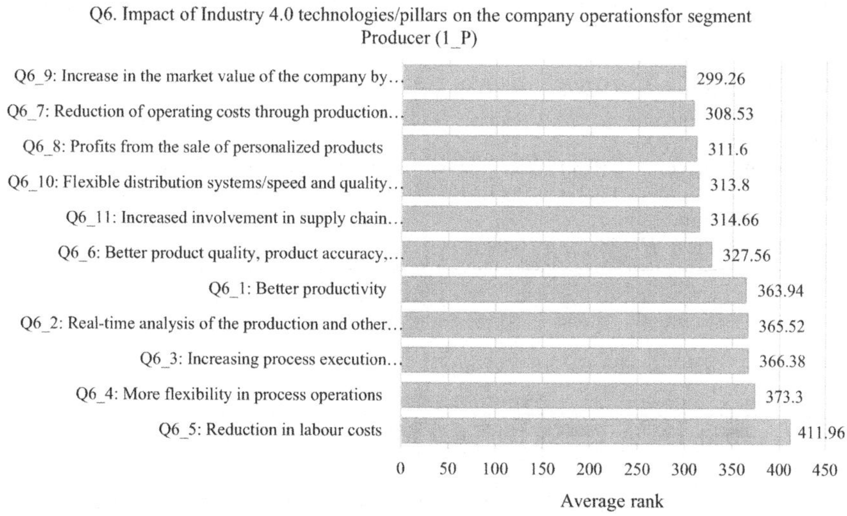

Figure 3.14 Detailed results of Kruskal-Wallis ANOVA test for Q6 in the segment: Producers (1_P).

a necessary of reduction in labour cost. The steel sector in Poland employs more than 24,000 people, of which about 70% are employed in production processes (Gajdzik, 2012). Reorganization of staff in steel enterprises is the challenge for managers in transformation to Industry 4.0 (Gajdzik, 2020). The second important factor (motivator) for implementing Industry 4.0 technologies in steel sector is the greater process flexibility that steel mills gain when they automate and computerize

Table 3.10 The response structure for question Q7: Areas of greatest opportunity for Industry 4.0 pillars (Q7_1...Q7_9) in the segment: Producers (1_P)

Q7. Areas of the greatest opportunities for the Industry 4.0 pillars:	*Segment: Producer (1_P) – n (% of row)*				
	Q7=1	*Q7=2*	*Q7=3*	*Q7=4*	*Q7=5*
Q7_1. Research and development/ product design/ services	0 (0%)	2 (3.23%)	17 (27.42%)	9 (14.52%)	34 (54.84%)
Q7_2. Supply chain	0 (0%)	2 (3.23%)	15 (24.19%)	29 (46.77%)	16 (25.81%)
Q7_3. Production/ manufacturing	0 (0%)	3 (4.84%)	17 (27.42%)	7 (11.29%)	35 (56.45%)
Q7_4. Warehouses/ logistics	0 (0%)	3 (4.84%)	17 (27.42%)	25 (40.32%)	17 (27.42%)
Q7_5. Sales and marketing/ consumer advice/ commercial negotiation	0 (0%)	3 (4.84%)	13 (20.97%)	32 (51.61%)	14 (22.58%)
Q7_6. Customer services (pre- and post-sales)	0 (0%)	2 (3.23%)	14 (22.58%)	28 (45.16%)	18 (29.03%)
Q7_7. Business management and administration	0 (0%)	0 (0%)	10 (16.13%)	14 (22.58%)	38 (61.29%)
Q7_8. Maintenance	0 (0%)	2 (3.23%)	14 (22.58%)	10 (16.13%)	36 (58.06%)
Q7_9. Communication	0 (0%)	1 (1.61%)	11 (17.74%)	30 (48.39%)	20 (32.26%)

Kruskal-Wallis test: H=28.25; p<0.001.

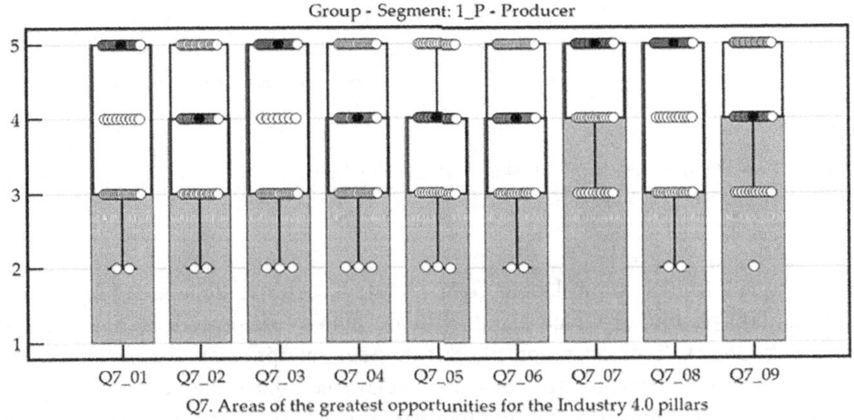

Figure 3.15 The response structure for questionQ7: Areas of greatest opportunity for Industry 4.0 pillars (Q7_1...Q7_9) in the segment: Producers (1_P).

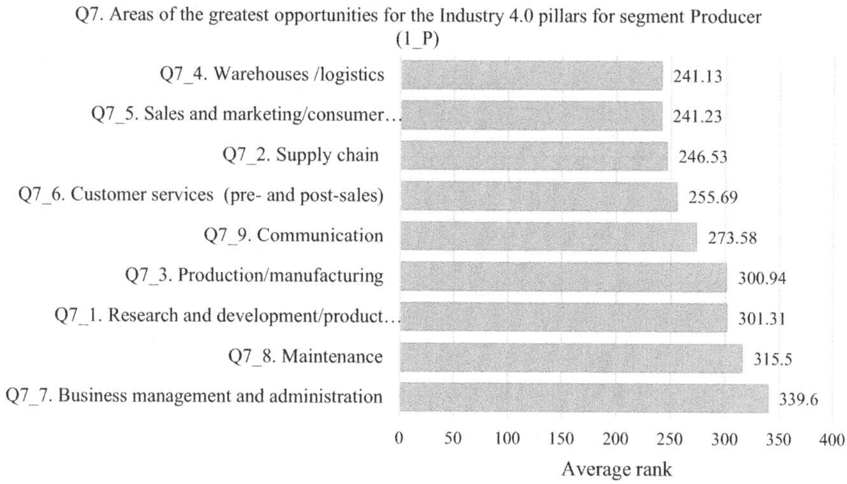

Figure 3.16 Detailed results of Kruskal-Wallis ANOVA test for Q7 in the segment: Producers (1_P).

processes. Modern technologies are an opportunity for steel mills to improve process optimization.

The next scope of research (field of study) was the areas (functions) in the company that need a strong focus on the development of Industry 4.0 technologies. The results of the research are shown in Table 3.10 and in Figures 3.15 and 3.16.

Respondents in the Producers segment (1_P) said that Q7 areas such as:

- Q7_7. Areas of the greatest opportunities for the Industry 4.0 pillars: Business management and administration
- Q7_8. Areas of the greatest opportunities for the Industry 4.0 pillars: Maintenance
- Q7_1. Areas of the greatest opportunities for the Industry 4.0 pillars: Research and development/product design/services
- Q7_3. Areas of the greatest opportunities for the Industry 4.0 pillars: Production/ manufacturing

Industry 4.0 offer the greatest opportunities for the development of in the steel sector. However, the development of the technologies, or pillars, of Industry 4.0 in steel mills in Poland faces barriers, which are:

- Q8_1. Lack of qualified staff (digital skills)
- Q8_2. High cost of technological investments/uncertain return on investment
- Q8_3. Market situation / economic situation
- Q8_4. Sectoral governmental policy
- Q8_5. Impact of foreign business groups on the domestic market
- Q8_6. High cost of reorganization

Results of research are presented in Table 3.11 and on Figures 3.17 and 3.18.

Table 3.11 The response structure for question Q8: Barriers to the Industry 4.0 pillars (Q8_1...Q8_6) in the segment: Producers (1_P)

Q8. Barriers to the Industry 4.0 pillars:	*Segment: Producer (1_P) – n (% of row)*				
	Q8=1	*Q8=2*	*Q8=3*	*Q8=4*	*Q8=5*
Q8_1. Lack of qualified staff (digital skills)	0 (0%)	1 (1.61%)	14 (22.58%)	12 (19.35%)	35 (56.45%)
Q8_2. High cost of technological investments/ uncertain return on investment	0 (0%)	1 (1.61%)	14 (22.58%)	13 (20.97%)	34 (54.84%)
Q8_3. Market situation / economic situation	0 (0%)	2 (3.23%)	16 (25.81%)	30 (48.39%)	14 (22.58%)
Q8_4. Sectoral governmental policy	0 (0%)	2 (3.23%)	15 (24.19%)	30 (48.39%)	15 (24.19%)
Q8_5. Impact of foreign business groups on the domestic market	0 (0%)	0 (0%)	8 (12.9%)	16 (25.81%)	38 (61.29%)
Q8_6. High cost of reorganization	0 (0%)	0 (0%)	6 (9.68%)	19 (30.65%)	37 (59.68%)
Kruskal-Wallis test: $H=34.50; p<0.001$					

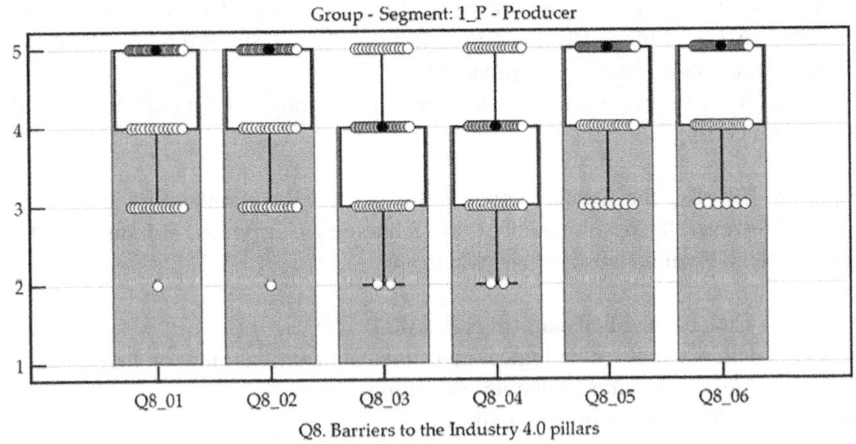

Figure 3.17 The response structure for questionQ8: Barriers to the Industry 4.0 pillars (Q8_1...Q8_6) in the segment: Producers (1_P).

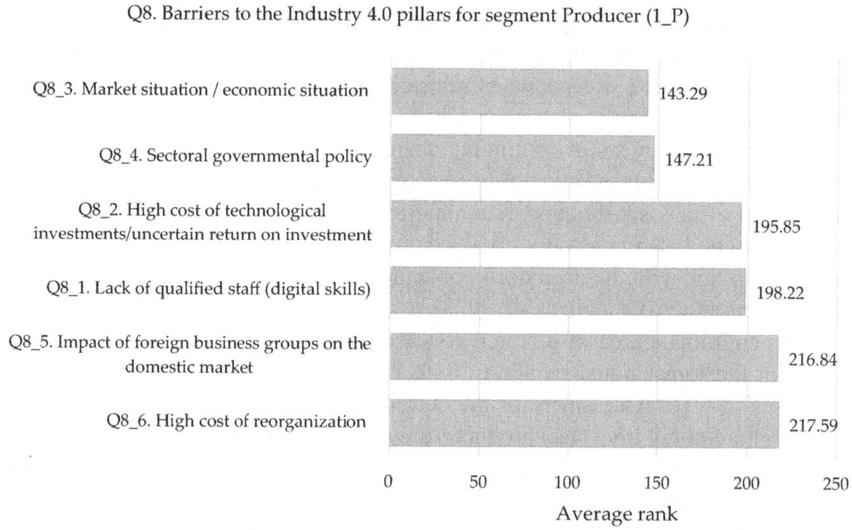

Figure 3.18 Detailed results of Kruskal-Wallis ANOVA test for Q8 in the segment: Producers (1_P).

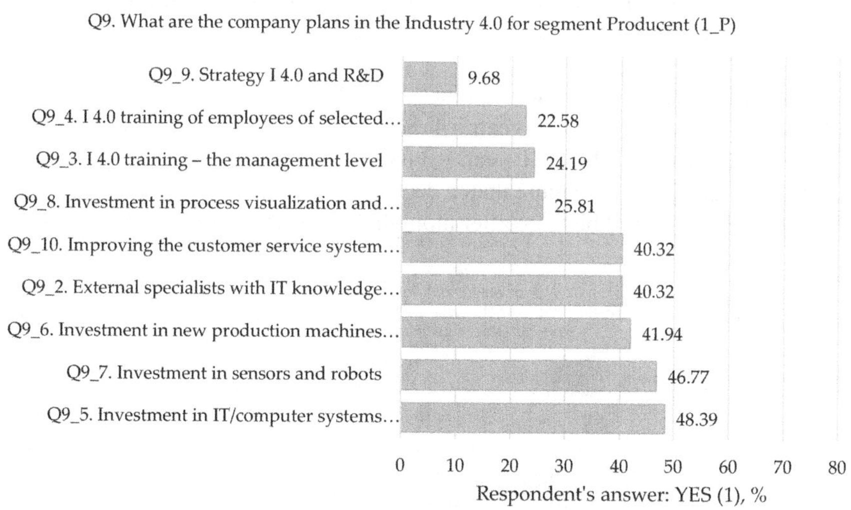

Figure 3.19 The response structure for the question Q9 in the segment Producers (1_P).

Respondents in the Producers segment (1_P) said that the biggest impediments to the introduction of the Industry 4.0 concept are caused by factors:

- Q8_6. High cost of reorganization
- Q8_5. Impact of foreign business groups on the domestic market

After completing the survey with questions in the form of a scale from 1 to 5, a question about the continuity of investment in key areas of change was introduced into the questionnaire. Respondents selected three key areas of continued investment (Figure 3.19).

Among the key areas of continuing change are investment in computer information systems and integration of used computer-operating systems at steel mills, installation of new sensors and autonomous robots in steel production and logistics. The second area is heavily involved in investments in new steelmaking technologies. In line with the deep decarbonization of the process, steel mills invest in clean technologies (Gajdzik et al., 2023).

The penultimate area of research concerned the assessment of the current situation in the topic: transformation of steel mills to Industry 4.0. The results of responses to Q10. Assessment of the current situation in the sector: steel sector (manufacture of pig iron, steel products) are presented in Figure 3.20. Based on the responses, the conclusion was drawn that steel mills (at the current stage of transformation to Industry 4.0) are characterized by gradual automation of production and related processes.

The last area of research concerned the time of changes (Q11) in the aspects of visible benefits of realized transformation to Industry 4.0). Time horizon for real opportunities to implement Industry 4.0 technologies in the company for all segments: Producers (1_P) are presented in Table 3.12. The following responses were available for selection:

- Q11_1. We see benefits now=5 point
- Q11_2. Benefits will be in 5 years=4 point
- Q11_3. Benefits will be in 10 years=3 point
- Q11_4. Benefits will be more than a decade later=2 point
- Q11_5. Benefits will be there after more than a decade and maybe even later -1

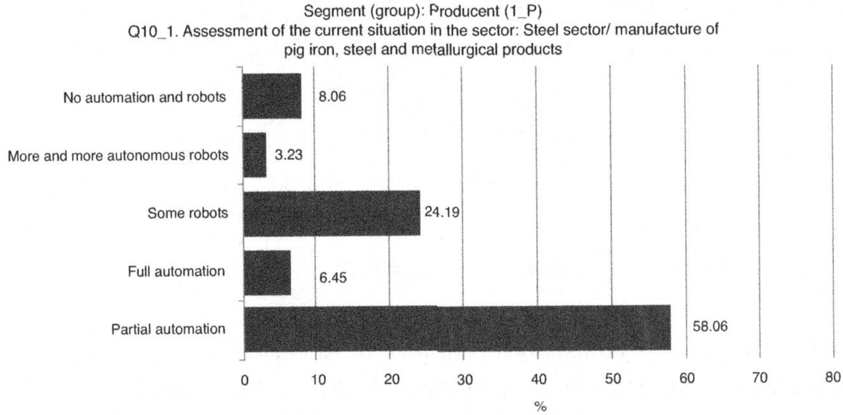

Figure 3.20 The response structure for question Q10. Assessment of the current situation in the sector: Steel sector/production of pig iron, steel and steel products in segments: Producers (1_P).

Table 3.12 The response structure for question Q11: Time horizon of real possibilities of implementing Industry 4.0 technology in the company in the segment: Producers (1_P).

Segment	Time horizon for real opportunities to implement Industry 4.0 technologies in the company				
(Group)	Q11_1=5 point	Q11_1=4 point	Q11_1=3 point	Q11_1=2 point	Q11_1=1 point
Producent (1_P) – *n* (% of row)	8 (12.9%)	11 (17.74%)	14 (22.58%)	11 (17.74%)	18 (29.03%)

Conclusion to the Table 3.12: depending on the type of technologies implemented, the effects of changes are visible in the short, medium, or long term.

Final conclusions of the field research:

The objective of the research, which was to determine (establish) the scope of change in the surveyed companies from the perspective of the development of Industry 4.0, was fulfilled. All the steel sector companies surveyed invested in solutions belonging to the industrial innovations of the fourth revolution. Changes in the steel sector (research segment: steel producers) confirmed the main hypothesis of the research about the accession of companies (steel section) to the transformation towards Industry 4.0. Technological solutions, classified into the various pillars of Industry 4.0, were identified in all surveyed companies. With regard to the adopted main hypothesis, the following was established:

- Representatives of the surveyed companies were knowledgeable about the concept of Industry 4.0 and its technologies. Familiarity with the concept of Industry 4.0 proved to be sufficient to conduct research in the subject area.
- The breakthroughs of Industry 4.0, according to those surveyed, are an opportunity for the development of steel companies. Companies are implementing new technologies to optimize processes and reduce labour costs.
- The companies surveyed relied on the quality, speed and precision of new technologies. Information technology and the Internet have supported the collection and processing of data needed to optimize processes, and have simplified and facilitated communication between people and machines.
- Changes are implemented gradually, from simple organizational projects to complex technological investments, and in stages on individual sections of primary and support processes.
- Barriers to the development of new technologies in the surveyed companies were primarily economic, technological and personnel factors.
- Transformation to Industry 4.0 is implemented continuously in the surveyed companies, albeit segmented (island) on selected processes. The intensification of the scope of changes with the visibility of their results is gradual in the short, medium and long term, depending on the type of investment and project schedule.

3.4 Pillars of Industry 4.0/5.0 in the steel industry

In our research described in last chapter we identify identifies several key pillars of Industry 4.0 in the context of the steel industry, including interconnectivity (IoT), information transparency, technical assistance (AI and robotics), decentralized decision-making, digitalization of products and services, and integration of the value chain. These pillars are driving advancements and changes in the sector.

Industry 5.0 represents a forward-looking paradigm in contrast to Industry 4.0, which emphasizes efficiency and productivity. Industry 5.0 is concerned with worker well-being and sustainability, aiming to ensure the long-term viability of businesses. Key aspects of Industry 5.0 include human-centrism, focusing on improving the work environment by promoting talent, diversity, and training. The goal is to shift the traditional industrial-economic paradigm, making organizations serve people rather than the other way around (Caricato and Grieco, 2024).

Resilience is another crucial component, addressing the need for businesses to adapt and withstand adversity at both local and global levels. Recent challenges like the Covid-19 pandemic, supply shortages, and conflicts like the war in Ukraine highlight the importance of being prepared to react and adapt, ensuring stable and sustainable operations.

Sustainability is the third pillar of Industry 5.0, acknowledging the limitations of planetary resources and the need to move away from the unrealistic pursuit of infinite growth. It seeks to foster sustainable and viable development, allowing for a lasting future for generations to come (Palazhchenko et al., 2024).

In the Table 3.13 there is a description of implementation of Industry 4.0/5.0 pillars in the steel industry.

In the steel industry, Big Data and Analytics play a crucial role in collecting and analysing data from various sources, such as sensors and machines on the shop floor. This data is used for real-time monitoring, predictive maintenance, and quality control. Advanced analytics are employed to identify trends, anomalies, and optimization opportunities, leading to improved production processes and product quality. Autonomous robots and AI are used in the steel industry to automate various tasks, such as material handling, welding, and quality control. These technologies are integrated into the broader framework of Cyber-Physical Systems (CPS), where machines and systems collaborate in real time. This integration enhances efficiency, reduces manual labour, and ensures safer and more precise operations (Tolettini and Lehmann, 2020).

Horizontal integration connects different stages of steel production, starting from raw material procurement to finished product delivery. This ensures seamless information flow and coordination across the entire value chain. Vertical integration links the shop floor with enterprise-level systems, enabling data exchange between operational and managerial levels for better decision-making and resource allocation. The Internet of Things (IoT) and Industrial Internet of Things (IIoT) technologies are implemented in the steel industry through the deployment of sensors and devices on machinery and equipment. This enables real-time data collection and remote monitoring, allowing for immediate responses to equipment issues, supply chain tracking, and inventory management (Dai and Zuo, 2020).

Table 3.13 Implementation of Industry 4.0/5.0 pillars in the steel industry

Pillar	*Implementation in the steel industry*
Big data & analytics	• Collection of data from various sensors and machines on the shop floor. • Advanced analytics to identify trends, anomalies, and optimization opportunities. • Predictive maintenance models to reduce downtime and maintenance costs. • Real-time quality control and defect detection using AI-driven algorithms.
Autonomous robots and AI	• Integration of autonomous robots for material handling and logistics within steel plants. • AI-driven robotics for intricate and precise tasks, such as welding or cutting. • AI-powered demand forecasting and supply chain optimization for streamlined production.
Systems integration towards CPS	• Integration of manufacturing systems, including machinery and production lines, into a unified CPS. • Real-time data sharing among machines, enabling collaborative decision-making. • Implementing middleware and protocols for seamless communication between different components.
Horizontal and vertical system integration	• Horizontal integration connecting the entire steel production process, from mining raw materials to delivering finished products to customers. • Vertical integration bridges the shop floor with enterprise-level systems, allowing data exchange for better decision-making.
IoT / IIoT	• Installation of IoT sensors and devices on machinery, furnaces, and equipment for monitoring and data collection. • IIoT-enabled remote monitoring and control of steel production processes, with real-time data accessibility. • IoT for supply chain tracking and inventory management.
Cyber-physical systems (CPSs) and cybersecurity	• Implementation of CPS for real-time control, monitoring, and synchronization of steel production processes. • Robust cybersecurity measures to protect against cyber threats, including firewalls, encryption, and regular vulnerability assessments. • Continuous cybersecurity training for employees to prevent cyberattacks.
Cloud computing	• Storing vast amounts of data in the cloud for scalability and accessibility. • Cloud-based analytics tools for real-time decision support, enabling remote access to data and analysis. • Scalable computing power for running complex simulations and models.

(*Continued*)

Table 3.13 (Continued)

Pillar	*Implementation in the steel industry*
Additive manufacturing	• Utilizing 3D printing for rapid prototyping and custom component manufacturing. • Application of additive manufacturing for complex, low-volume, or specialized steel parts. • Developing material specifications and quality control standards for 3D-printed steel components.
Virtual and augmented reality	• VR and AR technologies for training and simulating steel production processes, enhancing worker skills and safety. • Remote assistance and maintenance using augmented reality, allowing experts to provide guidance from a distance. • Integration of AR in maintenance and repair tasks, with overlaid data and instructions in real time.
Sustainability	• Implementing eco-friendly and energy-efficient technologies to reduce the carbon footprint of steel production. • Recycling and circular economy practices to minimize waste and promote sustainable resource use. • Optimizing supply chain logistics for reduced energy consumption and emissions.
Human-centricity	• Fostering a work environment that emphasizes the well-being, safety, and development of employees. • Implementing AI and robotics to complement human workers and enhance safety and productivity. • Training programs and upskilling opportunities to empower the workforce in adapting to advanced technologies.
Resilience	• Developing disaster recovery plans and redundant systems to ensure continuous steel production in the face of disruptions like natural disasters or supply chain interruptions. • Creating digital twins of critical processes for simulation and real-time monitoring to enhance operational resilience. • Embracing agile manufacturing practices that enable quick adaptation to changing market demands and unforeseen challenges.

Source: Own elaboration on basis: (Mishra et al., 2023; Hajoary, 2022; Pourmehdi et al., 2022; Sverko et al., 2022; Dai and Zuo, 2020; Tolettini and Lehmann, 2020; Govender et al., 2019).

Cyber-Physical Systems (CPSs) are integrated to provide real-time control, monitoring, and synchronization of steel production processes. Robust cybersecurity measures are implemented to protect these systems from cyber threats, including firewalls, encryption, and regular vulnerability assessments. Cybersecurity training for employees is conducted to prevent cyberattacks and data breaches. The steel industry leverages cloud computing to store and process large volumes of data for scalability and accessibility. Cloud-based analytics tools are used for real-time decision support, enabling remote access to data and analysis. Additionally, cloud resources are employed for running complex simulations and models to optimize production processes (Mishra et al., 2023).

Additive manufacturing, particularly 3D printing, is used in the steel industry for rapid prototyping and custom component manufacturing. It is applied to create complex, low-volume, or specialized steel parts. Efforts are made to establish material specifications and quality control standards for 3D-printed steel components. Virtual and Augmented Reality (VR and AR) technologies are adopted for training and simulating steel production processes. VR enhances worker skills and safety through immersive training, while AR is used for remote assistance and maintenance tasks. It overlays real-time data and instructions, enabling experts to guide on-site workers from a distance (Pourmehdi et al., 2022).

The implementation of the pillars of Industry 5.0 in the steel industry involves a holistic approach that focuses on sustainability, human-centricity, and resilience. These pillars are integral to shaping the future of the steel industry, making it more environmentally responsible, people-oriented, and adaptable to unforeseen challenges.

Bibliography

Arens, M., Neef, Ch., Beckert, B., Hirzel, S. (2018). Perspectives for digitising energy-intensive industries – findings from the European iron and steel industry. In: ECEEE Industrial Summer Study Proceedings. Industrial Efficiency, pp. 259–268.

Bauernhansl, T., Krüger, J., Reinhart, G., Schuh, G. (2016). *WGP-Standpunkt Industrie 4.0*. Wissenschaftliche Gesellschaft für Produktionstechnik.

BCG: Boston Consulting Group (Hg.) (2015). *Industry 4.0: The Future of Productivity and Growth in Manufacturing Industries*. München.

Bogner, E., Voelklein, T., Schroedel, O., Franke, J. (2016). Study based analysis on the current digitalization degree in the manufacturing industry in Germany. *Procedia CIRP*, 57, 14–19.

Branca, T.A., Fornai, B., Murri, M. M., Streppa, E., Schröder, A.J. (2020). The challenge of digitalization in the steel sector. *Metals*, 10(2), 288; (This article belongs to the Special Issue Challenges and Prospects of Steelmaking Towards the Year 2050). https://doi.org/10.3390/met10020288, online: https://www.mdpi.com/2075-4701/10/2/288/htm, [access data 10.10.2023].

Caricato, P., Grieco, A. (2024). *Optimization Patterns Enabled by Industry 4.0/5.0 Data*, 32nd International Conference on Flexible Automation and Intelligent Manufacturing, 601–608.

Cheng, J., Westman, J. (2020). Effects of Digitalization in Steel Industry Economic Impacts & Investment Model. Degree Project in Industrial Engineering and Management, Second Cycle, 30 Credits Stockholm, Sweden 2020, KTH. https://www.diva-portal.org/smash/get/diva2:1460881/FULLTEXT01.pdf, [access data 12.10.2023].

Dai, H., Zuo, X. (2020). Industry 4.0 boosts the steel industry into a new era of digitalization and smart technology. In: AISTech – Iron and Steel Technology Conference Proceedings, 3, pp. 1829–1841.

ESTEP. The European Steel Technology Platform. Publication: ESTEP Highlights. (2021). https://www.estep.eu/assets/Uploads/ESTEP-AR2021-Final-v2.pdf, [access data: 12.10.2023].

Gajdzik, B. (2012). *Przedsiębiorstwo hutnicze po restrukturyzacji.* Politechnika Śląska: Gliwice.

Gajdzik, B. (2020). Industry 4.0 as the challenge for employment change and for restructuring process. *ZN WSH Management*, 2, 123–135.

Gajdzik, B. (2021). Knowledge of the pillars of Industry 4.0 in the Polish steel industry. In Proceedings of the 37th IBIMA Conference. Cordoba. Spain. 30–31 May 2021.

Gajdzik, B. (2022a). *Diagnoza kierunków transformacji przemysłu stalowego w Przemyśle 4.0*, Title in English: *Diagnosis of the Steel Industry Transformation Direction in the Industry 4.0*. Monograph 945. Silesian University of Technology: Gliwice, 468pp.

Gajdzik, B. (2022b). Frameworks of the maturity model for Industry 4.0 with assessment of maturity levels on the example of the segment of steel enterprises in Poland. *Journal of Open Innovation: Technology, Market, and Complexity*, 8(2), 77. https://doi.org/10.3390/joitmc8020077.

Gajdzik, B. (2022c). How steel mills transform into smart mills: Digital changes and development determinants in the Polish steel industry. *European Research Studies Journal*, 25(1), 27–42.

Gajdzik, B., Grabowska, S., Saniuk, S. (2021). A theoretical framework for Industry 4.0 and its implementation with selected practical schedules. *Energies*, 14(4), 940. https://doi.org/10.3390/en14040940.

Gajdzik, B., Wolniak, R. (2021). Transitioning of steel producers to the steelworks 4.0-literature review with case studies. *Energies*. https://doi.org/10.3390/en14144109.

Gajdzik, B., Wolniak, R., Grebski, W. (2023). Process of transformation to net zero steelmaking: Decarbonisation scenarios based on the analysis of the Polish steel industry. *Energies*, 16, 3384. https://doi.org/10.3390/en16083384.

Govender, E., Telukdarie, A., Sishi, M.N. (2019). Approach for implementing Industry 4.0 framework in the steel industry. In: Proceedings of the 2019 IEEE International Conference on Industrial Engineering and Engineering Management (IEEM). Macao. China. 15–18 December 2019; pp. 1314–1318.

Hajoary, P.K. (2022). Industry 4.0 maturity and readiness – A case of a steel manufacturing organization. *Procedia Computer Science*, 217, 614–619.

Herzog, K., Winter, G., Kurka, G., Ankermann, K., Binder, R., Ringhofer, M., Maierhofer, A., Flick, A. (2017). The digitalization of steel production. *BHM*, 162(11), 504–513. https://doi.org/10.1007/s00501-017-0673-9.

Iannino, V., Colla, V., Denker, J., Göttsche, M. (2019). A CPS-based simulation platform for long production factories. *Metals*, 9, 1025. https://doi.org/10.3390/met9101025.

Jenabi, H. (2023). Revolutionizing the iron and steel industry with blockchain technology. *Mining & Metals*, 28 June 2023. https://www.linkedin.com/pulse/revolutionizing-iron-steel-industry-blockchain-hamed-jenabi, [access data: 10.10.2023].

Lin, L., Zeng, J.Q. (2021). Consideration of green intelligent steel processes and narrow window stability control technology on steel quality. *International Journal of Minerals, Metallurgy and Materials*, 28, 1264.

Liu, W.Z. (2020). Current situation and thinking of intelligent manufacturing in China's iron and steel industry. *China Metallurgical*, 30, 1.

Machin, D., Campbell, M.J., Tan, S.B., Tan, S.H. (2009). *Sample Size Tables for Clinical Studies*. 3rd ed. Wiley-Blackwell: Chichester.

McKinsey & Company. (2016). Industry 4.0 after the Initial Hype: Where Manufacturers Are Finding Value and How They Can Best Capture It. https://przemysl-40.pl/wp-content/uploads/2016-Industry-40-after-the-initial-hype.pdf, [access data: 08.11.2023].

Mishra, R., Singh, R.K., Gunasekaran, A. (2023). Adoption of industry 4.0 technologies for decarbonisation in the steel industry: Self-assessment framework with case illustration. *Annals of Operations Research*, 7(4), 15–34.

Miśkiewicz, R., Wolniak, R. (2020). Practical application of the Industry 4.0 concept in a steel company. *Sustainability*, 12(14), 5776.

Mori, L., Saleh, T., Sellschop, E., Van Hoey, M. (January 2018). Digital opportunity map for a metal payer. In: *Unlocking the Digital Opportunity in Metals*. Metals and Mining Practice. McKinsey & Company: Beijing, 4.

Naujok, N., Stamm, H. (2018). Industry 4.0 in steel: Status, strategy, roadmap and capabilities. In: Proceedings of the Future Steel Forum. Warsaw. Poland. 6–7 June 2018; https://futuresteelforum.com/content-images/speakers/Dr-Nils-Naujok-Holger-Stamm-Industry-4.0-in-steel.pdf, [access data: 20.12. 2019).

Neef, Ch., Hirzel, S., Arens, M. (2018). Industry 4.0 in the European Iron and Steel Industry: Towards an Overview of Implementations and Perspectives Working document. Karlsruhe, 05 September 2018. Fraunhofer Institute for Systems and Innovation Research ISI. Karlsruhe, Germany. https://www.isi.fraunhofer.de/content/dam/isi/dokumente/cce/2018/Industry-4-0-Implementation-and-Perspectives_Steel-Industry_Working%20 document.pdf, [access data: 12.10.2023].

Palazhchenko, Y., Shendryk, V., Ivanov, V., Hatala, M. (2024). *Industry 5.0: Aspects of Collaboration Technologies*. 32nd International Conference on Flexible Automation and Intelligent Manufacturing, 609–617.

Phuyal, S., Bista, D., Bista, R. (2020). Challenges, opportunities and future directions of smart manufacturing: A state of art review. *Sustainable Futures*, 2, 100023. https://doi.org/10.1016/j.sftr.2020.100023.

Polish Steel Association, Katowice, Poland. (2022). Report Polish Steel Industry. https://www.hiph.org/ANALIZY_RAPORTY/raporty/, [access data: 10.10.2023]. Available after logging in for members of the Association.

Pourmehdi, M., Paydar, M.M., Ghadimi, P., Azadnia, A.H. (2022). Analysis and evaluation of challenges in the integration of Industry 4.0 and sustainable steel reverse logistics network. *Computers and Industrial Engineering*, 163, 107808.

Rüßmann, M., Lorenz, M., Gerbert, P., Waldner, M., Justus, J., Engel, P., Harnisch, M. (2015). *Industry 4.0. The Future of Productivity and Growth in Manufacturing Industries*. The Boston Consulting Group (Issue April).

Rudy, V., Rusnák, J., Mares, A. (2018). Application of Industry 4.0 tools in metallurgy processes. *Transfer Innovation*. Kosice TU, 38, 57–59.

Statistical Yearbook of Industry – Poland. Central Statistical Office, Warsaw. https://stat.gov.pl/, [access data: 10.10.2023].

Sverko, M., Grbac, T.G., Mikuc, M. (2022). SCADA systems with focus on continuous manufacturing and steel industry: A survey on architectures, standards, challenges and Industry 5.0. *IEEE Access*, 10, 109395–109430.

Tihinen, M., Käriäinen, J., Teppola, S., Parviainen, P. (2017). Tackling the digitalization challenge: How to benefit from digitalization in practice. *International Journal of Information Systems and Project Management*, 5, 63–77.

Tolettini, L., Di Maria, E. (2023). The impact of Industry 4.0 on the steel sector: Paving the way for a disruptive digital and ecological transformation. *Recycling*, 8(4), 55. https://doi.org/10.3390/recycling8040055.

Tolettini, L., Lehmann, C. (2020). Industry 4.0: New paradigms of value creation for the steel sector. *Knowledge Management and Organizational Learning*, 9, 179–206.

World Steel Association. The White Book of Steel (2013). https://worldsteel.org/publications/bookshop/the-white-book-of-steel/ (access data: 10.3 2022).

World Steel Association. (2023). Paper: Smart Manufacturing. https://worldsteel.org/about-us/smart-manufacturing/.

Yao, L., Wang, J.S. (2020). Goal and realization of intelligent manufacturing in steel industry. *China Metallurgical*, 30, 1–4.

Zeman, P. (2017). Industrie und Stahlbau 4.0- ein paar Gedanken! *Stahlbau* 86(1), 84–86.

Zhou, D., Xu, K., Lv, Z., Yang, J., Li, M., He, F., Xu, G. (2022). Intelligent manufacturing technology in the steel industry of China: A review. *Sensors*, 22(21), 8194. https://doi.org/10.3390/s22218194.

4 Sustainable Industry 4.0/5.0

4.1 Concept of sustainability in industrial transformation

Sustainable development is an action plan that meets the needs of the current generation without jeopardizing the well-being of future generations. The United Nations developed the 2030 Agenda for sustainable development. There are 17 sustainable development goals with specific assessment indicators for each of the goals (United Nations, 2015).

1 No poverty
2 Zero hunger
3 Good health and well-being
4 Quality education
5 Gender equality
6 Clean water and sanitation
7 Affordable clean energy
8 Decent work and economic growth
9 Industry innovation and infrastructure
10 Reduced inequalities
11 Sustainable cities and communities
12 Responsible consumption and production
13 Climate action
14 Life below water
15 Life on land
16 Peace, justice, and strong institutions
17 Partnerships for the goals

A last progress report on the assessment of *Sustainable Development Goals* was released in 2023. The results of this report were very alarming (United Nations, 2023). COVID-19 pandemics and military conflicts negatively affected many sustainability goals. The effects of the pandemic have impact on the following problems:

- Poverty levels have increased.
- Deaths from tuberculosis and malaria have increased because of disruptive health services.

DOI: 10.4324/9781032697611-4

- Many young people never returned to school after the disruption related to COVID-19.
- Around 100 million people in the world were displaced because of military conflict.
- Global greenhouse gas emissions are still increasing.
  (However, these emissions are expected to decrease by 43% between 2024 and 2030.)
- Many countries are experiencing high inflation and increasing interest rates.

After the recovery from COVID-19, the public is more aware that our health, prosperity, and lifestyle cannot be taken for granted. Climate change and environmental degradation have become a serious threat to humans. Production and manufacturing are needed to satisfy our consumption needs. At the same time, manufacturing is a major contributor to our environmental problems. Sustainability Goal 12 (United Nations, 2015) is asking for responsible consumption and production. Many customers indicate that they are considering the environmental impact of the products they are purchasing. This is very encouraging customer behaviour. We all need to work together to protect the environment and natural resources (Munoz-La Riveria et al., 2020). We need to develop a new circular economy to reduce waste and pollution. Governments of all countries should be leading us in that direction. There is an opportunity at the end of every crisis. The current COVID-19 crisis created an opportunity to develop a sustainable economy that satisfies the needs of the current generation and at the same time protects the planet for future generations.

Many of the sustainability goals are related to and can be achieved through industrial transformation. Industrial transformation is often referred to as the Fourth Industrial Revolution (Industry 4.0). Advancements in computer technology (cognitive computing and artificial intelligence) allow machines to learn and communicate with each other without human intervention (Oztemel and Gursey, 2020). This revolutionized the manufacturing industry to an extent like never before in the last 50 years. During the manufacturing process, a large amount of real-time data is collected and processed. By manipulating real-time data, the manufacturing process can be optimized (Dubey et al., 2019; Ghobakhloo, 2020). The digital revolution in the manufacturing industry is still in progress and creates great opportunities, as well as challenges.

Industry 4.0 technology combined with the need for sustainable development created new opportunities for the manufacturing industry. Smart manufacturing by applying artificial intelligence and Internet of Things allows for optimization of manufacturing processes. The criterion for optimization is to minimize the negative environmental impact (Piccarozzi et al., 2022; Olah et al., 2020). This negative environmental impact can be minimized by the following.

- Conservation of energy
- Conservation of raw materials
- Improvement of manufacturing safety as well as product safety
- Use of fewer production steps
- Optimization of the supply chain by using local suppliers and bulk shipping methods

Prior to smart manufacturing in Industry 4.0, optimization like this was not possible. Optimization can also be applied to the designing process for a sustainable product (Dahmani et al., 2021). The criterion for that optimization is also environmental impact. Environmental impact of a new product being designed is measured by combining the environmental impact of manufacturing the product with the environmental impact of using the product (for the lifespan of the product). The goal is to minimize the combined total environmental impact. Sustainable products need to meet the following criteria.

- Be repairable.
  We need to manufacture products that can be repaired and will last for a long period of time. Production of poor-quality products which are disposable is not sustainable.
- Be disassembled and remanufactured.
  Using the parts from disassembling one product to make a new product saves raw materials and energy.
- Be part of industrial symbiosis.
  Discarded materials and parts can be repurposed and used for other applications. These practices lead to a circular economy. By eliminating inefficiency and waste businesses can stay competitive in the new sustainable environment.

This leads to the transition from *a linear economy* to *a circular economy*. In a circular economy, we consume less but better-quality products. Long-lasting products cost more but the customer is saving money in the long term. Establishing businesses that can handle repair work as well as the recycling of discarded products can stimulate economic growth. In a circular economy, the manufacturing industry does not rely entirely on natural virgin materials. A circular economy reduces the use of natural resources while also reducing waste.

The great opportunities in Industry 4.0 are optimization and streamlining of the manufacturing processes to increase efficiency. Optimization accomplished the following: saved raw materials, saved energy, and water, as well as reduced costs by increasing efficiency, streamlined the supply chain, provided production flexibility.

Optimization can also be performed to increase the efficiency of the entire supply chain to make it more sustainable. Using local suppliers and arranging bulk shipments are more efficient from the perspective of saving energy (fuel) and lowering pollution (Fallahpour et al., 2017).

4.2 The impact of Industry 4.0/5.0 on environmental sustainability

The manufacturing industry is needed to maintain our lifestyle, prosperity, and economic development. It also provides employment for a significant number of people. At the same time, industry is responsible for degradation of natural resources because of (Ghobakhloo et al., 2021) air pollution, water pollution, and soil pollution as well as land degradation, hazardous wastes, acid rain, climate change/global warming, and excessive use of energy.

The priority of industry was always to generate profit and satisfy the expectations of the stockholders (Goodman et al., 2017). Environmental protection and sustainability were never a high priority for the manufacturing industry. Practices protecting the environment need additional investments. Government agencies were always placing some restrictions related to air pollution, discharge of polluted water, etc. Industry was trying to satisfy the government requirements with minimum investments. Industry was willing to pay the penalty for not complying with the requirements (Zhang et al., 2020). Paying the penalty was less expensive than complying with government regulations. The reason for these practices was the low profit margins because of competition. The Fourth Industrial Revolution and automated manufacturing are gradually changing the priorities of industry related to sustainability. Those changes are because of the following (Salim et al., 2019):

- The cost of raw materials is increasing. Some of the raw materials are being depleted or are hard to find.
- The United Nations promotes sustainability goals supported by governments of most developed countries.
- The public became environmentally conscious and willing to support products and businesses protecting environmental sustainability.
- Government offers grants for the modernization of the manufacturing processes and implementation of *smart manufacturing*. Those grants, however, are linked to environmental responsibility and ecofriendly practices (Xu et al., 2018; Xie et al., 2019).
- Profit margins of the manufacturing industry increased because of automated manufacturing and the implementation of Industry 4.0 principles. Industry is now financially able to support environmental and sustainability initiatives.
- There is social pressure for implementing sustainable practices. Society is more aware of unsustainable consumption, distribution of wealth, poor working conditions, etc.

The technology that is part of Industry 4.0 allows for tracking of raw materials and energy used in production as well as the waste, water and air pollution, created by the manufacturing process. Industry 4.0 technology also allows for the optimization of the manufacturing process. Sustainability and environmental impact are normally the criterion for optimization. The manufacturing process can be adjusted to increase the environmental sustainability of the product. The design process of the product being manufactured is also part of the optimization cycle. Using advanced internet connections between machines participating in the production process, all data are being recorded as *big data*. This *big data* can be analysed and used for optimization purposes. The general rule to achieve sustainability is called *The Rule of Four Rs* (reduce, reuse, recycle, replace). In Industry 4.0 production is only done on demand with minimal defects in the product. This increases the efficiency of the process. Industry 4.0 encourages sustainable practices by promoting the following: (Stock et al., 2018; Xie et al., 2019) circular economy, sustainable business model, sustainable lifecycle of the product, sustainable manufacturing of the product, and sustainable supply chain.

Even in Industry 4.0, there is still too much attention on profit making at the expense of compromising sustainability. Smart manufacturing is, however, an efficient alternative that tries to protect our planet against climate change (Melander, 2017; Gmelin and Seuring, 2014).

In the 21st century, more businesses are sustainability oriented. Industrial transformation requires all businesses to consider environmental as well as social and economic opportunities and threats. Business leaders understand the importance of sustainability in managing any business. Literature analysis indicates that Industry 4.0 is conducive towards supporting sustainability and sustainable innovations by supporting the following (Aboelmaged and Hashem, 2019; Awan et al., 2020; Song et al., 2019):

- Innovativeness related to the development of green products.
- Innovativeness related to the development of green and cleaner processes.
- Innovativeness related to multidisciplinary collaboration in the process of the development of sustainable products.
- Innovativeness extending the lifecycle of a product.
- Innovativeness related to sustainable collaboration and the development of processes, materials, and technology which are environmentally friendly.

Technology in Industry 4.0 enables manufacturing companies to introduce environmentally friendly practices into the production process. Automated Industry 4.0 influences sustainability and eco-friendly production technology as well as business practices (Khan et al., 2021; Chiarini, 2021). The process of product design became more efficient and led to environmentally friendly products. Cognitive computing and artificial intelligence allow for comprehensive optimization of the new products being developed. Comprehensive optimization also includes the manufacturing processes of the new product as well as end-of-life disposal of the product. The criterion for this optimization is to minimize environmental impact. Prior to cognitive computing and Industry 4.0, comprehensive optimization like this (combining designing, manufacturing, and disposal of discarded products) was not possible. All three elements of the lifecycle of a product (designing, manufacturing, and disposal of discarded products) have a negative influence on the environment.

By combining those three elements affecting the environment, we can assess better the eco-friendliness of the product. Industry 4.0 allows for the improvement of the design process, implementation of cleaner production while still increasing productivity and generating a profit (Cillo et al., 2019). There are many ways Industry 4.0 contributes to the sustainability of the manufacturing industry (Di Valo et al., 2020). This is usually done by sustainable innovations.

4.3 Sustainable business practices in Industry 4.0/5.0 implementation – case studies

One of the core tenets of sustainability is the efficient use of resources, and Industry 4.0/Industry 5.0 technologies are ideally suited for achieving this goal. Smart manufacturing processes can significantly reduce resource waste by optimizing energy consumption, minimizing material usage, and reducing downtime through predictive maintenance. These technologies enable businesses to make the most of their resources while simultaneously lowering their environmental footprint.

In an era where consumers demand greater transparency, Industry 4.0/Industry 5.0 offers tools like blockchain and IoT devices to provide real-time tracking and tracing of products within the supply chain. This not only helps in preventing fraud and counterfeit goods but also ensures ethical and sustainable sourcing of materials. Businesses can demonstrate their commitment to sustainability by sharing data on the environmental and social impact of their supply chain. Industry 4.0/Industry 5.0 encourages the integration of renewable energy sources into manufacturing processes. Smart grids and energy management systems can optimize the use of clean energy, making production more sustainable. Businesses can reduce their carbon footprint by harnessing solar, wind, or hydropower, thus contributing to a greener future (Gajdzik et al., 2019).

The circular economy model, which aims to minimize waste and maximize the reuse and recycling of resources, aligns well with Industry 4.0/Industry 5.0. Technologies like the Internet of Things (IoT) and data analytics can enable products to be tracked throughout their life cycles. This data can inform decisions about refurbishing, repurposing, or recycling products, reducing the volume of waste in landfills and conserving resources.

Industry 4.0/Industry 5.0 supports the concept of decentralized or localized manufacturing. By embracing small-scale, localized production facilities, businesses can reduce the environmental impact associated with long-distance transportation of goods. This not only enhances sustainability but also creates jobs and promotes economic development in local communities. As Industry 4.0/Industry 5.0 technologies permeate urban environments, the concept of smart cities gains momentum. These cities leverage technology to optimize infrastructure and resource use, leading to cleaner and more efficient urban living. Sustainable infrastructure, smart transportation, and resource-efficient urban planning are all vital components of this transformation.

Data analytics is a cornerstone of Industry 4.0/Industry 5.0, and it plays a crucial role in sustainability efforts. Businesses can use data to identify areas where they can improve efficiency, reduce waste, and lower their environmental impact. It also helps in setting clear sustainability goals and measuring progress, fostering a culture of continuous improvement.

Case study 1

Many organizations in the world use sustainable business practices. The first case study we use to analyse is an example of industrial organization from Gremany – South Africa branch.

Organization in this case study is a prominent German-based technology organization with a global reach. The organization specializes in manufacturing in the context of water management and offers engineering solutions, power station management, mining, automation, service, and consultancy services. This indicates a diverse portfolio of services related to technology and water management. The company is based in Germany and has a subsidiary located in Johannesburg, South Africa. This indicates an international presence and operations in multiple countries. The organization values professionalism, proactivity, commitment, responsibility, and technological success, reflecting its commitment to excellence and innovation (Claude-Helene and Osthuizen, 2022).

Workers view Industry 4.0 sustainable business practices as driven by technologization, job retrenchment, automatization, artificial intelligence, smart systems, robots, and robotics. However, they emphasize that true sustainability can only be achieved when technology is combined with the "human touch" and the knowledge of individuals involved (Claude-Helene and Osthuizen, 2022). Managers in this company identify three positive and constructive ways to navigate the transition to Industry 4.0: pursuing speed and technological advancements, developing and managing employee skills, and addressing the challenges posed by Broad-Based Black Economic Empowerment (BBBEE) policies in South Africa (Shai et al., 2019).

The study shows that speed and effectiveness are essential in Industry 4.0 practices, achieved through technological advancements. Participants highlight the benefits of machines taking over routine work, freeing up time for more important tasks. They also stress the need for organizations to catch up with global technological advancements. Managers recognize the importance of upskilling employees to cope with Industry 4.0, emphasizing the need for training programmes and knowledge development. They believe that employees should adapt to new challenges, improve communication skills, and contribute to training and educating others (Claude-Helene and Osthuizen, 2022).

Participants have mixed views on the compatibility of BBBEE policies and Industry 4.0 sustainability. Some see BBBEE as hindering business operations and job quality, while others believe it can provide training and opportunities for previously disadvantaged groups (Sackey and Bester, 2016). Managers stress the importance of creating a meaningful workplace that ensures the survival and well-being of employees. They see sustainability as intertwined with personal and professional development, not just in terms of technological advancements but also in terms of personal growth and mindset transformation (Schutte, 2015).

The case study highlights the complexity of achieving sustainability in the context of Industry 4.0 within South Africa. It emphasizes the need to balance technological advancements with a human touch, address skill development and training, navigate the challenges posed by BBBEE policies, and create meaningful work environments. The study suggests that sustainability in the Industry 4.0 era should encompass not only technological innovation but also holistic well-being and development for employees.

Case study 2

In this case study, we have analysed the case of Nokia company. Nokia is actively engaged in the implementation of Industry 4.0 and 5G technology, leveraging its expertise in telecommunications, networking, and digital solutions to play a significant role in advancing Industry 4.0. Nokia is a major player in the development and deployment of 5G networks. 5G technology is a fundamental enabler of Industry 4.0, providing the high-speed, low-latency connectivity required for various applications, including IoT, robotics, and automation. Nokia's expertise in 5G infrastructure positions them as a key contributor to Industry 4.0 (Janke and Misler-Bher, 2015).

Organization provides a range of Internet of Things (IoT) solutions and platforms designed to connect and manage devices and sensors. These IoT solutions are crucial for Industry 4.0 applications, enabling real-time data collection and analysis for smart manufacturing, logistics, and asset management. Nokia offers private wireless networks for industrial customers. These networks are tailored for specific applications in manufacturing, logistics, and other sectors, allowing businesses to have dedicated, secure, and reliable connectivity for their Industry 4.0 initiatives.

Analysed firm is involved in cloud and edge computing solutions, which are integral to Industry 4.0. These technologies enable real-time data processing and analytics, supporting automation, predictive maintenance, and other critical functions in smart factories. Nokia is exploring the concept of digital twins, which involves creating virtual replicas of physical assets, systems, and processes. This technology is invaluable in Industry 4.0 for simulating and optimizing operations, predicting issues, and enhancing decision-making (Muller and Bevan-Dye, 2017).

Security is a paramount concern in Industry 4.0, and Nokia offers network security solutions to protect critical infrastructure and data. These solutions help safeguard against cyber threats and ensure the integrity of connected systems. Nokia provides digital transformation services to help businesses transition to Industry 4.0. These services include consulting, system integration, and managed services to support the deployment and operation of Industry 4.0 solutions.

Sustainable business practices in Industry 4.0, as applied by Nokia, involve adopting environmentally and socially responsible strategies and technologies that align with the principles of sustainability while leveraging the capabilities of the fourth industrial revolution. Nokia can implement energy-efficient solutions as part of Industry 4.0 initiatives. This includes optimizing the energy consumption of their network infrastructure, data centres, and manufacturing processes. Energy-efficient technology choices, such as low-power devices and green data centres, can reduce the environmental impact of operations (Agrawal et al., 2018).

Nokia can focus on designing products and systems that have longer lifecycles and are easier to upgrade or recycle. By extending the life of their equipment and minimizing electronic waste (e-waste), they contribute to a more sustainable approach to manufacturing and product management. Embracing a circular economy model, Nokia can design products with the intent of reusing materials and components. This approach can lead to reduced resource consumption and waste generation while promoting the recycling and repurposing of equipment.

Nokia can implement sustainability principles in its supply chain management. This includes sourcing materials responsibly, reducing transportation emissions, and ensuring that suppliers adhere to environmental and social standards. By promoting a green supply chain, Nokia can reduce its overall environmental footprint. Utilizing Industry 4.0 technologies, Nokia can implement remote monitoring and predictive maintenance solutions. This reduces the need for physical maintenance visits, decreasing carbon emissions associated with travel, and improving the efficiency and longevity of equipment.

In Industry 4.0, Nokia can collaborate with partners and customers to share data and insights. This sharing can lead to more sustainable practices by optimizing operations, reducing waste, and collectively working towards common sustainability goals. Nokia can innovate with sustainability in mind. This involves creating solutions that not only enhance performance and connectivity but also prioritize energy efficiency and environmental impact.

Nokia can actively engage with local communities where they operate to ensure that their Industry 4.0 initiatives do not have adverse social or environmental impacts. They can contribute to the development of greener and more inclusive communities. Ensuring adherence to environmental regulations and industry sustainability standards is crucial. Nokia should actively monitor and meet or exceed these requirements to demonstrate their commitment to sustainable business practices. Analysed organization can also maintain a strong focus on corporate social responsibility, including ethical practices, fair labour standards, and community support. This enhances their reputation and contributes to sustainable business practices in Industry 4.0 (Abu-Raed, 2021).

Case study 3

In this case study, there is a description of United States Steel Corporation. The United States Steel Corporation (US Steel) is one of the largest steel producers in the United States and has a long history in the steel industry. US Steel is likely implementing Industry 4.0 principles in its manufacturing processes. This involves the use of data analytics, the Internet of Things

(IoT), and automation to enhance the efficiency and flexibility of its steel production. Sensors can monitor equipment conditions, track product quality, and optimize energy consumption in real-time. Industry 4.0 enables predictive maintenance for machinery and equipment. US Steel can use data analytics and machine learning to predict when equipment might fail and schedule maintenance before costly breakdowns occur, ensuring smoother and more efficient operations (Kim, 2021).

Sustainable business practices in the context of Industry 4.0 and potentially Industry 5.0 are essential for companies like the United States Steel Corporation (US Steel) as they navigate the challenges of the modern industrial landscape. These practices align with the growing global emphasis on environmental responsibility, social consciousness, and economic viability. US Steel can invest in advanced technologies like smart manufacturing, AI-driven process optimization, and IoT (Internet of Things) sensors to enhance energy efficiency and reduce carbon emissions in their operations. The company should focus on transitioning to cleaner energy sources, such as renewable energy, to power their facilities.

US Steel can adopt a circular economy model by implementing efficient recycling and reusing processes for steel products. This not only reduces waste but also minimizes the need for new resource extraction. Leveraging Industry 4.0/5.0 technologies, US Steel can create a smart and efficient supply chain that optimizes routes, minimizes wastage, and reduces the environmental impact of logistics. Exploration of innovative materials and production techniques with a reduced environmental footprint, such as the utilization of recycled steel or adoption of green manufacturing processes (Peters, 2022), fostering diversity and inclusivity within the workforce, prioritizing employee well-being, and providing avenues for skill enhancement to adapt to evolving industry demands. Implementation of real-time monitoring systems to ensure adherence to environmental regulations and proactively identify and address potential issues. Investment in research and development to explore sustainable alternatives and develop new technologies aimed at minimizing the environmental impact of steel production. Engagement with diverse stakeholders, including local communities, environmental organizations, and regulatory bodies, to cultivate trust, exchange best practices, and ensure alignment of US Steel's sustainability initiatives with societal expectations. Publication of comprehensive sustainability reports to underscore US Steel's dedication to sustainability, transparently communicating progress, objectives, and key performance indicators (Tolettini and Di Maria, 2023). Formulation of a clear, long-term sustainability strategy integrated into the company's overarching business plan, thereby embedding sustainability as a foundational element of US Steel's operations.

Summing up US Steel, like many traditional industrial companies, faces a significant challenge in transitioning to more sustainable practices.

However, embracing Industry 4.0/5.0 technologies and sustainable business practices is crucial for ensuring the company's viability in the face of increasing environmental and social pressures. This transformation can not only reduce its environmental impact but also enhance its competitiveness and resilience in a rapidly changing global marketplace (Moravec et al., 2023).

In Table 4.1, there is a comparison of those three case studies. All three case studies are actively implementing Industry 4.0/5.0 principles, but their approaches to sustainable business practices vary based on their industry focus and specific challenges. While Case Study 1 emphasizes the "human touch" and skill development, Case Study 2 focuses on energy efficiency and circular economy principles. Case Study 3, a traditional steel company, is adapting to cleaner energy and sustainability while facing environmental and social pressures. Each case study reflects the unique challenges and opportunities within their respective industries and regions.

Table 4.1 The comparison of case studies about sustainable business practices in Industry 4.0/5.0

Aspect	*Case study 1*	*Case study 2*	*Case study 3*
Organization type	Technology company with global reach	Telecommunications and digital solutions provider	Steel production company
Industry focus	Water management, engineering, automation, etc.	Telecommunications, 5G technology	Steel production
Implementation of Industry 4.0	Yes	Yes	Yes
Sustainable practices	Balance technology with the "human touch", skill development, BBBEE policies	Energy-efficient solutions, circular economy, green supply chain	Energy efficiency, cleaner energy sources, recycling, diverse workforce
Technology integration	Emphasize the human element in Industry 4.0, skill development, and technological advancements	Utilizes 5G technology, IoT, digital twins, network security	Uses data analytics, IoT, and predictive maintenance
Sustainability strategies	Focus on personal and professional development, holistic well-being	Focus on energy-efficient solutions, circular economy, and green supply chain	Transition to cleaner energy, recycling, diverse workforce

(*Continued*)

Table 4.1 (Continued)

Aspect	*Case study 1*	*Case study 2*	*Case study 3*
Engagement with stakeholders	Emphasizes the importance of personal growth and mindset transformation	Engages with local communities, regulators, and environmental groups	Engages with local communities, stakeholders, and publishes sustainability reports
Long-term sustainability strategy	Not explicitly mentioned	Not explicitly mentioned	Emphasizes the need for a long-term sustainability strategy
Main challenges and opportunities	Balance between technology and human elements, BBBEE policies	Environmental responsibility, energy efficiency	Environmental and social pressures, competitiveness

Source: Own elaboration on basis: Claude-Helene and Osthuizen, 2022; Muller and Bevan-Dye, 2017; Abu-Raed, 2021; Moravec et al., 2023; Tolettini and Di Maria, 2023.

Bibliography

Aboelmaged, M., Hashem, G. (2019). Absorptive capacity and green innovation adoption in SMEs: The mediating effects of sustainable organisational capacities. *Journal of Cleaner Production*, 220, 853–863.

Abu-Raed, N. (2021). Predictive maintenance Industry 4.0: Case Nokia. Master's thesis, LUT University. https://lutpub.lut.fi/bitstream/handle/10024/163034/Predictive_maintenance_industry_4.0_case_Nokia.pdf?sequence=5&isAllowed=y, (access data: 27.10.2023).

Agrawal, A., Schaefer, S., Funke, T. (2018). Incorporating Industry 4.0 in corporate strategy. In Brunet-Thornton, R., Martinez, F. (Eds), *Analyzing the Impacts of Industry 4.0 in Modern Business Environments*, IGI Global: New York, 161–176.

Awan, U., Arnold, M.G., Golgeci, I. (2020). Enhancing green product and process innovation: Towards an integrative framework of knowledge acquisition and environmental investment. *Business Strategy and the Environment*, 30(2), 1283–1295.

Chiarini, A. (2021). Industry 4.0 technologies in the manufacturing sector: Are we sure they are all relevant for environmental performance? *Business Strategy and the Environment*, 30(7), 3194–3207. https://doi.org/10.1002/bse.2797.

Cillo, V., Petruzzelli, A.M., Ardito, L., Del Giudice, M. (2019). Understanding sustainable innovation: A systematic literature review. *Corporate Social Responsibility and Environmental Management*, 26(5), 1012–1025. https://doi.org/10.1002/csr.1783.

Claude-Helene, M. Oosthuizen, R.M. (2022). Sustainability in Industry 4.0 business practice: Insights from a multinational technology company. *Frontriers Sustainability*, 3. https://doi.org/10.3389/frsus.2022.886986.

Dahmani, N., Benhida, K., Belhadi, A., Kamble, S., Elfezazi, S., Jauhar, S.K. (2021). Smart circular product design strategies towards eco-effective production systems: A lean eco-design Industry 4.0 framework. *Journal of Cleaner Production*, 320, 128847.

Di Valo, A., Palladino, R., Hassan, R., Escobar, O. (2020). Artificial intelligence and business models in the sustainable development goals perspective: A systematic literature review. *Journal of Business Research*, 121, 283–314. https://doi.org/10.1016/j.jbusres.2020.08.019.

Dubey, R., Gunasekaran, A., Childe, S.J., Papadopoulos, T., Luo, Z., Wamba, S.F., Roubaud, D. (2019). Can big data and predictive analytics improve social and environmental sustainability? *Technological Forecasting and Social Change*, 144, 534–545.

Fallahpour, A., Olugu, E.U., Musa, S.N., Wong, K.Y., Noori, S. (2017). A decision support model for sustainable supplier selection in sustainable supply chain management. *Computer Industry Engineering*, 105, 391–410. https://doi.org/10.1016/j.cie.2017.01.005.

Gajdzik, B., Oleksiak, B., Pustějovská, P., Tkadlečková, M. (2019). Environmental protection in Industry 4.0. Opportunities and threats in selected areas. *New Trends in Production Engineering*, 2(2), 184–194.

Ghobakhloo, M. (2020). Industry 4.0, digitization, and opportunities for sustainability. *Journal of Cleaner Production*, 252, 119869.

Ghobakhloo, M., Iranmanesh, M., Grybauskas, A., Vilkus, M., Petraite, M. (2021). Industry 4.0 innovation and sustainable development: A systematic review and a roadmap to sustainable innovation. *Business Strategy and the Environment*, 30(8), 4237–4257.

Gmelin, H., Seuring, S. (2014). Achieving sustainable new product development by integrating product life-cycle management capabilities. *Journal of Production Economics*, 154, 166–177. https://doi.org/10.1016/j.ijpe.2014.04.023

Goodman, J., Korsunova, A., Halme, M. (2017). Our collaborative future: Activities and roles of stakeholders in sustainability-oriented innovation. *Business Strategy and the Environment*, 26(6), 731–753. https://doi.org/10.1002/bse.1941.

Janke, A., Misler-Behr, M. (2015). Identifying the disruptive potential of the sustainable innovation in the case of e-mobility. In: 2015 World Congress on Sustainable Technologies, WCST 2015; pp. 63–64, 7415119.

Khan, I.S., Ahmad, M.O., Majava, J. (2021). Industry 4.0 and sustainable development: A systematic mapping of triple bottom line, circular economy and sustainable business models perspectives. *Journal of Cleaner Production*, 297, 126655. http:doi.org/10.1016/j.jclepro.2021.126655.

Kim, H.Y. (2021). Pollution control and productivity growth: Some unusual evidence from the U.S. steel industry. *Review of Economics and Finance*, 19, 80–96.

Melander, L. (2017). Achieving sustainable development by collaborating in green product innovation. *Business Strategy and the Environment*, 26(8), 1095–1109.

Moravec, R., Schlichting, W., Ruf, J., Mantooth, F. (2023). Initial experience with new round caster operation and improvements at U. S. Steel – fairfield works. In: AISTech – Iron wand Steel Technology Conference Proceedings, May; pp. 1163–1171.

Muller, R.-A., Bevan-Dye, A.L. (2017). Reliable Nokia-brand personality perceptions of the Finnish communication giant. *Eurasian Studies in Business and Economics*, 5, 785–796.

Muñoz-La Rivera, F., Hermosilla, P., Delgadillo, J., Echeverría, D. (2020). The sustainable development goals (SDGs) as a basis for innovation skills for engineers in the Industry 4.0 context. *Sustainability*, 12(16), 6622.

Oláh, J., Aburumman, N., Popp, J., Khan, M.A., Haddad, H., Kitukutha, N. (2020). Impact of Industry 4.0 on environmental sustainability. *Sustainability*, 12(11), 4674.

Our World in Data Team. (2023). SDG Tracker: Measuring Progress towards the Sustainable Development Goals. https://ourworldindata.org/sdg.

Oztemel, E., Gursev, S. (2020). Literature review of Industry 4.0 and related technologies. *Journal of Intelligent Manufacturing*, 31(1), 127–182.

Peters, G. (2022). Clean Air Council v. U.S. Steel: Cooperative federalism or regulating in the dark? *Ecology Law Quarterly*, 49(2), 583–589.

Piccarozzi, M., Silvestri, C., Aquilani, B., Silvestri, L. (2022). Is this a new story of the "Two Giants"? A systematic literature review of the relationship between Industry 4.0, sustainability and its pillars. *Technological Forecast and Social Change*, 177, 121511.

Sackey, S.M., Bester, A. (2016). Industrial engineering curriculum in Industry 4.0 in a South African context. *South African Journal Industrial Engineering*, 27, 101–114. https://doi.org/10.7166/27-4-1579

Salim, N., Ab Rahman, M.N., Abd Wahab, D. (2019). A systematic literature review of internal capabilities for enhancing eco-innovation performance of manufacturing firms. *Journal of Cleaner Production*, 209, 1445–1460. https://doi.og/10.1016/j.jclepro.2018.11.105.

Schutte, C.S.L. (2015). The Status and Challenges of Industrial Engineering in South Africa. Inaugural lecture delivered on 19 October 2015, Department of Industrial Engineering, Stellenbosch University. Sun Media.

Shai, L., Molefinyana, C., Quinot, G. (2019). Public procurement in the context of Broad-Based Black Economic Empowerment (BBBEE) in South Africa—Lessons learned for sustainable public procurement. *Sustainability*, 11, 7164. https://doi.org/10.3390/su11247164.

Song, M., Fisher, R., Kwoh, Y. (2019). Technological challenges of green innovation and sustainable resource management with large scale data. *Technological Forecasting and Social Change*, 144, 361–368. https://doi.org/10.1016/j.techfore.2018.07.055.

Stock, T., Obenaus, M., Kunz, S., Kohl, H. (2018). Industry 4.0 as enabler for a sustainable development: A qualitative assessment of its ecological and social potential. *Process Safety and Environmental Protection*, 118, 254–267. https://doi.org/10.1016/j.psep.2018.06.026.

Tolettini, L., Di Maria, E. (2023). The impact of Industry 4.0 on the steel sector: Paving the way for a disruptive digital and ecological transformation. *Recycling*, 8(4), 55.

United Nations. (2023). *Sustainable Goals Report 2023: Special Edition (Towards a Rescue Plan for People and Planet)*. Ross, J., Ed. ISBN: 978-92-1-101460-0. https://unstat.un.org>sdgs/report>2023.

United Nations: Department of Economic and Social Affairs. (2015). Sustainable Development: The 17 Goals. Sdgs.un.org/goals.

Xie, X., Huo, J., Zou, H. (2019). Green process innovation, green product innovation, and corporate financial performance: A content analysis method. *Journal of Business Research*, 101, 697–706. https://doi.org/10.1016/j.jbusres.2019.01.010.

Xie, X., Zhu, Q., Wang, R. (2019). Turning green subsidies into sustainability: How green process innovation improves firms' green image. *Business Strategy and the Environment*, 28(7), 1416–1433. https://doi.org/10.1002/bse.2323.

Xu, L.D., Xu, E.L., Li, L. (2018). Industry 4.0: State of the art and future trends. *The International Journal of Production Research*, 56, 2941–2962.

Zhang, J., Liang, G., Feng, T., Yuan, C., Jiang, W. (2020). Green innovation to respond to environmental regulation: How external knowledge adoption and green absorptive capacity matter? *Business Strategy and the Environment*, 29(1), 39–53. https://doi.org/10.1002/bse.2349.

5 Innovations in the transformation of the steel industry to Industry 4.0/5.0

5.1 Concept of innovation in industrial transformation

Historically every industrial revolution was a result of a major disruptive revolutionary innovation. At the same time, every industrial revolution introduced new technology. This created opportunities for many additional innovations improving and changing applications of the newly developed technology. This is especially true during the Fourth Industrial Revolution.

The word *innovative* was used first in the early 17th century. Innovators were described as *heretics* because they were questioning the status quo (Wolniak and Grebski, 2018). During the First Industrial Revolution innovativeness became a very valuable trait and attribute. During the Second Industrial Revolution Thomas Edison started a *modern research and development company*. Thomas Edison was recruiting highly innovative individuals from all over the world. (Nikolai Tesla was one of those individuals.) Many patented inventions came from Thomas Edison's laboratory. High-profile inventors like Thomas Edison and Nikolai Tesla were becoming celebrities.

Computer technology started the Third Industrial Revolution. Many disruptive inventions and technologies were introduced during that timeframe. The development of computer technology led to the introduction of the Internet of Things (IoT), cloud computing, cognitive computing, and artificial intelligence.

This led to the Fourth Industrial Revolution. During the Fourth Industrial Revolution, many jobs with repetitive predictable tasks became automated. Industry 4.0 is responsible for many positions being eliminated, but it is also responsible for creating many new positions.

Positions created by Industry 4.0 require knowledge and innovativeness. Presently we live in a knowledge-based economy. Innovativeness became more important than ever before (Matt et al., 2021). However, innovativeness cannot exist in isolation. Most of the attributes and skills needed for an individual to be innovative are developed through their life experiences. There are many components of the innovativeness ecosystem (Wolniak and Grebski, 2018): families, elementary and secondary schools, institutions of higher education, local industry, local government and regional policymakers, and international cooperation.

DOI: 10.4324/9781032697611-5

Very often the school system (from elementary to higher education) discourages students from being innovative or challenging the teachers. Often the system of education is encouraging conformity (Wolniak and Grebski, 2018). This is counter-productive from the perspective of developing much needed innovativeness skills and attributes (Gajdzik and Grebski, 2022). Innovativeness and creativity need to be nurtured and rewarded in all components of the innovativeness ecosystem. Innovative individuals need other innovative people around them to intellectually stimulate each other. Innovative individuals tend to cluster in cities where modern high technology industries are located. Those cities are becoming *innovative cities* with the number of patents/thousand residents/year reaching fifty times the national average.

Industrial transformation cannot be accomplished by any one stand-alone company. Progress in industrial transformation requires the interaction between industry partnering and different institutions and organizations. These innovativeness ecosystem partners include the following (Matt et al., 2021; Oh et al., 2016): manufacturing companies, government agencies, business associations, universities as well as industrial research and development centres. In the Europe, companies have problem with generation gap (Gajdzik and Szymszal, 2015). There are many workers aged 50+ in the steel mills. There is a gap between the old and the new generation. This gap is the result of the falling birth rate and the new expectations of generation Z.

Interaction between innovativeness ecosystem partners as well as supply chain partners accelerates the implementation of the Industry 4.0 concept (Matt et al., 2018). The role of educational institutions is also very important. Higher education institutions need to develop continuing education programmes using state-of-the-art teaching and learning methods and technologies. Continuing education courses need to focus on digitalization, cognitive computing, data processing, artificial intelligence, etc. (Kurdve et al., 2020; Markkula and Kune, 2015).

There are effective strategies to incorporate new innovations into Industry 4.0 (Edquist, 2005): agile approach, rapid alterations, intelligent fast failure approach, continuous learning and upskilling as well as recognition and celebration of successes, listening to the voice of the workers, and empowerment of the employees.

Digitalization is being considered a catalyst for improvement. Digital transformation generates sustainability benefits and increases productivity as well as resilience (Benitez et al., 2020).

The role of government is to build secure and reliable *high-bandwidth connectivity*. This is important for digital transformation of the manufacturing industry, government agencies, public sector, and healthcare (Reischauer, 2018). Digitizing transport and modernizing the energy grid is also important in implementing Industry 4.0. Earlier implementation creates a bigger impact (Kahle et al., 2020). Industry 4.0 has been shown to have an impact on the economy.

Innovations related to cognitive computing, artificial intelligence (AI), augmented reality as well as 5G and 6G networks are presently shaping the future of industry. There is an industry network for collaboration and implementation of the new innovations (Dedehayir et al., 2018).

A wide range of partners representing the smart manufacturing industry work together on building state-of-the-art technology solutions. This collaboration is happening in the following areas (Pino and Ortega, 2018; Rocha et al., 2019).

- Internet service providers working on linking together the range of different devices and machines.
- Cloud computing experts and consultants customizing the network according to the needs of individual customers.
- Manufacturing industry partners and experts assisting in implementing automated manufacturing to specific company needs.

The digitalization and automated manufacturing processes have gained popularity. It is expected by the end of 2023 approximately 72% of manufacturing companies will be digitized, automated and working in the Industry 4.0 mode. (In 2018, those numbers were 33%.)

In the area of computer technology, numerous innovative projects are contributing to the advancement of smart manufacturing, making it more accessible and user-friendly. These projects are centred around several key topics, each of which plays a significant role in shaping the future of manufacturing.

Augmented reality (AR) and virtual reality (VR) technologies are transforming the way manufacturing processes are executed. They provide interactive, immersive experiences that enhance training, maintenance, and design activities. The concept of digital twins involves creating virtual replicas of physical systems, enabling real-time monitoring, analysis, and simulation. This technology offers insights into equipment performance and facilitates predictive maintenance. IoT connects physical devices and sensors to the Internet, allowing for data collection, analysis, and control. This connectivity optimizes equipment performance, streamlines processes, and provides valuable insights for decision-making.

AI technologies, including machine learning and deep learning, empower machines to make autonomous decisions, analyse data, and improve manufacturing processes. AI enhances predictive maintenance, quality control, and production optimization. Collaboration tools and platforms enable teams to work seamlessly across different locations and time zones. These technologies enhance communication and coordination, fostering collaborative efforts in product design, development, and production. Integrated platforms that consolidate various manufacturing and data management functions provide a comprehensive solution for Industry 4.0 adoption. These platforms simplify the transition by offering a unified environment for managing processes and data.

The adoption of these technologies paves the way for a smooth transition to Industry 4.0, the Fourth Industrial Revolution. This transition is marked by improved productivity and efficiency, as processes become more streamlined and optimized. Additionally, safety standards are enhanced through real-time monitoring and predictive maintenance, reducing the potential for accidents. Furthermore, sustainability gains importance as smart manufacturing allows for better resource utilization and waste reduction, aligned with broader environmental goals. In summary, these innovative projects in computer technology are instrumental in driving the transformation of manufacturing towards increased productivity, efficiency, safety, and sustainability.

5.2 Innovations in the steel industry

The steel industry has seen several significant innovations over the years, aimed at improving the efficiency, sustainability, and quality of steel production. Some of the key innovations in the steel industry include (Zanoli et al., 2023; Attarpour and Nasri, 2023; Mallet and Pal, 2022; Ryan, 2022; Explore, 2023; Wang, 2022; Skoczkowski et al., 2020):

- Electric Arc Furnaces (EAFs) which are becoming increasingly popular for steel production, especially for recycling scrap steel. They are more energy-efficient and produce fewer greenhouse gas emissions compared to traditional blast furnaces. EAF technology has improved over time, making it a more viable option for steel manufacturing.
- Researchers and companies are developing alternative ironmaking processes that produce steel with lower carbon emissions. Some of these technologies include direct reduction, hydrogen-based reduction, and novel smelting processes. These methods aim to reduce or eliminate the reliance on carbon-intensive coke and coal.
- The steel industry is adopting Industry 4.0 principles, incorporating automation, data analytics, and the Internet of Things (IoT) to optimize production processes, increase efficiency, and reduce downtime. Advanced sensors and real-time data analysis help in predictive maintenance and quality control.
- The development of advanced steel alloys has led to materials with superior strength, corrosion resistance, and other desirable properties. These advanced alloys find applications in industries such as aerospace, automotive, and construction.
- Additive manufacturing, or 3D printing, is being used to produce intricate steel components with reduced waste and faster production times. This technology enables the creation of complex, lightweight structures that were previously challenging to manufacture.
- Steel manufacturers are increasingly focused on sustainability. They are working on recycling and reusing steel products, reducing waste, and implementing eco-friendly processes. Additionally, some companies are exploring carbon capture and utilization (CCU) and carbon capture and storage (CCS) to mitigate carbon emissions.
- The integration of digital technologies and artificial intelligence is being used to optimize the entire steel production process, from raw material handling to finished product quality control. This results in energy savings, reduced waste, and enhanced product quality.
- Green steel is produced using renewable energy sources and technologies that significantly reduce carbon emissions. This involves using hydrogen produced

from renewable sources and electricity from sustainable grids. Several companies and initiatives are working on scaling up green steel production.

- The development of nanostructured steel materials has led to stronger and more durable products. These materials have applications in various industries, including automotive, construction, and energy.
- Combining steel with other materials, such as composites or polymers, can result in lightweight, high-strength materials with applications in aerospace and transportation industries. These composites offer improved fuel efficiency and performance.

In Table 5.1, there is a presentation of various types of innovations in the steel industry with division into: technological innovation, process, innovation, sustainability innovation, and product innovation.

Technological advances in the steel industry involve the development of advanced steel alloys with improved properties, such as strength, corrosion resistance, and weight reduction. 3D printing is being used to create intricate steel components and enable customization. Nanotechnology is applied to enhance steel properties, and advanced coatings are developed to improve corrosion resistance and thermal properties (Fichera et al., 2020).

Process innovations focus on optimizing steel production methods. Electric Arc Furnaces (EAFs) are being fine-tuned for greater efficiency and sustainability. Direct reduction processes, including hydrogen-based methods, are employed to reduce carbon emissions and enhance energy efficiency. Recycling processes are improved to recover more steel from scrap, and Industry 4.0 technologies, such as automation and data analytics, are integrated to enhance production processes (McDonald, 2018).

Product innovations in the steel industry include customization to meet the specific needs of various industries and applications. Steel composite materials, created by combining steel with composites or polymers, are developed for lightweight, high-strength applications. Smart steel products with embedded sensors and real-time monitoring features are designed to monitor performance and provide data for maintenance and quality control (Zanoli et al., 2023; Gajdzik and Wolniak, 2021).

The very interesting and important from Industry 4.0/5.0 development point of view is a category of sustainable innovations. Sustainable innovations in the steel industry focus on reducing the environmental impact of steel production while maintaining economic viability. These innovations are crucial in addressing climate change and resource conservation (Bhaskar et al., 2022).

Green steel is produced using renewable energy sources, such as wind and solar power, and clean hydrogen produced from renewable sources. This approach significantly reduces carbon emissions associated with steel production. Carbon Capture and Storage (CCS) involves capturing carbon dioxide (CO_2) emissions from steel production processes and storing them underground to prevent their release into the atmosphere. This helps reduce the industry's carbon footprint (Souza Filho et al., 2023).

Table 5.1 Examples of innovations in the steel industry in main categories of innovation

Category	*Innovation*
Technological innovation	Advanced steel alloys with improved properties (strength, corrosion resistance, weight reduction).
	Utilization of 3D printing for intricate steel components and customized designs.
	Application of nanotechnology to enhance steel properties.
	Development of advanced coatings for steel.
Process innovation	Optimization of Electric Arc Furnaces (EAFs) for efficiency and sustainability.
	Implementation of direct reduction processes, including hydrogen-based reduction.
	Advancements in recycling processes to recover more steel from scrap.
	Integration of Industry 4.0 technologies for automation and data analytics.
Sustainability innovation	Carbon Capture and Storage (CCS) to reduce carbon emissions.
	Carbon Capture and Utilization (CCU) for value-added product creation.
	Transition to green steel production using renewable energy and hydrogen.
	Waste reduction practices to minimize environmental impact.
Product innovation	Customization of steel products to meet specific industry and application needs.
	Development of steel composite materials (steel with composites or polymers) for lightweight, high-strength applications.

Source: Own elaboration on basis: (Mallet and Pall, 2022; Gajdzik and Wolniak, 2021; Explore, 2023; Ryan, 2022).

Carbon Capture and Utilization (CCU) is an innovation that involves using captured CO_2 emissions as a feedstock for the production of valuable products, such as chemicals and building materials. This transforms a waste product into a resource. Enacting waste reduction strategies and embracing the circular economy concept through the design of steel products for reuse, remanufacturing, and recycling. This minimizes waste and conserves resources (Kawabata, 2023).

Innovations in water management help reduce water consumption and minimize environmental impacts. Water recycling and treatment systems are implemented to ensure efficient and sustainable use of water resources. Innovations in material use and resource efficiency aim to reduce the consumption of raw materials and energy in steel production. Improved process control and better utilization of scrap steel contribute to resource conservation (D'auria, 2023).

Development and implementation of low-carbon technologies, including hydrogen-based reduction methods and alternative ironmaking processes, reduce the carbon footprint of steel production. Eco-labelling and certification programmes help consumers and businesses choose steel products that meet specific sustainability criteria, fostering responsible consumption (Pham, 2023).

Ensuring that raw materials, such as iron ore and coal, are sourced from suppliers with sustainable practices reduces the environmental impact of the entire supply chain. Collaborations between steel manufacturers, government agencies, research institutions, and environmental organizations promote the sharing of knowledge, technologies, and best practices to drive sustainability in the steel industry (Theuringer, 2022).

In the steel industry, new innovations can be connected with Industry 4.0/5.0-based solutions. For example, it is possible in the steel industry the use of IoT in monitoring various aspects of the steel production process. This includes monitoring mobile people and machines using Radio Frequency Identification (RFID) technology, tracking vehicles through ground penetration radar (GPRs), and using wireless sensors to monitor equipment and processes (e.g. vibration, temperature, pressure). These technologies aim to collect and record information to optimize raw material handling and control interactions with the external environment.

The steel industry is exploring the use of advanced materials and nanotechnology to create products with specific properties. This is especially relevant for producing materials that are lighter and more resistant, catering to the needs of the environment and customers. These innovations focus on developing new materials and improving product quality.

Artificial intelligence is applied in specialized sintering/pelletizing systems, offering online chemical analysis of sinter and blending of raw materials. Additionally, artificial neural networks are used for prediction and control of steel production parameters, enhancing the control of the final product's temperature and chemical composition. These technologies enable predictive manufacturing and real-time intelligent planning (Santos et al., 2021).

These innovations are applied at different stages of the steel production process, with a focus on refining and rolling mills, which offer opportunities for cost reduction, predictive maintenance, and greater equipment and raw material efficiency. However, the text also notes that these technologies are still being tested, and some need further development to gain the necessary robustness for industrial applications. Mentioned innovations aim is to optimize the steel industry rather than revolutionize it, reinforcing existing technological trajectories while increasing operational efficiency and productivity. It also highlights that the diffusion of these technologies varies across different clusters, and some, like Nanotechnology, are still at an early stage of adoption.

5.3 Industry 4.0/5.0 as a boaster of innovations in the steel industry

Industry 4.0 characterized by the integration of digital technologies into manufacturing and production processes has the potential to be a significant booster of innovation in the steel sector. Industry 4.0 technologies, such as the Internet of Things (IoT), allow for real-time monitoring and control of the steel production process. Sensors and data analytics can track the condition of equipment, the temperature of molten steel, and the quality of the final product. This leads to increased efficiency and a dramatic reduction in defects and waste.

Smart sensors and data analytics can predict when machinery and equipment are likely to fail. This enables steel manufacturers to schedule maintenance at the most convenient times, reducing downtime and ensuring the smooth operation of steel mills. The use of robots and automation in the steel sector is not new, but Industry 4.0 takes it to the next level. Robots can perform tasks in high-heat and high-risk environments, enhancing worker safety and increasing productivity. Automation also allows for consistent and precise production, resulting in high-quality steel products (Mishra et al., 2023).

The steel industry relies on a complex global supply chain for raw materials and distribution. Industry 4.0 enables end-to-end visibility and optimization of the supply chain. From tracking the availability of raw materials to real-time monitoring of logistics, steel manufacturers can make informed decisions that minimize costs and reduce environmental impact. With the adoption of digital technologies, the steel sector can meet the growing demand for customized steel products. Using advanced software and machinery, manufacturers can easily adjust production to meet specific customer requirements, leading to greater customer satisfaction and market competitiveness (Hajoary, 2022).

Industry 4.0 allows steel mills to optimize their energy consumption by analysing data and making real-time adjustments to the production process. This leads to reduced energy costs and a smaller environmental footprint. The enormous amount of data generated in the steel industry can be harnessed for innovation. Advanced analytics and machine learning can identify trends and opportunities for improvement. For instance, data analysis can reveal new alloy compositions, production techniques, or quality control methods that were previously hidden (Miśkeiwicz and Wolniak, 2020).

The digital age enables collaboration between steel manufacturers, suppliers, and customers in ways previously unattainable. Sharing data and insights can lead to innovations that benefit the entire sector. Industry 4.0 can help the steel sector reduce its environmental impact. By optimizing processes, reducing waste, and enhancing energy efficiency, the industry can move towards more sustainable production methods (Pourmedi et al., 2022).

The steel industry, a cornerstone of modern infrastructure and manufacturing, is continuously evolving to embrace the transformative potential of Industry 4.0. This industrial revolution is characterized by nine key pillars, each offering a unique set of innovations that can revolutionize the steel sector. The steel industry can harness vast amounts of data to optimize operations. Predictive maintenance using data analytics reduces downtime and increases machinery reliability. Real-time data analysis improves product quality by monitoring and controlling variables, while demand forecasting ensures a seamless production process aligned with market trends. Robots and AI systems are becoming integral to steel manufacturing. Autonomous robots handle material handling and logistics, reducing labour costs, and enhancing efficiency. AI-driven predictive maintenance optimizes machinery performance and safety, with robotic systems often deployed for hazardous tasks (Dai and Zuo, 2020).

Systems Integration towards CPS (Cyber-Physical Systems) focuses on integrating equipment and processes into unified systems. For the steel industry, this means real-time monitoring and control of production processes, ensuring greater precision and responsiveness. Seamlessly integrating supply chain partners and vertically integrating production processes ensures a holistic approach. It enhances supply chain efficiency and enables end-to-end control, which is critical in steel production (Tolettini and Lehmann, 2020).

Real-time monitoring of equipment using IoT sensors is essential for maintenance and control. IoT sensors also track product quality and process parameters, providing critical data for continuous improvement. Implementing CPS enhances control and automation within steel production. However, with this increased connectivity comes a need for robust cybersecurity measures to protect sensitive data and operations from cyber threats.

Cloud-based data storage and analytics offer remote access and collaboration opportunities. This is particularly beneficial for storing vast datasets and sharing data with partners across the supply chain. Also known as 3D printing, additive manufacturing is revolutionizing steel production. It allows for the creation of complex steel parts with minimal waste, rapid prototyping, and tooling, enhancing design flexibility and reducing lead times.

VR and AR are employed in the steel industry for training, simulation, and maintenance procedures. These technologies create a safe and immersive environment for workers to learn, visualize complex processes, and simulate scenarios before execution. Virtual prototyping and design in 3D space further improve product development (Govender et al., 2019).

Industry 5.0 implementation in the steel industry is poised to undergo a profound transformation. To embrace this new era, it can harness innovations deeply connected with the three pillars of Sustainability, Human-Centricity, and Resilience.

Sustainability is at the forefront of the steel industry's evolution. To reduce its environmental footprint, steel manufacturers are implementing green technologies that significantly curtail carbon emissions. This includes adopting energy-efficient production processes and transitioning to sustainable sourcing of raw materials. A key aspect of sustainability is recycling and reusing steel scrap in the production process, thus promoting circular economy principles. Additionally, integrating carbon capture and storage (CCS) technology can further minimize the industry's environmental impact (Sverko et al., 2022).

Human-Centricity emphasizes placing the workforce at the heart of operations. In the steel industry, this entails rethinking traditional processes and work environments. Ergonomically designed workstations are becoming more prevalent, enhancing worker comfort and reducing physical strain (Saniuk and Grabowska, 2024) and safety (Gajdzik et al., 2015; Gajdzik, 2021). Training and upskilling programmes are equipping employees with the necessary skills to operate alongside advanced technologies. Collaborative robotics are being introduced to improve both worker safety and productivity. Moreover, feedback mechanisms and employee wellness programmes are fostering a more caring and supportive work culture (Caricato and Grieco, 2024). Decision-making in smart manufacturing is also facilitated. Leaders have statistical methods at their disposal, including prediction tools (Szymszal et al., 2016). Technology is increasingly supporting them in

Table 5.2 Innovations in the steel industry based on Industry 4.0/5.0 solutions

Industry 4.0/5.0 pillar	*Innovations for steel industry*
Big data & analytics	Predictive maintenance to reduce downtime by analysing machine data. Data-driven quality control to identify defects in real-time.
Autonomous robots and AI	Autonomous robotic systems for material handling and logistics. AI-driven process optimization for energy efficiency and production.
Systems integration towards CPS	Integration of production systems to create a seamless workflow. Real-time monitoring of equipment and processes.
Horizontal and vertical system integration	Horizontal integration between different steel production units. Vertical integration with suppliers and customers for supply chain optimization.
IoT / IIoT	IoT sensors on equipment for condition monitoring and performance tracking. IIoT for real-time inventory management and supply chain visibility.
Cyber-Physical Systems (CPSs) and Cybersecurity	Implementation of CPS to control and optimize steel production. Robust cybersecurity measures to protect sensitive data and production processes.
Cloud computing	Cloud-based data storage and analytics for real-time insights. Remote access to production data and systems for off-site monitoring.
Additive manufacturing	3D printing for rapid prototyping and tooling. Customization of steel products through additive manufacturing.
Virtual and augmented reality	Virtual training and simulation for workers. Augmented reality for maintenance and repair guidance.
Sustainability	Implementation of green technologies to reduce carbon emissions. Recycling and reusing steel scrap in the production process. Sustainable sourcing of raw materials. Energy-efficient production processes. Implementing carbon capture and storage (CCS) technology.
Human-centricity	Ergonomically designed workstations to improve worker comfort. Training and upskilling programmes for the workforce. Collaborative robotics to enhance worker safety and productivity. Worker feedback systems to improve work conditions. Employee wellness and mental health support programmes.
Resilience	Diversification of supply chains to ensure a steady flow of raw materials. Robust disaster recovery plans and crisis management strategies. Predictive maintenance to reduce unplanned downtime. Implementing digital twins for better process optimization and resilience. Resilience against cybersecurity threats through advanced cybersecurity measures.

Source: Own elaboration on basis: (Mishra et al., 2023; Govender et al., 2019; Tolettini and Lohmenn, 2020; Dai and Zuo, 2020; Pourmehdi et al., 2022; Sverko et al., 2022).

decision-making and process optimization. Leaders 4.0 are relieved of the notorious process control. The creative leader knows the possibilities of Industry 4.0/5.0 technologies and how to apply them effectively (Kwiotkowska et al., 2022).

Resilience is paramount in a world where unpredictability is a constant. To ensure the steel industry remains robust in the face of unforeseen challenges, diversifying supply chains is essential. This helps ensure a steady flow of raw materials even in times of disruption. Robust disaster recovery plans and crisis management strategies are being fine-tuned to swiftly respond to unexpected events. Predictive maintenance is also playing a pivotal role in reducing unplanned downtime, thereby fortifying operational resilience. Furthermore, the implementation of digital twins offers a powerful tool for process optimization and resilience, enabling manufacturers to simulate and prepare for various scenarios. Lastly, guarding against cybersecurity threats through advanced cybersecurity measures is vital for protecting sensitive data and maintaining the integrity of production processes (Palazhchenko et al., 2024).

Table 5.2 give some examples of innovations which can be implemented in steel industry which are based on Industry 4.5/5.0-based solutions.

References

Attarpour, M.R., Nasri, A. (2023). The most effective technological learning mechanisms for innovation: Evidence from Iran's steel industry. *International Journal of Technological Learning, Innovation and Development*, 15(1), 90–113.

Benitez, G.B., Ayala, N.F., Frank, A.G. (2020). Industry 4.0 innovation ecosystems: An evolutionary perspective on value cocreation. *International Journal of Production Economics*, 228, 107735.

Bhaskar, A., Abhishek, R., Assadi, M., Somehesaraei, H.N. (2022). Decarbonizing primary steel production: Techno-economic assessment of a hydrogen based green steel production plant in Norway. *Production*, 350, 131339.

Caricato, P., Grieco, A. (2024). *Optimization Patterns Enabled by Industry 4.0/5.0 Data.* 32nd International Conference on Flexible Automation and Intelligent Manufacturing, pp. 601–608.

Dai, H., Zuo, X. (2020). Industry 4.0 boosts the steel industry into a new era of digitalization and smart technology. In: AISTech – Iron and Steel Technology Conference Proceedings, 3; pp. 1829–1841.

D'auria, M. (2023). The journey towards EU green steel. *Steel Times International*, 47(3), 35–37.

Dedehayir, O., Makinen, S.J., Ortt, J.R. (2018). Roles during innovation ecosystem genesis: A literature review. *Technological Forecasting and Social Change*, 136, 18–29.

Edquist, C. (2005). Systems of innovation: Perspectives and challenges. In Fagerberg, J., Mowery, D.C. (Eds), *The Oxford Handbook of Innovation.* Oxford University Press: New York, 181–208.

ExploretheTop10SteelIndustryTrends.(2023).https://www.startus-insights.com/innovators-guide/steel-industry-trends/, [access data: 27.10.2023].

Fichera, S.S., Arfò, S., Huang, Y.L., Matarazzo, A., Bertino, A. (2020). Circular economy and technological innovation in steel industry. *Procedia Environmental Science, Engineering and Management*, 7(1), 9–17.

Gajdzik, B. (2021). Machine and equipment operator in Industry 4.0 — introduction to the topic. *Material Economy and Logistics Journal*, LXXIII(5), 1–7. http://dx.doi.org/10.33226/1231-2037.2021.5.1

Gajdzik, B., Grebski, M.E. (2022). Human factor in Industry 4.0: About skills of operators in steelworks 4.0. Scientific papers of Silesian University of Technology. *Organization and Management* Series no. 157, 119–132.

Gajdzik, B., Szymszal, J. (2015). Generation gap management in restructured metallurgical enterprises in Poland. *International Journal of Management and Economics*, 47, July–September, 107–120. http://www.sgh.waw.pl/ijme/.

Gajdzik, B., Wolniak, R. (2021). Digitalisation and innovation in the steel industry in Poland—Selected tools of it an analysis of statistical data and a case study. *Energies*, 14(11), 3034.

Gajdzik, B., Zwolińska, D., Szymszal, J. (2015). Behavioural determinants of work accidents and absenteeism in a metallurgical enterprise. *Metalurgija*, 54(4), 741–744.

Govender, E., Telukdarie, A., Sishi, M.N. (2019). Approach for implementing Industry 4.0 framework in the steel industry. In: IEEE International Conference on Industrial Engineering and Engineering Management; pp. 1314–1318, 8978492.

Hajoary, P.K. (2022). Industry 4.0 maturity and readiness – A case of a steel manufacturing organization. *Procedia Computer Science*, 217, 614–619.

Kahle, J.H., Marcon, E., Ghezzi, A., Frank, A.G. (2020). Smart products value creation in SMEs innovation ecosystems. *Technological Forecasting and Social Change*, 156, 120024.

Kawabata, N. (2023). Evaluating the technology path of Japanese steelmakers in green steel competition. *Japanese Political Economy*, 32(5), 25–37.

Kurdve, M., Bird, A., Lage-Hellman, J. (2020). Establishing SME-University collaboration through innovation support programmes. *Journal of Manufacturing Technology Management*, 31(8), 1583–1604.

Kwiotkowska, A., Wolniak, R., Gajdzik, B., Gębczyńska, M. (2022). Configurational paths of leadership competency shortages and 4.0 leadership effectiveness: An fs/QCA study. *Sustainability*, 14, 2795. https://doi.org/10.3390/su14052795

Mallett, A., Pal, P. (2022). Green transformation in the iron and steel industry in India: Rethinking patterns of innovation. *Energy Strategy Reviews*, 44, 100968.

Markkula, M., Kune, H. (2015). Making smart regions smarter: Smart specialization and the role of Universities in regional innovation ecosystems. *Technology Innovation Management Review*, 10(5), 7–15.

Matt, D., Bolzano, I., Molinaro, M., Orzes, G., Pedrini, G. (2021). The role of innovation ecosystems in Industry 4.0 adoption. *Journal of Manufacturing Technology Management*, 32(9), 369–395.

Matt, D.T., Rauch, E., Riedl, M. (2018). Knowledge transfer and introduction of Industry 4.0 in SMEs: A five-step methodology to introduce Industry 4.0. In Brunet-Thornton, R., Martinez, F. (Eds), *Analyzing the Impacts of Industry 4.0. In: Modern Business Environments*. IGI Global: Hershey, PA, 256–282. EISBN13: 9781522534693.

McDonald, C. (2018). Materials processing Institute innovation for the global steel industry. *Ironmaking and Steelmaking*, 45(5), 394–396.

Mishra, R., Singh, R.K., Gunasekaran, A. (2023). Adoption of industry 4.0 technologies for decarbonisation in the steel industry: Self-assessment framework with case illustration. *Annals of Operations Research*, 7(4), 15–34.

Miśkiewicz, R., Wolniak, R. (2020). Practical application of the industry 4.0 concept in a steel company. *Sustainability* (Switzerland), 12(14), 1–21, 5776.

Oh, D.S., Phillips, F., Park, S., Lee, E. (2016). Innovation ecosystems: A critical examination. *Technovation*, 54, 1–6.

Palazhchenko, Y., Shendryk, V., Ivanov, V., Hatala, M. (2024). *Industry 5.0: Aspects of Collaboration Technologies*. 32nd International Conference on Flexible Automation and Intelligent Manufacturing, pp. 609–617.

Pham, Q. (2023). Green iron, green steel. *Steel Times International*, 47(3), 72–73.

Pino, R.M., Ortega, A.M. (2018). Regional innovation systems: Systematic literature review and recommendations for future research. *Cogent Business and Management*, 5(1), 1463606.

Pourmehdi, M., Paydar, M.M., Ghadimi, P., Azadnia, A.H. (2022). Analysis and evaluation of challenges in the integration of Industry 4.0 and sustainable steel reverse logistics network. *Computers and Industrial Engineering*, 163, 107808.

Reischauer, G. (2018). Industry 4.0 as policy-driven discourse to institutionalize innovation systems in manufacturing. *Technological Forecasting and Social Change*, 132, 26–33.

Rocha, C.F., Mamedio, D.F., Quandt, C.O. (2019). Startups and the innovation ecosystem in Industry 4.0. *Technology Analysis and Strategic Management*, 31(12), 1474–1487.

Ryan, M. (2022). Steel Industry in 2022: Most Promising Technologies to Keep an Eye on. https://www.abiresearch.com/blogs/2022/06/28/steel-industry-in-2022-most-promising-technologies-to-keep-an-eye-on/, [access data: 27.10.2023].

Saniuk, S., Grabowska, S. (2024). Skills and competencies of industrial employees in the Industry 5.0 environment. In: Burduk, A. et al. (Eds), *Intelligent Systems in Production Engineering and Maintenance III*. Conference Paper. Lecture Notes in Mechanical Engineering. Springer: Cham, 251–264. https://doi.org/10.1007/978-3-031-44282-7_20.

Santos, M.S., Mendes, G.P., Resi, M.B. (2021). Technological innovations and Industry 4.0 in the steel industry: Diffusion, market structure and intra-sectoral geterogeneity, Brasilian. *Journal of Innovation*, 20, e021006.

Skoczkowski, T., Verdolini, E., Bielecki, S., Kochański, M., Korczak, K., Węglarz, A. (2020). Technology innovation system analysis of decarbonisation options in the EU steel industry. *Energy*, 212, 118688.

Souza Filho, I.R., Ma, Y., Raabe, D., Springer, H. (2023). Fundamentals of green steel production: On the role of gas pressure during hydrogen reduction of iron ores. *JOM*, 75(7), 2274–2286.

Sverko, M., Grbac, T.G., Mikuc, M. (2022). SCADA systems with focus on continuous manufacturing and steel industry: A survey on architectures, standards, challenges and Industry 5.0. *IEEE Access*, 10, 109395–109430.

Szymszal, J., Gajdzik, B., Kaczmarczyk, G. (2016). The use of modern statistical methods to optimize production systems in foundries. *Archives of Foundry Engineering*, 16(3), 115–120. https://doi.org/10.1515/afe-2016-0061

Theuringer, M. (2022). How green steel finds its way into products. *Steel Times International*, 46(6), 27–28.

Tolettini, L., Lehmann, C. (2020). Industry 4.0: New paradigms of value creation for the steel sector. *Knowledge Management and Organizational Learning*, 9, 179–206.

Wang, L. (2022). Role of FDI and energy intensity in mitigating the environmental pollution in the Chinese steel industry: Does technological innovation makes a difference? *Environmental Science and Pollution Research*, 29(19), 28127–28138.

Wolniak, R., Grebski, M. (2018). *Promoting Creativity and Innovativeness in Education*. CreateSpace Independent Publishing: North Charleston.

Zanoli, S.M., Pepe, C., Orlietti, L. (2023). Synergic combination of hardware and software innovations for energy efficiency and process control improvement: A steel industry application. *Energies*, 16(10), 4183.

6 The summarization of research results on smart steel manufacturing

6.1 Characteristics of the triad: sustainability – smart steel manufacturing – human factor

During the Fourth Industrial Revolution, intelligent technologies are being developed, which represent an opportunity to create smart manufacturing. The concept of smart manufacturing is linked to various forms of intelligence, such as intelligent machines, intelligent production processes, intelligent devices, intelligent engineering, intelligent technologies, intelligent logistics, intelligent networks, and more. The Internet of Things (IoT), big data, and artificial intelligence (AI) are compelling traditional industrial structures to undergo rapid transformations. The scale, scope, and complexity of these changes will be unprecedented. Steelmakers are actively embracing advanced technologies to adapt to this massive paradigm shift. The leading steel mills will tailor technologies like AI and virtual factories and apply them to production sites. They will enhance integration across value chains by connecting clients and suppliers through smart factories.

6.1.1 How do steel mills prepare for the future of manufacturing?

The Fourth Industrial Revolution is making significant strides in the steel industry, and new changes are becoming evident. These changes affect many areas of steelworks operations and their value chains. The transformation of the steel industry into smart steel manufacturing is underway. Steel mills belonging to powerful (global) capital groups are increasingly investing in technologies that, first, represent an opportunity to create smart steel manufacturing and, second, to establish a strong digital ecosystem. Steel producers are aware of the challenges posed by the Fourth Industrial Revolution and its associated concepts such as Industry 4.0 and the subsequent Industry 5.0. The connection of steel production technologies (machines) to global computer networks has opened new possibilities for directly involving steel producers in the broader process of creating value for consumers of steel products.

Steel producers are becoming more closely linked to steel consumer markets, and with the latest technologies of the Fourth Industrial Revolution, they can enable consumers to co-create steel products. In the realm of economics, there is a strong shift from competitiveness to cooperation, stimulating the implementation of

DOI: 10.4324/9781032697611-6

innovative solutions in product and manufacturing technology from the "advanced technology" areas. The design and development of smart steel manufacturing require increasing collaboration across the group of steel product manufacturers and consumer markets.

In the context of Industry 4.0, smart steel manufacturing is an opportunity for every steel mill that intends to participate in creating new processes, products, and services. A key research area – the overall framework for intelligent steel production – is important for recognizing trends in industrial transformation. This book introduces the concepts of smart steel manufacturing, starting from the most general issues covered in literature review-based chapters, through the presentation of case studies and direct research results.

A three-segment system of transformational frameworks for the steel sector towards co-creating Industry 4.0 is characterized. This triad includes changes occurring in steelworks in sustainability, smart steel manufacturing, and the human factor. The described transformation directions, based on smart steel manufacturing, particularly emphasize the concept of Industry 4.0. Due to the complexity of technological processes and their impact on the natural environment, the ongoing industrial transformation must not neglect the sustainability segment. Steel mills are responsible for emitting over 7% of CO_2 into the atmosphere (Iron and Steel, 2020). This crucial environmental aspect has been considered in European industrial policy. By 2050, in the net-zero strategy, steel mills will replace current high-emission technologies with low-emission technologies and eventually with the latest climate-neutral technologies, currently in the testing phase.

Deep decarbonization of the steel industry is a strategic direction of steel mill transformation. Concurrently, changes towards smart manufacturing will accelerate. However, every change is accompanied by certain behaviours, often social, not so much related to the designed new solutions but rather caused by their consequences. Human-machine collaboration and the application of intelligent production change the human factor. People acquire new digital skills, sometimes unconsciously. In the near future, digital skills will dominate over others. Intelligent machines can assist people in performing most of their tasks through speech recognition, computer vision, machine learning, and advanced synchronization models.

The changes resulting from the use of Industry 4.0 technologies in the steel sector, such as cloud computing, the Internet of Things, big data analytics, artificial intelligence, and augmented reality, aim to decentralize control processes so that every intelligent element of the system can make self-adjusting decisions. For example, to maintain a synchronized production rhythm, intelligent components operating at each stage of steel production will be able to collaborate seamlessly. In addition to being flexible, a production system needs to ensure the visibility of real-time operational data and provide insight for better and faster decision-making along the value chain. One change is the integration of digital networks into value chains. Plants, companies, and even the entire steel industry can be integrated into a single digital ecosystem.

6.2 Model of pro-quality steel mill management in smart sustainable steel manufacturing

The conducted research work, titled "Sustainability, Smart Manufacturing, and Human Factors: The Transformation of the Polish Steelwork Industry", had an experimental nature. Its main objective was to develop a framework for the transformation of steelworks into Industry 4.0. This goal was achieved.

Based on the conducted research on the impact of Industry 4.0 and Industry 5.0 (concepts intersecting in recent years of transformation) on the functioning of steelworks, a progressive process of changes in the steel sector was observed. Advanced technologies, in conjunction with the requirements of sustainable development and responsibility towards the human factor, are incorporated into the strategies for the development of the steel industry. As our case study analyses have shown, powerful capital groups – major global steel producers – serve as benchmarks for these changes.

The final result of the research is a model of the transformation of the steel industry – an industrial reindustrialization model based on the pillars (key technologies) of Industry 4.0 and economic-social conditions. At the centre of this model is the triad of our research: sustainability – smart steel manufacturing – human factor. Key directions of changes were attached to each element of the triad. The model is presented in Figure 6.1.

This research work does not mark the end of considerations on the subject of Industry 4.0 in the steel sector; on the contrary, it represents the first step towards

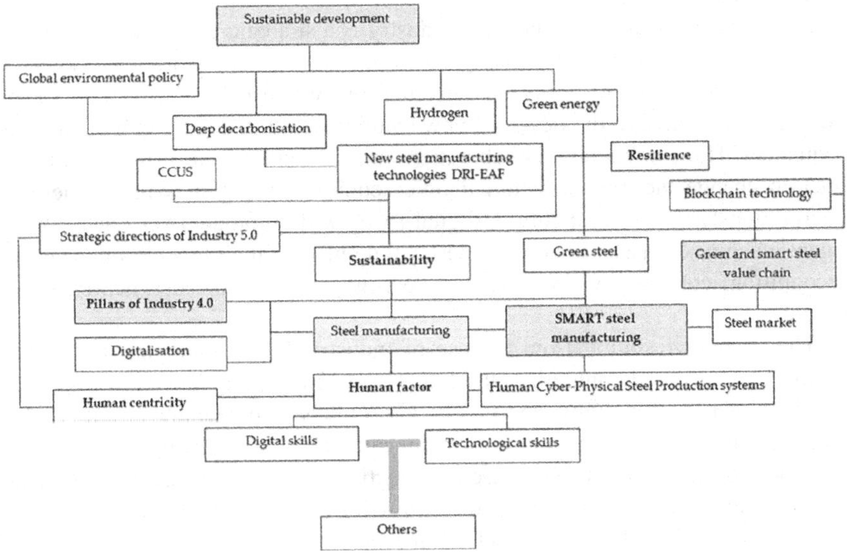

Figure 6.1 Model of transformation of the steel industry towards smart and sustainable steel manufacturing.

Source: Author's own study.

a comprehensive description of this multifaceted and complex issue. Continuing work in this area, it is recommended to consider using the developed methodology as a foundation for conceptualizing further research on Industry 4.0. Moreover, the involvement of scientists, experts, and practitioners in methodological work related to the smart steel manufacturing issue on the international stage is recommended. In further studies on the topic, it is suggested to expand the scope to include other participants in the value chain in the global steel market.

The main limitation of the study presented in this book is because the research focuses on the steel industry, specifically in the context of the Polish steelwork industry. The research primarily focuses on the steel sector. It may not provide a comprehensive view of the interactions and interdependencies between the steel industry and other sectors within the broader Industry 4.0 landscape.

Also the book primarily discusses the practices and transformations observed in major global steel producers. Generalizing these findings to smaller or region-specific steel mills may not accurately represent the diverse landscape of the entire steel industry. The research does not explicitly address cultural or regional differences, which can play a crucial role in the adoption and adaptation of smart manufacturing practices. Cultural nuances may impact how technologies are embraced and implemented in different contexts.

Bibliography

Iron and Steel Technology Roadmap towards More Sustainable Steelmaking. International Energy Agency. (October 2020). https://iea.blob.core.windows.net/assets/eb0c8ec1-3665-4959-97d0-187ceca189a8/Iron_and_Steel_Technology_Roadmap.pdf, [access data: 27.10.2023].

Index

Made in the USA
Monee, IL
13 September 2026

62980176R00092